REVOLT AGAINST THE PLUTOCRACY

By

Jay T. Baldwin

This book is a work of non-fiction. Names and places have been changed to protect the privacy of all individuals. The events and situations are true.

© 2004 by Jay T. Baldwin All rights reserved.

No part of this book may be reproduced, stored in a retrieval system, or transmitted by any means, electronic, mechanical, photocopying, recording, or otherwise, without written permission from the author.

First published by AuthorHouse 05/04/04

ISBN: 1-4184-5486-9 (e-book)
ISBN: 1-4184-5487-7 (Paperback)

This book is printed on acid free paper.

Table of Contents

About the Book v

Chapter 1 Past prosperity. Sharing the fruits of our labor 1

Chapter 2 Largest economic boom in history. Bourgeoisie only! 28

Chapter 3 Tin man. Cold hearted, ruthless corporate America. 60

Chapter 4 Designed by greed. New world economic & political order. 125

Chapter 5 The paradox. Big, plutocratic, capitalism, the new communism. 222

Chapter 6 Placid Outrage, Violent Apathy. Social conditioning, the silent enemy. 279

Chapter 7 Wake up America! Hello! Protest now or revolt later. 324

REVOLT AGAINST THE PLUTOCRACY! 420

BIBLIOGRAPHY 426

About the author 431

About the Book

In a continuing line of thought provoking, controversial, provocative books, REVOLT AGAINST THE PLUTOCRACY! is another weapon to be used as a counter force against laissez-faire, oppressive, destructive, undemocratic, greedy corporate big capitalism. It picks up where DELIGHT OF THE OVERCLASS DEMISE OF THE MIDDLECLASS leaves off, addressing an ongoing relentless assault against American middle class working Americans, the working poor, and American consumers by corporations, and corrupted politics. All of this to reduce employment, and production costs to maximize profits, for the past 20 years. Ironically, this has resulted in the longest boom period in America's corporate economic history, as well as the world's, eclipsing the Roaring Twenties, and the Robber-Barron era. Even after 20 years of corporate hay days, not much has ever trickled down to the average American blue, and white collar worker as Ronald Reagan had promised with Reaganomics. Even under two presidential administrations since Reagan, one Republican, one Democratic that ran for two terms, and another Republican, the rules have virtually stayed the same. The greed factor has remained king. This has resulted in a gradual decline of the average working American's income standards, living standards, hope and moral, and ultimately leading to the loss of the American Dream for the mass majority. Ironically, allowing the top 5%, the richest of the rich, the new American bourgeoisie, to continue into the new millennium reaping riches, and wealth unimaginable even 5 years ago. To our dismay, most of this at the expense of the remaining 90% of the people, and has lead to the destruction of the American Dream and the most conventional methods, handed down generation to generation, to access this American heritage. Could there be some mass conspiracy on behalf of this corporate elite, political elite, and the "Hear no evil," Speak no evil," "See no evil," federal government?

Revolt Against The Plutocracy! takes a more focused, philosophical view of society, causes, and counter measures the powerless masses can utilize to take the productivity, and profitability out of corporate America, as captive, until they get their share of this booming economy. An anticorporate terrorist kit, rich in methods of union style sabotage workers, and consumers can implement to hold profitability, and the economy hostage, unless corporations improve the income, safety, and product/service standards they offer to their employees and consumers. Finally, this book has useful, practical methods to counter social conditioning, and propaganda by corporate America, and the greedy, corrupted, unconcerned political powers of the land. Also a call to arms, as well as a moral booster for the oppressed, hard pressed American working class to halt America from further becoming an oppressive, undemocratic, autocratic plutocracy. The plutocracy has been waging war against the masses for twenty years, now the message has been received, and war has been declared!

Chapter 1 Past prosperity. Sharing the fruits of our labor.

The summer of 1957, 7:00 AM in a typical middleclass American neighborhood. The smell of bacon, and eggs is heavy in the air. The coffee percolator is making it's usual short burps and gurgles, with a strong sweet aroma of freshly perked grounds laying heavy in the kitchen. Honey! Breakfast is ready! I'll be down in a moment! The steady click clock coming down the stairs as if a two legged horse with new shoes was marching in step with an invisible drummer. Jim, I made you a chicken salad sandwich for your lunch with a banana. I made some of that yummy Maxwell house for your Thermos. Thanks, love! The faint giggles of children mixed with an occasional sharp "Stop that!" or "Let me have it!"

emanates from the bath room upstairs. What are you and the children going to do today? Well, I may take them later on this morning to Ed Smith's new Chevrolet lot, and check out that new improved Bel Air, and see what all the excitement is about. There is a short "Humm!" Let me know all about it this evening. Maybe, this Saturday we all can go and see it. I would like to see if it is what it's all cut out to be! After, all we could afford it now, since it's been six months since I got the generous raise at the plant, and orders are still picking up. It's keeping me on my toes, there is always some machine breaking down, and I am expected to have it up and running lickety split! Joe Baxter on the assembly line is the first to yell my name at the top of his lungs when his equipment malfunctions. He's an OK kind of guy though he takes his job seriously. After all, he has been at the plant for twenty one years or more! Last week I had to fill in for Benny right next to him on the assembly line. Benny took one of his sick days off to check on his father in Dushore. Joe said he would not have it any other way, even though on an extra hot summer day it can get a little stuffy in the plant. He said when his son gets old enough he will see about talking to Mr. Bird about letting him come to work to learn a little more about the business. If he likes it, he can join him in the future. Just passing the family trade on down the line. Jim, Didn't he mention something about putting air conditioning in his house, if that is the Joe you told me about last month? Yes dear!, his car is a lot newer than your old Buick. He will be spending some of his pay raise on other things this year. We will wait on the luxuries this year, and concentrate on getting you that new car. Thank God for the union, they were partially responsible for our pay raise. The boss was also partially responsible. He resisted the union's demand for a raise at first, but finally sided with them since company profits have been excellent due to this booming economy. He said with a half hearted smile, "Well, I guess all of you bums deserve a raise, you've earned it! Besides, I gave myself a good raise too." "What's good for the goose, is good for the gander!" "Keep up the good work men, this factory isn't going anywhere!" Bev!, Don't forget, if you go by the dime store today, get me a quart of oil, so I can keep a spare one in the Olds. Slurp!, gulp!, I've got to get going dear, so I am not late. I want to check one of the lathes, before it is warmed up today. Ok, honey, I will see you tonight a little after five. What do you want for dinner? Surprise me dear!

Later that evening. Honey!, I am home! Hello, daddy! Hey, daddy Two young children race toward the door. Jim, you're a little late today! It's five fifty. I know dear, It's all we can do to keep the orders filled. I am putting in some overtime this week again. People are buying home appliances like there is no tomorrow! The American Dream is wonderful Bev, isn't it? Yes it is my love, our dinner is getting cold! Hey children!, dinner is served! A delicious aroma of meatloaf and boiled mixed vegetables lingers still from a couple of hours cooking. Dinner is great dear! Thank you Jim, I am a little tired after running errands, a load of laundry, with the kids out of school for the summer. Did you have time to go by the car lot, and look at that new Chevrolet Bel Air. Yes my love, I brought home this pamphlet, and I took a few notes, even though the salesman gave me a cock eyed look. Boy, it went up a lot since last year. Two thousand three hundred and ninety nine dollars! Jim, that's brand spanking new! It's a hundred and five dollars more than last years model, Beverly! I know Jim, but you said by this time next year, you would be making at least a dollar more an hour. I said, if this economy keeps going like it has this year, I will have gotten a couple of raises by this time next year. Oh! Bev, we may be able to do it after all, Mr. Bird had mentioned, at the last company, meeting in trying profit sharing for all of the employees. I forgot to tell you. I was a little suspicious at this idea, since we wouldn't know if the company really did exceed the profit goal. He seemed truthful as he commented that most of us have been so loyal for so many years. This was on his own doing and had nothing to do with the union. If the company exceeds it's profit goal for the year, the extra left over would be split up evenly amongst the employees. Jim, lets pray the economy keeps doing so well. I guess, if the boss makes out like a bandit, he would feel guilty if he didn't share it with his workers. In fact Bev, if he didn't share the spoils, he would be considered a greedy no good for nothing. It's the ethics of running a good business. In fact, between the unions, the moderate government regulation, and the fact of those ethics amongst corporate owners, the future for every body, and our children will be brighter. Every body wins. Even if the economy took a dive, the company wouldn't think of giving anybody a cut in pay. The boss would be considered a poor leader, and would not be able to show his face in public. The company would have to be hurting, really bad, and would have to prove it before they would even consider a thing like that. We will go up there on Saturday, and make a decision. I will give the old Buick a good wash up before we go in, case we decide to trade it in. We could always go and check out a new Cadillac Fleetwood for around four thousand five hundred dollars. Bev, only if we go to Los Vegas, and hit the big jack pot! Danny and Karen, if you are finished with your desert, you can go and play for a little bit. Danny, I saved a jar for you to put your lightning bugs in tonight. Just do not let them out all over the house, Please! Do not even think of putting them down your sister's dress!

Jim, I was talking to Betty today while she was hanging the laundry out. She and George are thinking of selling the house. They want a slightly larger house. George got a pay raise at Sears and Roebuck. Betty makes a buck or two with the quilts, and pot holders she makes, and sells down town. What are they asking for the house Bev? She said it was appraised at twelve thousand dollars. I am sure glad we bought this house when we did. That is about two years salary at my current pay. Inflation Jim, just so your wages increase faster, like they have been doing for awhile. If not, I may find myself working a part time job somewhere, and then none of the house work would get done, and Mom and Dad would have to look after the kids in the summer. I do not think that will happen Beverly. We will have a man on the moon before that will ever happen, and we will have a color television instead. By the way Bev, some clown is tinkering around with the idea of a television with a color screen. Jim, I bet that contraption will cost as much as a new house! The few offered now with normal black and white screens, are too expensive as they are. They are only for the rich folks. Danny!! Danny! You didn't! I see lightning bugs blinking in the dark corners.

Well does that bring back memories or what! Well this was a slice of the American way of life in the late fifties. This was the third American economic boom period, which would last at least another decade. A code of ethics accepted as the thing to do existed in most work places. There were a few exceptions in corporate America. But most realized how important an employee/employer symbiotic relationship was. The work was hard, and most working husbands worked five days a week, and put in some overtime. A good percentage of working Americans had the weekends off! During holidays, towns looked like ghost towns. The post war period gave rise to the strongest most prosperous secure middle class the world has ever seen. Yes, my friends, most, not all American middle class families had one income. The proverbial Partridge family. Leave It To Beaver, Dennis The Menace scene. Mom home to run the house!

Well, we have returned from our little trip back in time, with our fictitious family Mr. and Mrs. Jim Bel Air, with actual statistical figures from the U.S. Dept. of Labor Employment and Earnings Statistics for the United States 1909-1968, and a few almanacs of statistical information for this period. Now let's get the old trusty almanacs out again and throw a few more figures around, to see roughly how life was at the incline of the journey to the American Dream. These figures are from the end of the war in 1947 through 1969. Non supervisory blue collar workers in the New England region saw an increase in average income of

35%. Mid Atlantic region saw a marginal increase of 30%. The South Atlantic region sky rocketed 100%. Our East South central region jumped 78%. The East North central region gained 50%. West South region shot up 95%. Our West North central gained 58% in wages. But the most prosperous was the Mountain region with a stellar 220% income increase. The next, to hold the second place, is the Pacific with a cosmic 210% increase in bacon and eggs. The nation, as a whole, enjoyed a 60% increase in income. These figures are for all trades, all lines of work from the floor sweeper to the CEO.

During this period, incomes from the Chief Executive Officer to the assembly line worker, rose more in unison with each other. Let's have a look at blue collar pay raises by trade category. The mining industry commanded a 65% salary raise from 1947 to 1967. The construction industry had a raise in pay from 1947 to 1967 of 60%. The manufacturing trades gained 28% in take home pay. Trade had a 50% rise of wages. Transportation and public utilities had the least amount of prosperity from 1947 to 1967 with a meager 5% raise.

Since the real significant period of prosperity didn't build up enough momentum until after 1950, we will further categorize the climb to the American Dream in more detail, but around the mid to late fifties. The following list of figures may become a little boring, but I feel it will be useful information to compare in later chapters. You have to build a foundation, and laying a slab is not the prettiest step in any construction's evolution. Please bear with me! The average non-supervisory weekly pay check increases

Jay T. Baldwin

from 1957-1967 in the non-agricultural U.S. private industries are as follows. The nation as a whole in 1957 earned an average $73.33 per week. By 1958 was $75.08. 1959=$78.78, 1960=$80.67, 1961=$82.60, 1962=$84.60, 1963=$88.64, 1964=$91.33, 1965=$95.06, 1966=$98.82, and 1967=$101.84. How would you like to have pay increases like that today? Only in your wildest American dreams, literally, only if you are a member of the working middle class, or the poor! In 2001, it is a whole different story, that we will go into a more detail later. By trade category it is as detailed. Durable goods production in 1957 earned $88.26 per week, per worker. In 1958 it was $89.27, 1959=$96.05, 1960=$97.44, 1961=$100.35, 1962=$104.70, 1963=$108.09, 1964=$112.19, 1965=$117.18, 1966=$122.09, 1967=$123.60. Lumber and wood products production in 1957 was $66.64, 1958=$69.09, 1959=$74.24, 1960=$73.71, a little step backwards, but in 1961 $76.83 re-gained lost ground and some. 1962=$79.20, 1963=$81.80, 1964=$85.24, 1965=$88.75, 1966=$91.80, 1967=$94.87. The furniture industry in 1957 earned $69.83 per week. By 1958=$69.95, 1960=$75.20, 1961=$76.40, 1962=$79.37, 1963=$81.80, 1964=84.46, 1965=$88.19, 1966=$91.72, and 1967=$94.13. The fabricated metal production industry earned $88.34 per week, per employee. By 1958=$89.78, 1959=$96.12, 1960=$98.42, 1961=$100.85, 1962=$104.81, 1963=$108.05, 1964=$111.76, 1965=$116.20, and finally in 1967=$123.67. The transportation production industry in 1957 earned a loyal assembly line worker in 1957 $97.51. In 1958 $100.40, and 1959 $107, 1960 $111.52, 1961=$113.40, 1962=$122.22,

1963=$126.72, 1964=$130.09, 1965=$137.71, 1966=$141.86, and last but not least $142.42 in 1967. You know what's ironic? After ten years of corporate down sizing, I was, on occasions, earning about $150 after taxes on a bad week. This was at one of my pest control companies on a commission salary, after it had been down sized, and we were taken off the hourly compensation plan. I used to earn three times that in the past! Let's get back to the subject, even though it is so tempting for me to make comments now. A food production worker in 1957 earned $75.48 per week. In 1958 $79.15, 1959=$82.82, 1960=$86.09, 1961=$88.75, 1962=$91.84, 1963=$94.30, 1964=$97.17, 1965=$99.87, 1966-$103.82, and finally $125.95 in 67. The retail stores with positions such as floor sales consultants, cashiers, stock boys, etc. paid at that time, the equivalent of a minimum wage retail position today in the department stores. In 57 it paid $59.60 per week, 1958 $61.76, 1959=$64.41, 1960=$66.01, 1961=$67.41, 1962=$69.91, 1963=$72.01, 1964=$74.28, 1965=$76.53, 1966=$79.02, and finally $82.13 in 67. Good God, you wouldn't see raises like that today in retail positions, unless the government legislated an increase in the minimum wage. Financial brokers, insurance agents, and real estate agents earned $67.53 in 57, $70.02 in 58, 1959=$72.74, 1960=$75.14, 1961=$77.12, 1962=$80.92, 1963=$84.38, 1964=$85.79, 65=$88.91, 66=$92.13, and $95.46 in 67.

Now for some weekly averages of construction trades, and how much prosperity gains they had in the decade from 57 to 67. We are almost finished with the boring part, but patience is a virtue as all of this will be the pieces of a grand puzzle. This puzzle will be the ground work for the rest of the book, and will be an excellent reference point to gauge future ideas, standards, and ultimately, where the American Dream has gone. A typical brick mason, plaster worker, or stone worker earned $100.68 per week in 1957. This climbed to $145.10 in 1967. An electrician earned $129.07 in 57. In 1967 he took home $190.42. A lumber yard worker had $66.64 in 1957, and by 67 had $94.87. In 57 a typical furniture builder or cabinet maker made $69.83, and by 67 and $94.13. Mattress and bedding makers earned $69.56 in 57, and by 67 earned $94.28. Panel and flat glass workers made $113.60 in 1957, and by 1967 had $153.72 per week in the bank. Concrete workers and pourers took home $87.48 in 57, and by 67 grossed $133.40 a week. A metal worker made $99.00 in 57, and 67 made $137.27. Hand tool and die maker/cutlery grossed $83.02 in 57 and by 1967 made $117.38. Plumbers earned $87.52 in 1957. A plumber made $113.08 in 1967. An aircraft mechanic made a whopping $103.34 in 57 and by 1967 made $143.95.. What the heck? Let's get it all out now, so we will not have to cross this bridge again. More weekly pay scales! A form equipment tech made $93.50 in 1957, then went up to $129.11. A crane and backhoe/ loader operator made almost as much as an aircraft technician at $92.90 in 57, and $135.72 in 67. Now one of the trades I am qualified for, a class A CDL truck driver was respected, with dignity, at $123.02 in 1967. I do not have info. for 57. A transmission mechanic earned almost as much as an aircraft mechanic at $95.58 in 1957, and by 1967 made $131.57. TV and radio repair techs. grossed $77.10 in 57, and by 1967 grossed 118.70. The dignified and respected auto assembly line worker earned $100.61 in 1957, then made a stellar $144.84 by 1967. The American Dream was a reality for these blue collar workers, however today, they would not get much more respect than a kid flipping burgers if it were not for the unions. Thank God for the auto workers union for saving some of their dignity. Aircraft assembly line workers earned $96.35 in 57, and by 67 made $144.84. A jeweler/watch repair made $72.34 in 57, and went up to $93.20 in 67. A butcher grossed $91.88 in 57, in 67 had $137.38. Textile and clothing workers made $68.23 in 57 and $94.78 in 67. Book bindery workers at a publisher earned $84.00 in 57, and $113.93 in 67. Local truck driver's wages were $87.29 in 57, and was glorified at $116.89 in 67. Warehouse and stock boys made $96.33 in 1957, and $134.37 in 67. The under appreciated utilities, gas workers, city workers, and sanitation workers/garbage men, were praised with $95.22 in 57, and $145.25 in 67. The taken for granted dept. store clerk made $64.29 in 1957, and made $85.20 in 67. Pharmacists took $83.37 in 57, and $119.89 in 67. A restaurant waiter pocketed $42.10+ tips in 57, and $49.77+ tips in 67. A bank teller took $88.40 a week in 67. I do not have 57. Last but not least, my wife's new profession, an elementary school teacher earned $6,850.00 a year in 1957, and went up to $10,002.00 a year in 67.

    Now that's all wrapped up, you will see why I spelled it all out. Let's see how good our parents might have had it then, compared to today. Most of these worked figures will be from the 1960s, as this is when the standard of living for the typical American with a blue collar secure job crested into the strongest, largest middle class life style the world has ever known. Let's throw a few fun things around! Do you like cars? Well I do! My dream car is a 1957 Chevy Bel Air convertible, in aqua, with white two tone. A brand new 57 Chevy Bel Air, right off the assembly line cost about $2,200, give or take $200 depending on the model and extras. Let's see how many months of some typical worker's salaries it will take to get a 57 Chevy in 1957, if this was his only expense, and all he had to pay. A non-supervisory auto production line worker with $100.61 a week, took 21.8 weeks of salary for that car. That's about 5.4 months. The modern day direct descendant is the Chevy Impala, at about $34,000 loaded. A typical assembly line worker might make $520 a week depending if the union has been successful at keeping pay scales to some respectable level. It would take 65.3 weeks of pay checks to own that same care in today's pay standards. That's 16.3 months of pay, not including interest. Even with two full time incomes, today's American family could not purchase this same car, at the cost to income buying power of the single income in 1957. The family would still be in the hole, by roughly, almost 20 weeks, almost another whole income. That's almost three full time incomes to own the same car! About $10,400 dollars still behind the 1957 family in today's purchasing power. Oops!, our minimum wage retail store clerk suddenly got the craving for a 57 Chevy, right off the assembly line. At $64.29 per week x 52 = $3343.08 per year in income for our store clerk. Now take $2200 the car's price in 1957 and divide it by the clerk's weekly pay of $64.29 which equals 34.2 weeks of salary. That's 8½ months of income to get that car. Now let's see if in today's store clerk wages, if he/she could buy the same car. The average store clerk makes minimum wage, that's about $6.25 an hour. Multiply by 40 which equals $250 a week. Now $250 x 52 weeks per year = $13000 a year, which is national income at poverty level. Divide $34,000.00 by $13,000.00 = 2.6. It will take 2 years 7½ months to buy this same car today. That's a whopping 134 weeks of income to buy an equivalent car. A far cry from the 8½ months of 1957 wages. Now do you begin to get the picture? If you are starting to get a little hot around the collar, continue to read this book! The roller coaster ride has only just begun! If you happen to be one of those greedy, loathsome, corporate plutocrats, and you feel a bit nervous, then it's obvious. **You can't handle the truth!**

    That is very scary, if a person at minimum wage in 1957, can purchase almost the same car as two full time professional trade incomes in 2001. Let's see how our working pair is doing ten years later in 1967, the pinnacle of the American Dream and middle class living standards. An auto assembly line worker in 1967 earned $144.84 per week. The Impala/Caprice Bel Air model in 1967 cost about $2,600.00, that's only $400 more than the same car in 1967. Ha!, inflation is practically negligible, and wages continued to flourish. That shoots down the idea that the conservative Republicans keep throwing around, that if wages are on the increase, then inflation must be out of control. Oh dear!, we can not give the American workers a pay raise! Inflation will send the economy spiraling out of control, and corporate profits will suffer, what ever shall we do? Oh Dear! What a bunch of lying, deceitful corporate suck ups! It's more like the boss can't give himself that 400% pay raise this year. They make me sick!!! The worker earns $144.84 per week x 52 = $7531.68 a year. Then divide $2,600.00 by $144, the weekly income in 1967 standards, which equals 18.05 weeks of income for the car. That's 4½ months of income, which is much better than his first purchase in 1957. Wages defiantly rose quicker than the inflation rate.

Let's have a little fun! Let's pretend that America had not become the world's largest plutocracy, and greed had not taken over wonderful capitalist America. Capitalism did what the founding fathers intended it to do, and capitalism had lived up to it's own inherent code of ethics!

Ok!, the current income to cost ratio remained exactly the same as that in 1967. The American middle class has seen three decades of continuous prosperity. The American society is the closest to the mythical utopia it will ever be. American families are the strongest in the world as mothers don't have to work if they don't want to, as one income has continued to keep an average family of three financially independent, and inflation, and wages rose parallel for three decades. Our auto assembly line worker currently has an hourly salary of $47.11. He makes $1884.62 per forty hour week. That's a modest blue collar wage with a yearly salary of $98,000.00. The Chevy Impala costs $34,000.00 Let's divide $34,000.00 by the worker's weekly income of $1884.61 which equals 18 weeks of income to purchase the car. That's 4½ months of salary to buy this mid range priced car. Ok!, all of you pencil neck geeks out there, cross check me, the figures speak for them selves! Well, my reader friends, take that and put it into your pipe and smoke it! Yes! all of my corporate greed meisters out there, I didn't forget about you, even in this mythical, hypothetical, America you to would be doing quit well! Your employees would be as loyal as the family Golden Retriever, and would move mountains for you. Your employee turn over would be minimal. Every body would be like family. Oh! Oh! Oh!, one small, small detail, I forgot to mention! You would probably be earning roughly $300,000.00 annually. A very generous income to live happily ever after, instead of the $5 million you make in reality, with the massive pay raises, and perks annually as part of your compensation package in 2001.

    Back to reality! The typical rent for an apartment in 1967 was about $110 a month, that's a middle sized apt. about a two bedroom one bath. Let's keep our original two friends, the auto assembly line worker and the retail store clerk, since this represents the income extremes from high and low. Our assembly line worker gets paid $144.84 per week. He paid for his rent in 30.47 hours of work. That's 3 days and 7 hours worth of work. Let's see how today's worker makes out with today's income to expense ratio. Our worker makes $13.00 an hour, providing the unions have done their job, and have kept his income at a respectable level. That's $104 per day, $520 a week, $27,040.00 per year. The average Two bedroom one bath apartment in South Florida is about $800 a month, give or take $100. I know because, I live here and have been bounced around by rising rents, for the last ten years. Soon, my family and I will have to have three full time incomes just to keep pace with rising rents. I thought, by listening to the radios, watching the news, and reading literature that there is no inflation. I guess somebody forgot to tell these folks down here, or these are reports from some other planet! It takes our guy 63 hours 24 minutes, or 7.69 days to pay for his rent. That comes to 1 week 7 hours and 24 minutes if you want to be like Spock on Star Trek. That's just about double the amount of hours worth of work to pay for his rent, compared to his counter part in 1967. So today in 2001, even with two full time incomes, a typical American married or co-habitating couple would be three hours in deficit, and could not live in the same apt. as their equals with one income in 1967 did. I am beginning to notice a pattern here. It seems that since women hung up the apron, gave up being a house wife, and started hitting the job market, corporate America took that as their opportunity to lower workers pay to ½ of there usual amount. Maybe, they are exploiting women and not paying them as much as men. Hey!, my pay has decreased by almost ½ since the late 1980s. I used to earn almost $30,000 a year in 1989, and by 1998 I was down to $16,000 a year, almost half. The same has happened across most of the South Florida's job market in a ten year span of time. Jobs that paid $19 an hour are now down to $10 an hour. Jobs that used to pay $12 an hour are now paying $7 an hour, and on and on. Or they figured since John Doe is earning $20,000 a year, and was doing just fine, suddenly his wife Jane Doe decided to come to work also to earn $20,000, so they could live much better with $40,000 a year, so now they would pay John

$10,000 and Jane $10,000, and pocket the rest for themselves. Corporate America wouldn't feel the least bit guilty, because John & Jane Doe just got by on $20,000 a year before. Get two for the price of one! Oh!!, what a bargain! Secret! Secret, just maybe I stumbled on to one of their little secrets, the American people aren't supposed to know about. You corporate big shots think you can fool all of the people. Better think again!

    Well let's get back to our store clerk, and find out how much of her income is needed in 1967 to rent the same apt. She earns $85.20 per week multiplied 4 = $340.80 per month. Multiple $85.20 by 52 = $4430.40 per year. Rent for the apartment is $110 a month. At $2.13 per hour she needs 51 ½ hours to pay her rent. That's 6 days 3½ hours, or one week, one day and 3½hours of work to pay her rent. Even at minimum wage in 1967, the amount of income needed to comfortably pay the rent is about adequate, a 24% of an employee's pay. That's government statistics for home ownership. Now let's see how today's store clerk fares. Her pay is $6.25 per hour. $6.25 x 40 equals her weekly income of $250.00 multiplied by 52 = $13,000.00 Federal poverty level. The average apartment is $800 a month, give or take $100. At $50 a day income, she needs 16 days, that's 2 weeks and two days, or 96 hours just to pay the rent. That is not 24% of her monthly income. After taxes, she just might have enough to buy one week's of groceries. She would starve to death. She also wouldn't have enough to own a car. Corporate America expects all employees to own a car. It's one of the questions on their employment applications, or asked in the interview.

Jay T. Baldwin

Guess what happens if you do not have a car, or can not afford one? You do not get the job! If you tell the boss, you do not have the money to own one because you need it for the rent and a little food, he most certainly will say; "That's not my problem!" I guess they think money grows on the trees in each employees back yard, or they can get blood out of a rock. If you are working for a boss, that cuts your pay to sub standard wages, which is totally not your fault, and you loose your car, he will say it's not his problem. That's the same as a thief, you asked how am I to get home without money, saying it's not his problem since he stole your wallet. The old blame the victim ploy, a conservative favorite!

Let's take our hypothetical, fantasy ride, which should be reality, if greed had not gotten in the way, and the United States had not become the world's largest plutocracy. Our store clerk, if the income to purchasing ratio had stayed the same as it was back in 1967, would be earning a very modest $16.66 per hour as minimum wage. That is a skimpy $666.70 per week without overtime, or $34,668.40 per year at a minimum wage. So a kid flipping burgers, at minimum wage, in a fast food restaurant, would earn $34,668.40 per year. Hey kids!, eat your heart out! Welcome to your new inheritance! You could really have a hell of a party, Friday nights, with a $666.70 a week pay check. Maybe, you could go down to the nearest Chevrolet dealer, and drive out with a brand, spanking, new Impala. That's only a car payment of $566.66 per month. Do not worry, remember you earn $16.66 per hour, or $666.70. per week! Per month, only 4.2 days of work for that "way cool" ride! Pissed off to the max? That's what you're being cheated out of because of insatiable corporate greed, and a government that only looks out for the interests of the rich guy!! Want to join me on a "way cool" revolution to snatch back your share of the American Dream, from the totally "not cool" plutocrats?

Now, to appeal to those young adults who are considering a home purchase. To own a home is one of America's finest qualities. It is the American Dream expressed through wood, bricks, mortar and glass. John Cougar Mellencamp had a song, "Little pink houses for you and me!" In 1967, the average single family home would run you about $15,016.00. I guess you want to know how much this house would cost our little friends in 1967! Well, our assembly line worker is making $7,531.68 per year, or $144.84 per week. That is $28.96 per day, or $3.62 per hour. He will have to work a total of 518½ days to own the house. That's 1 year, 5 months and 13½ days of income to own the house. Today, in 2001, the house would cost $180,000.00. Our worker at $13.00 an hour, $104.00 a day, $520.00 a week, and $27,040.00 per year, can own the house with a whopping 1,731 days of work. That's 4 years, 9 months and 19 days of wages to purchase the same home. Even if his wife, if he is still married, got a job at the same pay scale, they would be almost two full time incomes in deficit. With both of them working full time jobs, it would take 865½ days to buy the same house as one income in 518½ days in 1967. Even if the dog gets a job at the same pay, it would still take 577 days for all three of them to buy the same house as one income in 1967. Believe it or not, they are still 59 days in deficit! Technically speaking in 2001 earnings, if greed had not taken over, the U.S. had not become a plutocracy, and the house's price remained in proportion with the income to purchase ratio of 1967, it would now cost $36,360.00 in 2001. In reality 2001, the same house costs $180,000.00. Suck on that for awhile my American readers! Now you can see for your selves, why more young Americans are being turned down by mortgage lenders because of insufficient income. My wife and I with two full time incomes, an Exterminator's income, and an Elementary school teacher's income, only qualify for an $85,000.00 home. You know what kind of neighborhood we have to choose from? We will have to settle for a fixer-upper in the ghettos of Miami's, Liberty City. The American Dream is now out of our reach. As little as ten years ago, we could have easily purchased a three/two in a good neighborhood, at $79,000.00. The average prices of homes in South Florida are increasing $2,000.00 to $3,000.00 per month, and shows no signs of slowing. The mortgage lenders said each of us would have to literally double our income, to qualify for a home in a semi-decent neighborhood. That means I would have to take my current income of $18,000.00 per year and multiply it by 2 = $36,000.00 per year. My wife would have to take her $31,000.00 per year income, and multiply it by 2 = $62,000.00. Stunning!

Now for our 1967 retail store clerk, who earns $17.04 per day, $85.20 per week, or $443.40 per year. She will have to work 881 days to own the same house at minimum wage in 1967. The house is $15,016.00 divided by her daily earnings. Then we divide 881 by 365 = the total day count for a year. That's 2 years, 5 months and 11 days worth of earnings to own the same house. Today in 2001, our store clerk at $6.25 per hour, $50.00 a day, $250.00 a week, and $13,000.00 annually, could own the same house with 3,600 days of wages. That is a whopping, mind boggling 9 years, 11 months, and 7 days!

Today, my wife, and I would have to have a combined yearly income of $98,000.00. to buy the same house my wife's sister, and her husband bought in the early 1980s, for about $79,000.00. Her house has recently been appraised at $185,000.00. Soon, only millionaires will be capable of buying even the smallest home in a typical middleclass neighborhood. Here is a bone for you to chew on. If South Florida property values continue as they have for the past fifteen years, my in-laws house, and property will cost a dizzying $545,000.00 in ten years. With both of our combined incomes of $188.40 per day, if our income does not increase or decrease by 2011, it will take 2892.7 days to purchase her home. Ironically, my pay at the pest control company known for it's once a year visits, was reduced $2.00 an hour in December 1999. I went from $11.00 an hour, to $9.00, a month after I started with that company. That was our Christmas present from corporate America! My wife's pay went up $2.00 an hour after her first year of teaching. They told me they are not finished restructuring at my job, and we will see more pay cuts, to increase corporate profits in the future. They only have $2.75 left to cut before they reach minimum wage of $6.25. Hopefully we can get the minimum wage raised again, if we can keep the pressure on the government. In two more years, my wife will get about another $2.00 an hour raise. That is how I figured our income will stay about the same. So we will pay the over-inflated home in 2011 in 7 years, 11 months, and 1 days worth of combined income. To keep things simple, no tax or interest will be added, therefore, our monthly mortgage payment, if it was our only expense that we worked for, no living expenses, would be $1,513.80 without interest and taxes. With them, the payment would be roughly $2,500.00 a month, give or take $300. Still think you can swing a home purchase. Soon, we will all be living in cardboard boxes under a bridge!

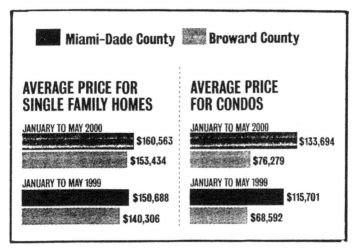

Illustration 1

"Fading dreams and lost memories" The average single family home cost has skyrocketed beyond imaginable limits, and beyond the typical working family's budget. Little by little the American Dream is being diverted to a wealthy privileged few, leaving the majority to settle for rentals, or to contemplate sharing a single family home purchase with other family members or friends and their families. Not a lick of difference between that of a third world country.

    The American way, once unique to America, is now adapting for the worse. Is this the price we all must pay for un-forgiving corporate and political greed?

    After reading this far, you probably feel all prosperity is gone now days. Greed is now the rule, not the exception. But, I will share an exception with you. All of you readers, who happen to be of the upper class, and have gained your infinite wealth through methods destructive to your employees, consumers, and American society, please read the next few pages carefully. You definitely have a lot to learn about sharing the fruits of your labor.

    I was thumbing through The Herald Miami's largest news paper, and found this little article. I thought, maybe, I was seeing things, and had to do a double take. The article by Sharon Cohen "Employees get millions when boss shares profits" printed on Sunday, September 12, 1999. A Bob Thompson owned a road construction firm called Thompson-McCully Co. He started his business with his school teacher wife, and $3,500.00 in the basement of a very humble house he has owned for 37 years. Forty years later, he has a profitable multi-million dollar firm. The firm employs some 550 workers. He sold the entire company for $422 million to a firm based in Dublin Ireland. He broke the good news that nobody would loose their jobs. Then he dropped the bomb shell, everybody will share in the $422 million. The article quoted "The big hearted boss divided $128 million among his 550 workers. And for more than 80 people he had a bonus beyond belief: They would become millionaires." Rusty Stafford one of the companies area managers opened an envelope from Mr. Thompson at his home. His wife Tammy commented, teary eyed, "Russ, I think the commas are in the wrong place," Russ recalls; "I looked at it, and kept looking, and thought the next thing I knew, Ed McMahon would be knocking at the door." Mr. Thompson had commented that people make millions in the stock market, then quoted; "but we're dependent on people, so it would just not be fair not to do it. They've allowed me to live the way I want to live." Mr. Thompson worked out a plan with his senior staff to distribute the proceeds. His hourly workers received $2,000 for each year of service. Some of the gift checks exceeded their annual salaries. Salaried workers, who were not given pensions, got annuity certificates they can cash in when they reach 55 or 62. These were $1 million to $2 million each. Then with a final heart felt gesture, Mr. Thompson paid all of the taxes on the gifts for the employees. Some of his workers, who tried to talk to him, became emotional, breaking down in tears, so Bob insisted they just drop him a note. A worker's wife wrote a response letter on behalf of her husband and quoted; "It is the stuff fairy tales are made of," "What do I say to you for changing our lives and handing us a future that we have never dreamed of?" An area manager, 48 year old Cheryl Lynn Angel Said; "Please know you have always been a success story to me," "I have watched and admired you. You will never be forgotten. There will not ever be a day that I don't thank God for you." "I don't think anyone's invented what I feel, a sense of serenity for the future."

Now this is an exception in a world of heartless greed mongers only looking out for numero uno! This is a sign that not all is lost. It's corporate heroes like Mr. Thompson, that had the American spirit to share there wealth resulting in the glory days of the fifties, and the sixties. They just did it more subtly by paying more to their employees on an hourly basis, and less to themselves. It was also not the fabulous press story as it is today, because now days it is almost unheard of, and not the kosher thing to do in the eyes of corporate America. There are a few corporate capitalists out there, that have the well-being of the country, and mankind in heart. These few deserve to be glorified higher than any petty movie star or sports hero. They should unite amongst themselves, and create a movement to reverse destructive corporate greed, and the plutocratization of America.

My challenge to you, my fellow readers, is to do a little home work your selves. Ask your parents or grand parents, right now, how much they were paid in the 1950s through 1960s. If you think this whole book, up to now, is nothing but pure rhetoric, you have been effectively socially conditioned by society. We will cover social conditioning in much more detail in later chapters. I dare you, I challenge you to do a little research your selves. You will see the truth!

AMERICAN ATTITUDES AND THE AMERICAN DREAM

Jay T. Baldwin

1995 Survey of Parents

(1) Do you expect your children will have a better life than you have had, a worse life, or a life about as good as yours?	Better life .... 46% Worse life .... 20% About as good .... 27% No children .... 6% Not sure 1%
(2) For most Americans, do you think the American dream of equal opportunity, personal freedom, and social mobility has become easier or harder to achieve in the past 10 years?	Easier to achieve ... 31% Harder to achieve .. 67% Not sure 2%
(3) And do you think this American dream will be easier or harder to achieve in the next 10 years?	Easier to achieve ... 22% Harder to achieve .. 74% Not sure 4%

Illustration 2

"The loss of the American Dream is now being accepted as the norm." This survey from The State of Americans is undeniable proof that the ideological social conditioning campaign by the power elites is very successful indeed. All of these proud

Americans identify this problem. Ironically, a scant few bother to even challenge the plutocratic system, much less attempt to become civically involved to attempt to change it. They accept it as the inevitable like some natural phenomenon totally out of their control.

Jay T. Baldwin

Chapter 2 Largest economic boom in history. Bourgeoisie only!

DEMISE OF THE MIDDLECLASS

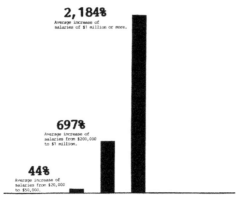

Illustration 3

Demise of the Middleclass as we once knew it! The Internal Revenue Service figures and the results of corporate deregulation in the decade of the 1980s. Ironically, this has resulted in a 2,184% increase in the salaries of the overclass, the largest increase of the richest incomes in recorded history. However, the middleclass has had only a 44% increase in the same period of time. If a family earning $13,000 a year at poverty level, had the same increase in their income as the rich, they would have had an unbelievable $283,920 annual income! Poverty would no longer exist! This is the beginning of the end of our middleclass culture. Is a class war inevitable????

The first economic boom in American history, to really make a mark on society, was the Post Civil War boom in the 1790s. Then, we had a second such economic bliss period known as the Guilded age. This was around the years of the 1880s. Then everybody knows about the Roaring Twenties. Marked by elite clubs, champagne nights, beautifully dressed fragrant wives to the first American bourgeoisie. The Post World War II period would be the first time capitalism, would be truly successful. The first three economic haydays were very exclusive indeed. They catered to the richest segments of society. This stirred up political visionaries such as Karl Marx to begin a campaign of bashing capitalism. In their minds, capitalism would be only for the elites. It seemed capitalism was designed to be very exploitative for the masses, because of a severe disparity in incomes. This brought back visions of Kings, and castles where there was a favored few, whom benefited off the sweat, and toil of a proletariat or serf class. Greed seemed to be the ruling factor. But the 1950s through the 1960s, would put this theory to rest, supposedly forever, and shame Karl Marx, his comrades, and communism forever. During this period, we did watch the rise of the strongest middleclass, and the smallest number of poor in the history of the world. Income differences were at their lowest. The rich made between ten and twenty times the lowest paid workers. A typical single family home would fetch about $15,000.00, give or take a couple of thousand. Yet, a mansion would not be that much more at about $30,000.00 and up. A typical family car would run $2,300.00, and a Cadillac Fleetwood of the rich, would run a whole two times the cost of the average family car. The lives of Americans would become the envy of the world. America would be changed forever. Hey you stupid facist commies, eat your hearts out!

Then came the 1980s, yes those 1980s! Laissez-Faire capitalism at it's greediest, most efficient best. The 1980s launched the fifth time in history the United States would experience an economic boom period. However, something happened, that would slowly, and methodically unravel the masterpiece of American capitalism for the common man, the average American. Like a giant Condor the economy soared, soared, and continues to rise on some invisible thermal to this day, eclipsing all of the previous prosperous periods, both in time span, and capital gains of those already with capital. Wednesday, December 1, 1999 in the Sun Sentinel page 31A, Frank Rich (not joking with the Rich part of his name) of the New York Times wrote an article "Who doesn't want to be rich?" hitting the nail right on the head. "When historians look back at America as it rang in the momentous year of 2000, what will they find? An outbreak of millennial spirituality? "Prosperity with a purpose"? Guess again. What they are going to see instead is a country drunk on a TV quiz show called Who Wants to Be a Millionaire?" It seems we have suddenly gotten a craving for all of these shows glorifying endless wealth dreams are made of. "All the stuff our parents told us didn't come true." quoted NBC executive Rosalyn Weinman. All of the shows like Inside Edition, Sixty Minutes, 20/20, and Hard Copy etc. seem to gravitate around famous stars, sports heroes, or the lives of rich corporate icons. These shows used to do stories mainly on events that effected the average American, from politics, economics to the heroic deed done by an average citizen. Now, they cover most things that have no bearing on our lives what so ever, and the average American shouldn't be the least bit interested in. Yet, we seem almost in a brain washed stupor cheering, and screaming at something that has no effect on our lives, and has as much of a chance of happening to us as an alien encounter, with a bonus ride in a flying saucer. Most popular magazines seem to cater to the elite few, with articles, and advertisements of expensive vacations to exotic lands, luxurious homes on the water, gorgeous sleek boats, fancy big automobiles, diamond clad watches, and stock brokerage firms requesting a $ million minimum for first time investors. You would think, if you were an alien visitor from another planet, by all of the hype about mass riches, and wealth that this country, and every single member of it's population were rolling in dough. That we wipe our _ _ es with hundred dollar bills, and flushed them down the toilet. We role our cigarettes with fifties, and each citizen has a cool $ million stashed away in the mattress. Frank Rich quotes; "If this country is so rich, why are so many coveting prosperity they already have? The answer is that most people don't have it, and the gap between the haves and the have-nots—-and the haves and the middle class—-is growing. While nearly half the country invests in stocks, 90 percent of the shares are held by the wealthiest 10 percent of the households according to studies cited by The Wall Street journal; meanwhile, stock options have pushed the ratio of executive pay to factory worker pay from 42 to 1 in 1980 to 419 to 1 in 1998." As you have learned in Delight Of The Overclass Demise Of The Middleclass somebody has to pay for this mass flood of wealth to the elite few. It has been proven that as wealth increases, in the hands of the elite minority, faster than it is generated by larger amounts of actual dollars in circulation, it has to be taken from the masses by cheaper products built, cheaper services, more scandals, more corruption, more corporate extortion, more mergers, more pay, and benefit cuts, longer hours, harder work for employees, and ultimately more plutocratization. Why the Sam h _ _ l isn't there mass civil disobedience? Why aren't we swamping talk shows with outrage? Is there an end of outrage in this country? Have we forgotten how to protest, or are we to scared to show our real feelings? Has social conditioning been that successful?

James Lardner in his article "The Rich Get Richer" page 39 U.S. News & World Report February 2, 2000, takes a wide angle more conservative view of today's bullish economy. President Clinton's Council Of Economic Advisors reported income increases for t hose in the bottom 20 percent from 1993 to 1998. The poorest fifth have prospered more than the richest fifth, and the gap between the rich and poor has narrowed since 1970. If this is actually true, why have I been taking pay cuts at record levels, even under the Clinton era? I would take this report from the Clinton Administration with a grain of salt. I will tell you why!!! Hey, maybe, the liberals want to look good on there way out, like they have something to take credit for, other than, corruption, scandals and Bill Clinton's insatiable sex drive! Conservatives, don't get your hopes up, I am by no means getting cozy with you either!!!

    Being on a pest control rout exposes me to all types of people, and all economic categories of income levels, but mostly, all different types of careers. Over the last 14 years of service in this field, I have also become sort of a make shift psychiatrist to my monthly customers. While I efficiently eradicate their homes of ants, roaches, fleas, rats, mice, and any other form of vermin that dares to show it's self while I am on the case, I also become the friend to spill the hardships of life on. I sort of become their Atlas, to take the weight of the world off of their shoulders for a few minutes. That trusty person who is all ears, and a smile to give a sense of security in a dog eat dog world. I learned the skill of inconspicuously interviewing them while I seem to be totally engrossed in the task of insect elimination. I would use opportunities, offered by a variety of sources, such as a news broadcasts on their TVs, or a comment about a good or service they have had. Then as they open up about their lives, I would take control of the conversation, asking them about their economic, political views, and job experiences. What they think about the latest current events. By the time I am finished ridding their home of all pests, I have a completed non-intrusive interview. Yes, I did get the service done accurately, and safely! In fact I still gave a far superior customer service, than most companies. No more bugs! I can promise you out of the thousands of Americans I have services over the last 14 years, 50 percent have suffered severe income, and compensation cuts at the hands of corporate America under both conservative, and liberal administrations. Out of the remaining 50 percent, 30 percent claim that their incomes have not increased at all in ten to fifteen years. Ten of the remaining twenty percent claim to have had fairly good increases. Of the last ten percent, the upper fifth have savored exorbitant income, and perk increases over the last ten to fifteen years. That last fifth, the top five percent, have literally been blessed with mind boggling income increases, and would not have it any other way. These select wealthiest few, on my rout, reside in the elite enclaves of Weston, or along the intercoastal waterways, the Isles of Las Olas Blvd. to the beach front in Ft. Lauderdale. Some have boasted such massive increases of incomes from their profitable corporations, or stock portfolio gains, that they are purchasing even larger homes, multiple homes, and homes overseas, with more expensive cars, and boats. Then expect a Christmas present from them! You would have a better chance of winning the lottery! Yes, I have even interviewed them, finding out how much they pay their employees, how often they get raises, and how they view employee rights. It takes a skillful hand with these elites. I have to pretend to be contemplating a career change, with interests in going to work for them to get the information I need, in the least intrusive, and non-intimidating manner as possible. After a few of these interviews, I have no problem seeing why the decline of the middleclass is under full swing. I am more inclined to believe actual interviews I have done, than those Poles of the Federal government. Yet, if you disagree with me please feel free to do your own polling, if you are in a position that exposes you to the public. You will discover the real truth!!! I wasn't lying!

Mr. Lardner quotes; "Americans first became worried about a class divide in the late 19th century, when the so-called robber barons amassed huge fortunes while immigrants toiled in sweat shops. But from the 1940's into the early '70s, incomes rose rapidly for Americans up and down the economic ladder-most rapidly, in fact, for those nearer the bottom. Then something happened, something economists are at a loss to explain. In 1979, average family income in the top 5 percent of the earning distribution was more than 10 times that in the bottom 20 percent. A decade later, the ratio had increased to nearly 16 to 1; by 1999, it stood at 19 to 1. That's the biggest gap since the Census Bureau began keeping track, in 1947. It's also the highest of the advanced industrial nations today. When it comes to concentration of wealth, too, the United States is generally believed to occupy the No. 1 spot, with 1 percent of the population holding roughly 40 percent of the nation's household wealth (up from about 19 percent in 1976)." "The best economy in 30 years ought to have lessened inequality."

The sociologists and economists claim they are at a loss to explain the sudden increase in income inequality. **Give me a break!!!** How lame can they be? Com on, it's as obvious as the noses on there ugly little primate faces! Pure, Grade A, un-processed raw unadulterated **GREED!** Nothing more, nothing less!

It seems that most economic reports still suggest that this booming economy has helped every body quit considerably. Here is some more supposed proof, based on supposed statistics, that incomes of all brackets are skyrocketing. In this Census report for October, 1999 the booming economy continues to generate more wealth for more Americans. The median household income rose in 1999 3.5 percent adjusted for inflation, the sharpest rise in three years. At $38,885.00, it's at an all time high. The Census bureau also reported that families living under poverty dropped 12.7 percent in 1998 from 13.3 percent in 1997 the lowest it has been since 1979. An article "Charting the Pain Behind the Gain", by the Wall Street Journal staff reporters Jacob M. Schlesinger, Tristan Mabry, and Sarah Lueck, In The Wall Street Journal Friday, October 1, 1999 quoted; "Gains were surprisingly widespread. Virtually every type of household-those headed by couples, by single mothers, old, young, immigrants, city dwellers, suburbanites-saw big gains. For the first time since 1975, every region of the country saw significant increases in income. Poverty in the South, long considered the country's economic backwater, plunged and is at a lower rate than in the West."

Hey, I live in the South, I think South Florida is in the South? Then why am I, and Millions of other blue collar Floridians, still receiving pay cuts at a record pace in 1999 and 2000?? **Hello! Is it our imagination, or did somebody forget to tell these jerks down here to follow the statistics.** It does seem that the information being thrown around is quite contradictory. Is somebody trying to hide something?? In the same paragraph it quotes; "Now the reality check. The Census study, one of the government's best annual snapshots of economic well-being, also offers stark proof that life is still a struggle for millions of Americans. All the fanfare about this record-breaking expansion-with tales of college dropouts turned IPO millionaires-masks statistics showing that overall, wages have barely budged for the decade as a whole. Last year's poverty rate was still 1.6 percentage points higher than it was in 1973, the twilight of America's last prolonged golden age." "The pretax median income in 1998-the dividing point between those households in the top half of the pay heap and those in the bottom half-was just $1,001 higher than it was in 1989. That translates into an average annual raise for the 1990s, adjusted for inflation, of $111.22, or a stingy 0.3%." "Second, the official statistics say that the fruits of prosperity in this decade have been even more heavily skewed toward the rich than in prior booms. The top 5% of households last year-those making $132,199 or more-had 21.4% of all income, well above the 17.5% earned by the top 5% in 1967. Income inequality rose sharply through the 1980s and early '90s, and the level has held roughly constant since 1994. That means the disparity has locked in at a historically high level." Rose Woolery, in Boston, a single mother quoted; "This country is still for those who have money." "For the people that don't have it, you're not going to get it." The Census Report seems to blur the real truth about rising living standards. It fails to mention the increase in work hours, responsibilities, and fatigue, families need to even see the smallest gains. Family work hours went up by 2% from 1989 to 1998. That's a shocking 3,149 hours per year now!!

    With feuding information like that, it's a wonder anybody believes anything these days! Who are we to believe? I am more likely to believe my own personal statistics gained by actual contact with the subjects. You know the old saying' "Get it right from the horses mouth." That is the best gauge to answer your questions. Here is another tidbit, I am more inclined to believe because of my own experiences. In the local employment news paper, the Employment Digest, Andy Golan does an article on the front page; "Wage differences growing among working class" "Despite what is popularly considered a robust economy, the salary gap is growing between the working class and the wealthy here in South Florida and across the nation." "Believe me, the average family is struggling to stay afloat. It does not have the income that it had five or six years ago. It has to dip into savings to meet monthly expenses," says Tony Russo a commercial banking and residential mortgage executive." "During the past 30 years, according to the federal agency, the national income of households in the bottom 20 percent of earners has risen less than one percent, while the average income of the top twenty percent has risen 44 percent. Perhaps more significantly, the nation's average hourly wages after accounting for inflation are $1.20 below their peak of $8.50 in 1973, according to the bipartisan federal advisory group created by Congress. Real median family income is lower now versus 20 years ago," says Jim Bills, an economist with the bank of Detroit." "Today, 32 percent of American working men aged 25 to 34 don't earn enough to lift a four person family out of poverty, according to studies cited by the National Center for Fathering." "Most Americans don't have it so good. They have jobs, but most wages and benefits are stuck or continue to drop." Says U.S. Secretary of Labor under the Clinton administration. "Wealth has exploded at the top, but the wages of people in the bottom half are lower today in terms of purchasing power than they were in 1989....."

How can something happen like this, in the richest country in the world, then on top of it all, in the most prosperous corporate economy in all history? You would think, if the United States government had detected such a grand scale national dilemma effecting at least half of the American population with the ferocity, and social destruction of an enemy invasion, evasive action would have been taken. Mind boggling! Freakin unbelievable, people don't seem to realize this assault on the livelihood of half of an entire nation's population will have the same exact impact as our country enduring a complete collapse of government resulting in a coup d'e'tat from some radical oppressive sect! Or imagine one hundred twenty five million of the two hundred fifty million people robbed at gun-point of $2,496.00. And the freakin government is basically sitting their with it finger up it's a _ _! I would hate to see, what would really happen, if a real enemy invasion of the main land did occur. The government should be on DEFCON 5 alert, implementing whatever was necessary to return the economy to it's rightful place. It should be headline news, on every TV station. It should have the same coverage as the bombing of Pearl Harbor.

Here is another tool the corporate overclass is using to it's advantage to create a bourgeoisie exclusive economy. Taxes! Yes I said taxes! In the 1950s and 1960s corporations had to pay their fare share of taxes. However, all of that changed under Ronald Reagan. Not only did Reagan's deregulation of corporate America result in the lifting of labor laws, environmental protection laws, consumer protection laws and protectioninst trade laws, but loop holes and tax breaks galore for the corporate scene. Some of the most powerful corporations pay practically ZERO, ZIPP, NADA, ZILCH, in taxes. This gives even more profits for the CEO, and his head cronies to laugh al the way to the bank with. In August of 1999, Congress completed another bill, giving billions and billions in more tax breaks, and incentives to corporate America, and the elites, resulting in businesses paying little or no federal tax. The income tax rate for American corporations is 35%. But it seems corporations have created endless legal ways to report less taxable income, while at the same time, quadrupling it's actual income. They utilize tax havens, and shelters so intricate, and complex that even the government's best

REVOLT AGAINST THE PLUTOCRACY

can not decipher them. And guess what? The corporations are still not happy with the potpourri of tax breaks given to them by Congress, so they dispatch more platoons of lobbyists to beg for more. It seems they will never be satisfied, give them an inch and they will take a mile. Who do you think pays for this? You and I!! That's who! They can make $ 1 million look like $ 1 on paper. That's like the equation $2 + 2 = 1$. It also reminds me of that odd form of talking in Georg Orwell's book 1984, known as "Newspeak", a form of contradictory speaking. Good means bad, white means black, etc. You can thank the Republicans for that!!!

Michael M. Phillips, Wednesday, August 4, 1999 in his article on the cover sheet "Taking Shelter" shares some eye opening information; "Out of 2.3 million U.S. corporations, more than half paid no federal income tax at all between 1989 and 1995, according to a General Accounting Office study using the most recent IRS data available. Many of these were mom-and-pop operations. But four of every 10 companies with more than $250 million in assets or $50 million in gross receipts paid less than $100,000 to Uncle Sam in 1995." At a time when corporations are reaping record profits, they are crying poor mouth to the IRS, claiming they are not making any money. Oh dear, I am a poor little, giant corporation, but I am not profitable, employee expenses, operating costs, competition and taxes are sinking the company. Oh dear God! What shall we ever do??? A bunch of lying, deceitful, crocodile tear crying con artists. Maybe they should give the CEO, and his overpaid stooges a fat pay cut if they think that business is going so bad! If a corporation is suffering from a money leak, then that is probably where it is, not the taxes, or employment expenses!

Illustration 4

"Sucking the life out of America." Like aphids, corporate greed is draining the very spirit out of America along with a prosperous American heritage.

Companies seem to be very hush-hush when it comes to reporting tax returns to the public. But, boy they are rare, and ready to flap their jaws about their annual reports to the shareholders, and how much taxes they must pay to Uncle Sam immediately, or else! I have a sneaking suspicion they do this so, they do not have to pay the shareholders as much in dividends, and they can pocket the rest for even more pay raises to the

REVOLT AGAINST THE PLUTOCRACY

greed meisters at the top. I can almost guarantee it! Also in this article; "Then there's the difference between the amount the company reported to it's shareholders, whom it wants to impress with high profits, and the amount the company reported to the IRS, which it hopes to keep at bay." Man, have the shareholders had the wool pulled over their eyes!

Mr. Phillips also quotes; "Congress has intentionally created ways for companies to put off tax payments and to collect tax credits that reduces future IRS bills. The tax code also lets companies take deductions for using up their equipment faster than it actually ages, a practice called accelerated depreciation." So let me get this straight, if a company can tell the IRS that it's equipment has fallen apart before it's time **they get a tax break!** Now we have opened up Pandora's box, **Oh boy!** Maybe if a company is looking for a few more tax breaks to fatten the wallet of the CEO, they might have a bribed individual sneak into the office, or plant after hours with a sledge hammer, and do a little repair work on the equipment. Or just possibly, a Molatov cocktail accidentally thrown through a nearby window to help speed things up a bit. It should be accelerated destruction instead. Oh yeah! Wait a darn minute! Now it is all coming together. How stupid could I have been? If you read my first book "Delight of The Overclass", "Demise of The Middleclass", you will remember I made a big stink about repair work never being done on the various types of equipment, I was operating at the various places I have worked. A quick brush up! I used to drive large eighteen wheeler semi-trucks with flat beds, and I used to haul prefabricated concrete structures over Florida. The supervisor told us how important it was to report any piece of equipment needing repairs. As drivers, we're responsible for the safety of our trucks and their loads, and if something happened, we would take the heat from the Dept. of Transportation, not the company. However, all of the drivers would report faulty equipment, but we were given every excuse under the sun as to why nothing was ever fixed. Ironically, we were ordered to continue to operate it in the unsafe condition. If we continued to fuss about it, we would be disciplined, or even fired. In several instances, drivers had incidents because of the neglected equipment, guess what?, they were fired. The company did this to show authorities it was taking action, and the driver was ultimately to blame for never reporting it to supervisors. At one of the pest control corporations, I worked at with a name that sounds a lot like porkin, the little pig, after they reorganized the company to increase profits and stock values, they became very adamant against repairing equipment. I am sorry, I have a bad memory, and can not remember the name exactly! Ironically, at the same time, we were all given a pay, and benefit cut. I had reported everything from leaky spray equipment to bad brakes, bald tires, to burned out headlights, and turn signal bulbs. Again, we were all ordered to use it the way it was, because corporate headquarters had not authorized repair work. We were also advised by our supervisors, if it is a minor repair, such as a burned out head lamp in the trucks, or a gasket, or any other small parts in the spray equipment, to repair it ourselves. Use your resourcefulness, or hit the bricks, as we were ordered. We were expected to eat the repair costs, as corporate headquarters no longer refunded employees through petty cash. It was our contribution to the corporate goals of becoming a billion dollar corporation by 2000. If you only knew what kind of service the customers were getting! A lot of excellent professional service with a new low cost insecticide, known as H20, one part hydrogen, two parts oxygen. They gave us an allotted chemical ration, for the whole week, and told us to cut the prescribed dosages into fourths. Basically to water it out. "Corporate headquarters in Atlanta said, "you guys are using to much chemical." The bugs were having a field day! Company wide, the customer complaint calls skyrocketed, and the service technicians, myself included, were ultimately blamed for not doing a thorough job. To rub salt into the wounds, we were expected to increase our service call loads by spending less time in the customer's homes. I was ultimately fired for uncovering a pay scam. I was not compensated, as I had been in the past, for home security system cross marketing leads for the branch company. I had teamed up with a couple of other employees to blow the whistle, but we were all terminated before we could make anything of it. I reported them to a variety of regulatory agencies, but I had under estimated the power of corporate big money. All investigations, to spite mass violations, were ended abruptly, with every excuse from lost documents, sudden lapses of memory, to superiors in Washington ordering a cease on all further investigations. Six years later, I was talking to somebody, who used to work with the government, claiming that a branch of the pest control responsible for security systems had a contract with the Government. I never did get the $600 or so owed me for the unpaid lead bonuses, because the Dept. Of Labor suddenly got cold feet with my case. What a kick in the teeth!

There seems to be a duel tax code, one for the normal everyday individuals, offering very little flexibility or mercy, and another offered to corporate American packed full of, flexibility, rewards, pardons, write offs, perks, and favors. Could you imagine having the same tax laws as corporations, the middle class, and the working poor would be a hell of a lot more prosperous. It sure seems, that our supposedly arch enemies, the federal government, and corporate America, whom fight like cats, and dogs by day, at night are cozy bed fellows. The fox has basically been given all rights to walk away with the hen house. The chicken run!! The tax situation, and some of these other deregulatory motions, so generously offered by government, are just the tips of the iceberg. That doesn't include the multiple experiences, more to come in later chapters, I have had with them.

Sue Reisinger's article "Brokaw: Prosperity dulls our quest for social change" pg. 1B in The Herald April 9, 1999 has this to say; "Since the mid-1970s, the top 1 percent of households has doubled its share of the national wealth to 40 percent; the top 5 percent have more than 60 percent of the wealth. The top 1 percent of households has more wealth than the entire bottom 95 percent combined." The article goes on to mention Tom Brokaw NBC news anchor quoting; "Yes, I'm concerned primarily about those at the very bottom,"

REVOLT AGAINST THE PLUTOCRACY

Tom Brokaw, in his weekly special "Fleecing of America" has done some wonderful work, uncovering some of corporate America's crimes against society in the past. However, he has toned down a little, reserving most of his attention on wasteful government pork barrel projects, smaller less known mom and pop firms or individuals running scams.

"A Paycheck Revolt in '96?" in Newsweek magazine pg. 52, February 19, 1996 by Jane Bryant Quinn had these few comments backing up the notion that America is becoming a thriving plutocracy. "Servant class: Maybe I've read too much Jane Austen, but attitudes seem to be taking a 19th-century turn. In Austen's time, the well-to-do were tended by a servant class. Today they're tended by hired services that they also keep in check. It's not just businesses that object to a higher minimum wage. The "overclass" doesn't want to pay more to it's day-care workers and household help, says economist Barry Boseworth of the Brookings Institution." If the overclass is supposedly making all of this money through their businesses in this robust economy, then why the hell aren't they parting with any of it. Has Scrooge fever bitten them or something? That takes me back to my pest control rout. During Christmas, I receive almost all of my gifts from the working poor, and the middleclass. The other thing I have noticed, is the amount of gifts did drop considerably from 1988 to the present. I used to get between $200 to $300 per year in the mid 80s, now, as of last year I got about $30 total. I was at a black man's house in a poor neighborhood one year, and upon completing his pest service, he whips out a twenty, shakes my hand, offering me a cola. He then says "go and have a steak dinner on me for Christmas!" I very rarely get a gift from the super rich in Weston, even though they boast record income gains. If I do get a gift from them, it is usually a card. I am always grateful for any holiday greeting, I am just using this as a measure of how the wealthier an individual is, the more likely he is to be stingy. Most of them treat you like a prole, low class commoner, like the wealthy do in England, with their nose in the air. Now I know why they are called high brows.

When I used to drive a furniture truck in the early 1980s, the middleclass, and poor would offer lunches and drinks, as the moves used to take several hours. If I had to use the bathroom, they would not hesitate to let me. They were not so demanding either. When we delivered new furniture to a home of the bourgeoisie, they almost always want us to do some home decorating. They want us to move this or that, then they expect us to stand there twaddling our thumbs, while they converse amongst themselves, deciding if they like it there or not. If not satisfied with it in that position, repeat steps one and two! Then when all is finally said and done, a big fat tip! **NOT!!!!** One would get a tip from a hobo before that.

It seems, that if you dig hard enough, you would find a modest amount of alarm, and concern about the rising disparity of income pushing the elites ever higher up the social ladder. But it's just a trickle compared to events that do not even effect us with a fraction of the impact. Gordon Williams on October 1996, pg. 20, "The Wealth and Health of Our Nation", throws this out; "A high growth economy suits the

REVOLT AGAINST THE PLUTOCRACY

American style of doing business and it certainly suits the American spirit. It feels wrong when our economy labors as it has the past half-dozen years. Jobs in certain sectors are hard to find these days. Consumer incomes don't seem to rise the way they used to. The gap between the rich and poor grows wider than it used to. Many Americans see themselves working harder than ever just to get by." Jill Smolowe's article pg. 45, Time magazine, February 5, 1996, "Reap As Ye Shall Sow", throws this side winder; "Pay-for-performance standards are a jackpot this year for executives, but not for workers."

Another strange transformation, that is the tell tale signs the overclass is gradually becoming the country's new overlords, in a new plutocracy. Single family homes, and the American Dream to own one. As you know, my wife and I, as of 2000, fall into the category of the houseless, with little possibility of ever owning one without outside help. This is because two full-time incomes couldn't even begin to purchase a single family home, in a half way decent neighborhood, outside of a ghetto. As you remember, the average single family home is appreciating at about $1,000 to $3,000 per month, and has been for the last 15 years. Here in South Florida, wealthy investors are buying up single family homes in record numbers. Sometimes they purchase several in one lower middleclass neighborhood, some right next to each other. Then they rent them out to people, who do not make enough money to swing a mortgage payment. This has been happening for about a decade now. Now we have a growing generation of Americans incapable of ever owning a home, unless some dramatic economic transformation returns the prosperous middleclass purchasing power of years gone by, back to the middleclass. Did you know that the right to own property, as stated in the Constitution of the United States, is not just a right to have a slice of America, but the access to power. That's right!, owning a property gives political and social power to the common man, through the process of building net wealth. Home ownership gives Americans more political, and social clout in local politics that effect economic trends. This could be another nail in America's coffin, purposely planned by the overclass to further sap power from the masses. A powerless population is a hell of a lot easier to control. As a property value increases, it's owner gains more net worth. As net worth increases, so does the owners ability to have access to more of the American Dream, financial clout, and the possibility of increasing his influence on political, and economic trends. Now multiply that by millions upon millions of homeowners. Now you see my jest. It's just like gun owners offer a counterbalancing force against a wayward government as planned by our founding fathers with the second amendment. What would be a more powerful method to further your slow stealthy invasion from within, if you are a member of the plutocracy planning an eventual heist of power. Hey, just maybe I am on to another little secret, the plutocrats do not want the American people to know about! In the new homes section of The Herald, Kenneth Harney's article pg. 5H Sunday, July 2, 2000 has this thought provoking information; "Do homeowners gains from the roaring '90s set them apart from those who don't own homes?" Dramatically so.

In terms of household wealth at the end of the decade, Americans are divided into two separate, and very unequal, economic societies-those who own homes and those who rent." "For homeowners 55 years of age and older, the contrasts are especially sharp. Home-owning households in the united states have a net wealth of $177,400 and home equity of $80,000. Renters in the same age bracket have a median net wealth of just $5,500 with zero equity." "The bottom line: Home ownership is a key to wealth in the American economy."

I just realized a most horrible paradox, as I finished this section of this chapter. It just smacked me up-side the head! It is so fantastic, and Orwellian it will leave your jaw on the ground, or it will make you laugh in disbelief. I have written it down to be introduced in future chapters.

Isn't it logical, if a society is having such a robust economy for such along period of time, that poverty would be on the decline rather rapidly? Again our economy defies all logic, and does not play by the natural laws. Why does our apple violate the laws of physics, and fall upward, when all other apples fall downward. Think about it a bit! If a family man, working a full time job, supporting a family of four, were to gradually receive pay increases, would he not share it with his family. The wife would get better and more expensive gifts. The family can get caught up on all of it's bills. The car would be repaired or replaced. And possibly, a second car purchased. God only knows we need one too, as we were forced to sell our second car due to my declining income in December 1999. For the first time we are a one car family. Being a one car family is not easy, and it only has minimum insurance on it, as that's all we can afford with two full-time incomes. They would start to enjoy the experiences of life, instead of just staying home all of the time because they do not have any money. The sleep, work, and eat if they had time, or money cycle would be broken. They would eat out more often, without worrying about not having enough money to go out, much less put the gas into the car for the excursions on the town. The children would enjoy new shoes and clothing. Maybe, they could save for a down payment on a house. Or just possibly, take that long overdue vacation not realized for over ten years. Then What's the beef? Why aren't any of these things occurring today in this supposedly roaring economy. Then that is a sign that something is seriously wrong. As with our hypothetical family man, if the income had increased, but none of it filtered it's way down to the other family members, that's a sign of an underlying problem. Maybe, he has a gambling problem, blowing his extra earnings. There is the possibility, God forbid, of another woman. Or worst of all, a serious drug problem. Something has to be responsible for gobbling up all of the extra earnings. The same goes for our corporate society. All of these supposed increases in family incomes are not filtering down to the working class wage-earner's family. Then what's the cause for the supposed decrease in poverty. How are there less people on social services, according to the statistics, if more people are slipping into lower income brackets? The same had occurred with the housing situation. However, we learned, that in fact, more houses were being purchased at a record pace, but by wealthy business investors making multiple purchases distorting the facts. Working class families were not the ones purchasing. This article in The Sun Sentinel Friday, January 16, 1998 by John Maines "Poverty in S. Florida: uphill battle of the '90s" backs my hypothesis up; "South Florida's poor population rose sharply during the early 1990s, according to figures the U.S. Census Bureau released on Thursday. In 1993, the latest year for which figures are available, 25 percent of Miami-Dade County residents were living in poverty-defined as earning less than $14,654 for a family of four that year. That compares to 17.9 percent in 1989. For children younger than 18, the situation was worse-one in three were poor, up from one in four in 1989." The article goes on to state Broward and Palm Beach county's poverty level as 12 percent of all residents, and 20 percent of all children. "The numbers [of poor children] do go higher every year," quotes Vera Ginn coordinator of special programs for Broward County School Board. Kay Scott, manager of the Title I program for Palm Beach County says this; "I'm seeing an increase, a very large increase, in the number of poor children we have coming into the school system," "We're seeing far more poor children than the census numbers seem to indicate."

Jay T. Baldwin

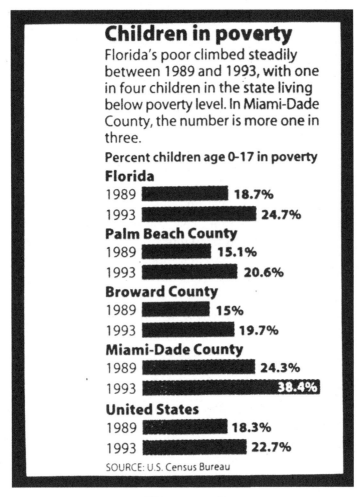

Illustration 5

Children in poverty Children growing up in poor families is on a rapid increase not just in Florida, but the entire nation According to the U.S. Census Bureau the percentage of children ages 0-17, nation

REVOLT AGAINST THE PLUTOCRACY

wide, has increased 4.4% in four years from 1989 to 1993. These are the most recent years done in the census. These figures are, more than likely, much higher now in 1998, as more families continue to slide below the poverty level due to diminishing after tax incomes, and/or diminishing purchasing power because of increasing inflation.

Again the Census figures clash considerably with reality. They appear to be false, or are being manipulated to down play the reality. Maybe its social conditioning (brain washing propaganda), again to be covered in later chapters.

Here is some more contradictory information indicating the economy is doing very well. Social services have watched their numbers of enrollees decline to record lows, but at the same time more people are in need of social service than ever before. Social conditioning once again!!!! "Drop in Food-Stamp Rolls Is Mysterious and Worrisome", an article pg. A20 in The Wall Street Journal Monday, August 2, 1999, by Shailagh Murray; "As the unemployed poor became the working poor, why are so many disappearing from food-stamp rolls-even though many still are eligible for the federal benefit?" Democratic Rep. Sandra Levin of Michigan adds; "There has been a breakdown, a misunderstanding of what moving from welfare to work is all about," "I don't understand it frankly," "We fought to make sure food stamps and child care and health care were part of welfare reform. And now kids are going hungry? What sense does that make?" According to the U.S. Dept. of Agriculture, there is no explanation as to the giant drop. It has launched an educational campaign to tell low income families, even if they are off of welfare, they are still eligible for food stamps. It seems people think if they are no longer eligible for welfare due to welfare reform, they are not eligible for anything. This leads to a serious dilemma. People are going hungry! The article goes on; "This is where the social-policy experts get worried: People are leaving the rolls, but clearly they are still in need. Catholic Charities reported that last year the demand for food assistance rose by an average of 38% in local parishes. A U.S. Conference of Mayors survey found that 1997 emergency requests for food rose by an average of 14% in 21 major cities. Enrollment in the National School Lunch Program, which has similar eligibility criteria, also rose by 6% from 1994 to 1997." "A recent Urban Institute study of former welfare recipients found that a third of families have had to skip meals or cut the size of servings in the past year because of inadequate money." "There may be some confusion around the country due to the welfare-reform laws," Says Agriculture Secretary Dan Glickman. "I think there may be some states and agencies who are not discouraging that thinking."

It seems that some states like the fact people are misunderstanding the laws, and not signing up for these services. Hey, ignorance is bliss according to t hose in power. That leaves more for the elites. Mr. Glickman also adds; "We've got so much food in this country-we've had four years now of record crop production," "It's just crazy that people eligible for food stamps are going hungry." This is a prime example of social conditioning. Propaganda, Soviet style, seems to rule!

REVOLT AGAINST THE PLUTOCRACY

With such a big deal as this economy is being made out to be, as purported by the press, all of the various polls, and Census figures, people tend to get a secure feeling. It's every where you look, in the papers, on the TV, in advertisements. They get a false sense of prosperity, even though nothing has changed in their take home pay. They think, by hearing news day after day, about this booming prosperous economy, they to have prospered, or will prosper soon, and can afford things they normally can not. Thus, a lot of working-class people go out on a spending spree, purchasing badly needed supplies, maybe a badly wanted luxury item, and run up a lot of debt. This, another testament of a dual economy, one for the rich, and one for everybody else. The question is, If the economy is so rosy, then why the hell are so many bankruptcy claims rolling in at record levels? There were not this many bankruptcy claims during the prosperous period between the 1950s and the 1960s, in fact they were down to their lowest then. Another example of our apple now falling upward. James Russel's article, "Dept pileup a dark cloud on a rosy economic horizon" pg. 4F, Sunday April 15, 1998 in The Herald. "Personal bankruptcy filings in the U.S. reached an all time high of 1.3 million last year, up about 20 percent from the 1996 level. This year is predicted to produce about 1.5 million." "By the end of 1998, there will be more bankrupts in the world's most prosperous country than armed servicemen," claimed the British weekly, The Economist.

In this chapter you have learned the fact there is a robust economy that has hung in there for 9 years and 3 months, the longest boom in history. We are also aware of the record amount of national income increases. There are the Census figures showing the entire country, the poor included, is seeing record increases in take home income. Poverty is down due to a steep decline in welfare applicants. Every thing seems the best it has ever been. Housing market is seeing record purchases. Durable goods are being purchased at record levels. The Republicans are boasting it was there last administration that's responsible, which a lot is definitely true for the worst, for the boom times. The Democrats are claiming they are responsible for it though it has been happening long before they took office. Then all must be hunky dory. **Then somebody please tell me along with nine out of every ten American workers, where the hell is this prosperous economy????? On another damn planet!!!!!**

REVOLT AGAINST THE PLUTOCRACY

Jay T. Baldwin

Chapter 3 Tin man. Cold hearted, ruthless corporate America.

The summer day of 1993 started like any other day. I had to take another load of concrete structures to their destination to a local construction site. My wife has to be to work at the large flower distribution firm, where she worked. She had worked there for a few years now. She had to drop off our six month old baby girl at Grandma's. Adriana was born with an underdeveloped set of kidneys, and an underdeveloped esophagus. She was pretty bad, if things got any worse, she would have had to go on to a dialysis machine. She could not keep food down either. My wife had to take her in for treatments at Miami Children's Hospital every two weeks for a battery of tests. This required she miss six hours twice a month. She worked out the missing time with her supervisor, and made up the missed hours through out the week. My wife was one of the most reliable employees there. She had received a letter of commendation for outstanding work.

    I was working at one of the truck driving jobs I had. I had been to several different jobs by now. It seemed that the average stay at any one job was about two months, and two to three weeks before they found a reason to terminate me. The same happened to just about everybody that worked at any of these jobs more than 90 days. These were eighteen wheeler truck driver positions, but didn't need a whole lot of training as we already knew how to drive the beasts. The only thing we had to learn was the product line we delivered. Ironically, these companies would run ads in the local papers 365 days a year. They would literally hoard stacks of applications, when the next round of firings, they would thumb through them. Next victim please!!! It was clearly apparent that there were more applicants than jobs. I finally figured out why they would fire employees after about 90 days. The probationary period of 90 days meant they did not have to pay holiday pay, vacation pay, or any portion of the employees' medical benefits. The state law happily gives these corporations this grace period to see if the employee works out. But what happens if the corporations find it cost effective to create an employee assembly line. In the front door and out the back! This way they can always keep a staff on hand to run the routs, but they didn't have to pay any full time expenses. Hey, these drivers are a dime a dozen these days! Who cares if they are human beings, and have families to feed. The only thing that counts is the bottom line. Yes, profits! Get them anyway you can, and the hell with everything else. The other thing I noticed while at some of these jobs, was the constantly declining starting pay. Even, in the short time I was there, I would eventually see some other driver reach his 90 day informal day of termination. They would always be terminated over the smallest things. The company would keep track of every little error from paperwork errors to fender benders. Then these things would be dug up and used as a reason for termination. This was a period of time when truck driver careers were loosing there standard of income, thanks to Ronald Reagan's deregulation of the trucking industry. Before, the deregulation the average semi-truck operator with a class A commercial drivers license with hazardous materials, doubles and tanker endorsements, would make between $14 to $16 an hour for a non-union company driver position. For the five or so years after 1990, the pay scale for these professional drivers plummeted. Then here comes the sneaky part. The replacement driver would almost always be hired 25¢ to $1 less an hour than the guy he just replaced. When his time was up, the next replacement would be hired even for less. This was a sneaky way for these greedy companies, to push the envelope, to see how little they could pay drivers, before the applicants would stop coming in. But, people would keep coming in! Oh, by the way, there other little thing, the lack of funds to repair the equipment went on un-hindered, and as accidents would occur due to neglected equipment, more drivers would be eliminated. The idiot who figured out how to manipulate the system like that, probably makes the salary equivalent of some kings.

Back to my wife. On one hot summer day, I came home from work at about 6PM or so after a 12 hour day, to find my wife crying. I said what's up? After about an hour of talking, I found out she was fired from her job. I asked why, and found out because she had to take our daughter to the hospital as usual. The supervisor, told her the company could no longer tolerate her brief absences. They told her she had to make a decision between her family, or her career. Even after my wife telling the supervisor the doctor's visits were a matter of life or death for our daughter, they un-sympathetically gave her a pink slip. By now I was seeing red, and contemplating some form of retaliation best not mentioned here. But, the real detonator to set off my anger, was the reason on the pink slip. Reason for termination; constantly tardy. Missing work. Poor performance. Now I was ready to explode!!! If you could only feel the rage we both felt, it's a miracle the evening news didn't have a story about another blue collar worker going postal, and shot his wife's employer. I was so close I tasted blood! Lucky for that supervisor, I happen to be a civilized person adamantly against crime.

The following weekend, I called a few attorneys, only to find out non of them would consider the case on contingency. Florida is a right to work state, and employees have no rights. I asked about the Family Leave Amendment of the Constitution, recently passed by Bill Clinton. I was again told those laws were merely paper tigers with no teeth. Isn't that sad, that underpaid American citizens are nothing but an exploitable natural resource, there to be used by corporate America as it sees fit, to make wealth beyond your wildest dreams for the elites. Welcome to a kinder gentler corporate totalitarianism!!

    Well after contacting the Dept. of Labor, we found out that several versions of the Family Leave Act were violated by the company, but our chances of winning were slim to non. They hesitatingly, gave us a formal complaint form to fill out, and turn in with any evidence, and they would review it. After about a month we finally got a letter of response. The letter basically stated there was not enough evidence to hold the company liable. My God Man, we had deposition letters from witnesses, and a letter from Adriana's doctor stating the reason for her missing work. Well, I saw red! What did they want us to have for evidence, a video-taped record of the whole thing? At that point, I decided to start a campaign of writing protest letters to the state Governor, the state Senator, all the way to the President of the United States, and his wife, since Hillary was so pro-women's rights. After about a couple of months, we received a letter from the oval office stating the case would be reopened. This is where I left off in Delight Of The Overclass Demise Of The Middleclass as the case was reopened, and still pending. Now we will pick up at that crucial point. We finally had our day in court but it didn't turn out like an old western where the good guy always wins. We were very early to the court and sat down to go through our paper work. When the corporate attorney entered with the CEO, and a few of the Executive officers one being my wife's supervisor, the Judge was very happy to see the company's attorney. They seemed to know

REVOLT AGAINST THE PLUTOCRACY

each other on a first name basis. That was just the beginning. After about two hours of opening statements, they started with the company presenting there case. We represented ourselves, as we didn't have money for an attorney. We were supposed to have our Dept. Of Labor case worker there at our side, representing us like an attorney. But that didn't happen, as he was on the twelve member review board acting as a jury member. The company had first crack at presenting their case. Now, my blood pressure started to rise as all of the supervisors degraded my wife as one of the worst employees ever to work there. They claimed the reason for termination was not the sick child. They presented documented evidence that my wife was always late. My wife looked at me and said that's not my time card! She had made copies of all of her time cards. Then several more time cards were presented. They even had her signature on them, but they were not the ones she had copies of. My wife stood up and said "Your honor those time cards are not mine they are in contempt of court. She proceeded to hand the real copies and said "Your honor here are the actual copies signed by me!" The Judge said in a stern voice, "Sit down Mrs. Baldwin, we will have a look at that after the trial!" Then the company had a couple of letters of discipline signed by my wife. My wife had received a letter a few months back, basically explaining she had to make up any time missed due to taking the child to the hospital, and she had to sign it. Well that letter was back, but didn't say the same stuff. My wife was smart and brought her copy of that very letter. The corporation started to read the letter to the court, and my wife had her copy in front of her. It started, half way through to sound like a totally different letter. It was basically written in a disciplinary, format dictating to her, that if the tardiness, substandard performance, and missed days didn't stop, termination would result. My wife stood up and again said "Your honor that is not the letter I signed, I have the original here!" Once again the judge said in a even sterner voice, "Mrs. Baldwin sit down, we will here it after the trial, or I will dismiss you for being in contempt of court!" Well, the corporation spent another 30 or so minutes bashing my wife. Well before the corporation could even finish their presentation, the judge just sat up and said, "I do not see why we have to drag this out for hours, but it's obvious that Mrs. Baldwin is just a disgruntled employee, and the claims brought by the corporation are warranted. I dismiss all charges brought against the corporation!" He then gavels. I looked at my wife, and said we didn't even have a chance to present our evidence. I then looked at our case worker, and said, "What the hell happened here?" He just shyly looked at us, as he proceeded to walk away saying, "I am at no liberty to comment. Thank you!" I noticed that there were microphones in the center of the tables. I said your honor, "what about our evidence?" He said, "My decision is final! Thank you!" As a flurry of emotions ran through my head, I then asked him as, he was putting his papers into stuffy folders, I would like a copy of the court tapes. He murmured, not even looking at us, "Write a formal letter requesting them!" Then he walked away. As my wife and I gathered up our paper work, we both over heard the lawyer of the corporation, as he patted the CEO, and some of the senior officers on the back, remarked, "I told you we would have this case won!" "These guys are just like the County Commission, give them enough to spend a few days on a sunny beach in the Caribbean somewhere, and you will get your way most of the time!" I then realized, we would have never won the case, even though all we were asking for was $60,000. It was pre-set who would come out victorious. The one who has the money would win! What kind of justice is that, in a land that claims to be a land of laws? This is the most prominent sign a society has become a plutocracy! You can buy justice! Freedoms, rights and privileges are reserved to the highest bidder. If you do not have any money, you do not have any justice.

I probably gave you a brief story about the pest control company I worked for, where there was no justice. Big corporations can not be defeated head on. There is a method you can use to defeat them, but I had to learn it through trial and error. I will discuss this in later chapters.

In 1997 I worked for a small mom and pop pest control company. The owner was well known for his participation in the pest control industry in South Florida. He was a very kind gentle man, always there to talk to if you needed. He compensated us very well by the hour. Again I had found a company that paid close to what I used to make in the 1980s. I worked there about 1 year. One day we had a company meeting, with the owner, and his wife. They broke the news that the company had been sold to a large nation wide company. This company is known for having a name like termite, and nicks, that's all I can say legally. I new right away that, things would change dramatically, probably for the worst. Well, we went on under the old name, and old pay system for awhile, before things were to transfer. The big corporation that had bought our company was in an acquisition mode, and had recently gobbled up two other local pest firms. It wasn't a month before they bought up two more. But by then, we had suffered a complete change in pay. I used to get an hourly pay of $10.50 an hour. They switched us over to commission only per job completed. That gave us almost a two hundred dollar per week pay cut. Our staff, up till that time, consisted of career family men with an average age of about 40. Everybody, was a close knitted family. But that all changed, that day. After the pay cut, we lost about 50 percent of the employees. Even the sales Dept. lost most of there middle-aged professionals, because the base salary of $350 per week, which was added to their commissions each week, was eliminated. That was a $350 per week pay cut! How the hell are working men expected to adjust their lifestyle, that much, to handle a pay cut of that size? I had no choice, along with about five other technicians, but to stay. I had no other jobs lined up to fall back on. We were paid bi-weekly under the new company. We got one check on the 12th of every month, and another on the 24th. On the 12th I went to get my check, and to my surprise, they claimed the checks never came in. We would have them tomorrow Well everybody, got the news. Tomorrow came and no checks. The excuse was "we do not know where they could be!" "Sorry!" Well I am starting to see red, along with the other employees. They said they would find out what happened to them and let us know then. Well a day went by. Two days. Three days,

REVOLT AGAINST THE PLUTOCRACY

and no check! We finally got a reply, "The checks will be in next week, there was a bad storm in Tennessee, where the main headquarters are located. There was a tornado, and a lot of damage in Memphis. Well next week came. Guess what? No check! The excuse for the day was "The checks were sent to the wrong branch." "It will be another week!" By now, we had some very angry people! We lost a few more at that point. Now, I hardly recognized anybody, as everybody had been replaced with a new much younger crowd. The average age was now about 21. A completely inexperienced ignorant crowd. Guess what? I was one of the few remaining with any experience at all, and I was commissioned to train the young guns, but of course with no more pay than my skimpy, $350 per week, when I used to earn an average of $550 per week.

Next week came, as usual, no checks! We were told that new checks had to be printed, and it would be two more weeks. The next morning was a Wednesday, the day of our weekly tech meetings. Well, the first thing discussed was the check situation. The mood was like a tinder box waiting for a spark to go off! The usual excuses came up again. Several technicians had families, and explained they had no more food and had not paid the rent. I was one of them, thankfully, the food part was tight but we did eat. My wife's parents let us eat over quit a bit, and my mother helped out with food for Adriana. But the rent went unpaid, and the car payments were very late. One technician, and his wife were on the verge of being thrown out of their apartment. Then we had one of the last remaining middle aged men, besides myself, break the silence in the meeting with a sharp, "If I do not get my pay k, a lot of people will be sorry!" He was a stocky , short New York Italian. He was a cab driver in oklyn New York. He had a very heavy New York ent, with the flare of a Mafia God father. I then said myself, now there's somebody I can get to Know a ttle better, as an ally. Because, I was just waiting to et at least one more person, who would not hesitate to join me on a nice little drive over to the Dept. Of Labor to fill out a formal compliant against the company. Well, the tech. meeting finally came to an end. Most of us including some of the sales people, secretaries, and termite tent crew guys all just kind of walked, in a big pack, to the break room, and smoking area in the back of the building. I took this opportunity, as every body was on the subject already, to feel each person out to see how much rage was true and honest. Most of the younger new employees were not very concerned, as most of them were still living with Mom and Dad, and had no real responsibilities. Most of them went to their trucks to prepare for the day. But us seniors, from all departments, started tossing ideas around about what to do. I made my move with an arm around the shoulder of our Italian cabby. I said, "lets all go down to the Dept. Of Labor and fill out a class action complaint!" I immediately got at least three immediate Ok's. A couple said "It won't do a bit of good!" I immediately replied, "That's exactly what they are banking on!!!!" "That's what most people would probably respond like!" It was hard to undo decades of social Conditioning in one break period. I did win at least two more supporters. The rest said they were already looking for other jobs, and did not want to waste their time. Well six was plenty, and we did what we had to do! Well, one call, and a letter from the Dept. Of Labor, a couple of days later brought the house down! We came into work as usual one morning, and the Big Cheese greeted us at the door. He said, "Good morning!" in a rather calm voice. Then he said do not leave just yet, but to call any customers that we might be late. He said he had to see each of us privately in his office. Well, as employees came out, they had a slight look of surprise, and some quietly chuckled under there breaths while looking down. Everybody was interrogated! Well my turn came! I went into his office like a kid entering the principal's office in elementary school. He calmly said, "Take a seat." "We received a call from the Dept. Of Labor yesterday, and got a letter from them about the pay checks!" "We do not know who called them, but we would appreciate if anybody has got a problem, they need to come to me!" "They are not to take matters into their own hands!" "We will find the person/persons responsible for this!!!!" I calmly said, "I couldn't imagine who would do something like that!" Quietly, I said to myself, *"Take that you son of a bitch!"* "How does a dose of your own medicine taste?" "I bet your family didn't have to go hungry, and you have been getting your pay all of those weeks!" I was on cloud nine! David did beat Goliath for a change.

    Well, that got immediate attention on the pay check situation. The very next day, they had our pay checks. We were paid for every single day up till that point. Only one sales rep. got some of his commission short changed, but would get it at the next pay period. We eventually found out why our pay was held up for so long. One of the senior secretaries, that stayed on during the ownership change, that we all trusted, said they plain didn't have the money. They had spent so much purchasing the last two small companies, they cut themselves short, and needed what little was leftover to compensate the upper management. Apparently they thought we were a herd of farm animals, the last ones to get food in the times of drought. Just pee-ons, there to be exploited. I stayed about 3 more months, until I found another job in the same industry for a lot more money! How do these companies think they have every right to do hard working people this way? Don't they have any kind of civility and heart???? Is the bottom line more important than the well-being of their work force? These are the real events in the daily lives of the working class, right from the horses mouth.

My first real memory of cold hearted, ruthless and cruel corporate America dates back to 1985. My mother used to work at a large Florida department store called Luria's for almost ten years. I can use their name as they do not exist anymore! She was one of the center Island jewelry clerks. She spent 9 hours a day on her feet, six days a week. She had a problem with her bladder causing frequent trips to the girl's room for some time, and needed some treatments. She decided to get the treatments, but the side effects were even more trips to the lavatory. She even got a doctor's note to present to the employer, explaining the situation. The store manager started to ridicule her almost immediately. He said that no employee was allowed more than three breaks a day, that was one at 10 Am, one at Lunch time and one at Three in the afternoon. My mom couldn't help it! If she held it, there could be dangerous results like a severe bladder infection or worse, bladder injury. No!, that didn't matter in the eyes of the boss! The bottom line is all that counts!!! What a jack a _ _!

She was terminated about a week later after 9 years, one year before she was eligible for retirement. She immediately went to the Dept. Of Labor, and filled a formal complaint. A few weeks later she got a letter from them, with bad news. There was not a thing the agency could do to help her, as there was not enough evidence that she was fired for the medical reason. The corporation said, she had been eliminated as part of a scale back, in that particular department, and the job was no longer open. Lies work almost every time for corporate America. One day they will pay dearly for their crimes against humanity. I was too young, and naïve to even get involved back then. I was a diamond in the rough, and had not been through the grinder yet.

I have heard of just about every story of corporate crimes from the clients on my pest control rout. Some have been harmed by faulty equipment, and had long drawn out battles in court that still have not been settled. Meanwhile, there whole lives have been turned up-side down. Some have gotten fired for getting to old. Some have gotten fired for getting pregnant. Some have gotten fired for having heart attacks. One even got terminated for taking time off from work, to bury her husband who died. I thought funeral leave was a law, but I think I am wrong. Some employees are used as scape goats for internal problems. Many can vouch the getting pregnant reason. Many were harmed by hazardous situations, and chemicals, and were terminated when they started to need medical care under Worker's Compensation. Hey, he's no good any more, and could possibly become a legal liability, just get his a _ _ out of here! Used just like a piece of toilet paper, and flushed down the toilet!

Let's briefly divulge into the reason that most corporations are so cold hearted, mean, inhumane, and rude with no morality. Why?, capitalism has placed profit, and the bottom line above all else. And the all that counts, the hell with you, the hell with me, and the hell with them attitude corporations seem to have. Haven't you wondered why most bosses are usually U.S. prime grade A jerks? And why, those who have these qualities, with serious attitude problems always seem to get promoted to positions of authority before courteous, kind, honest, and understanding guys do? You can graciously thank Nicclo Di Bernardo Machiavelli (Mack-ee-ev-elly), 1469-1527. Prince Machiavelli, Italian philosopher, statesman, and author known for political expediency being placed above humanity and morality. He was characterized by cunning, unscrupulous, deception, and dishonesty. Basically, your glorified run of the mill a _ _ hole! Just a serious jerk in his days. Another bad apple child, who probably was a dominant bully in school, and grew up to be the abomination he was.

It seems corporate America glorifies, and places individuals with Machiavellian qualities above the rest. They must think they are strong leaders or something. Haven't they ever heard of the old saying, "You can draw more butterflies with honey, than with vinegar."

Here is a brief sample of just some of the experiences I have had with Machiavellian supervisors. Back, when I was working for a pest control company in 1990, I had been performing lawn sprays which required the use of long rubber gloves to be worn during the whole treatment. This is to prevent any possibility of chemicals leaching into your skin. However, I seemed to have an allergic reaction to the resins in the gloves. I had gone to a doctor to have a culture done on the what looked a lot like athlete's foot of the hands. The doctor was to call me back during the day to let me know of his findings, that meant calling me at work. Well, I waited to have the supervisor page or call me on the truck's radio. This supervisor had been a service technician before he became a field supervisor. He had not been with the company that long. In fact most of the other techs had many more years experience than he had. I myself had 4 years more years than he had. We all wondered why he got promoted so fast, when a lot of other people had more experience. They must have seen some quality in him they respected. He had been known to be rather antisocial as a technician, staying rather to himself, and had a cocky attitude about him. The next day came, and I remembered the doctor should have called me the prior day. I called him, and was notified by his nurse that they left multiple messages at my work. I mentioned I had not received any massages from him. I came into work later that day to get some chemical. Well, I asked this supervisor why he had not been giving me my messages. The response was "We cannot be concerned with employees personal lives." I said it was a doctor trying to contact me with some important medical information. "That doesn't matter!", he said. Well, I left the room, and said on my way out, "I would appreciate receiving my messages." "Thank you" I immediately headed for one of the phones in the front office by the rout coordinators to call my doctor. As I was speaking to the doctor, our little friend came into the room, and stood, while staring at me. The first words out of his mouth were, "You can not use the company phone for personal business!" He then came over trying to grab the phone out of my hand, while I was talking to the doctor. I excused myself from the doctor saying, "Excuse me Dr. Meyers, There is a very rude person here trying to hang up the phone. After a literal tug of war with the phone, he managed to get it out of my hands, and hung it up. I have not been so humiliated before in my life, I said. I then screamed, "You do not do that again!" "That's very rude!" "If I have to call a doctor or something, it's my right!" I started to recall the doctor, and he seemed totally shocked, that I would openly defy him right in front of his face. He said, in a screaming voice, "You will not use that phone or you are fired!" I replied, "Fire me you a _ _ hole!" "You will have the biggest lawsuit buddy!" well he left the room, and I called the doctor back apologized, and explained what had just happened. Even he could not imagine the Gaul my supervisor had. Well, I never got fired.

    I used to work at a rock quarry driving a large 20 cubic yard dump truck for a mere $7 an hour. I chose this job because, the tractor trailer jobs didn't pay much more than this job. I was not going to drive the giant semi-trucks, with all of the responsibilities for the same wage as these easy to operate straight dump trucks. I believe in the economic law of supply and demand, and two can play the game when dealing with corporate America. Corporate America gets what it pays for!! If they only pay me $7 an hour, I will only give them $7 an hour worth of production. If they pay me $11.27 an hour as they once did, I will move mountains, giving them $11.27 an hours worth of quality production. An eye for an eye, and a tooth for a tooth! If every American worker believed, and did as I do, we would not be in the fix we are in today. We have allowed the decline of the American dream for the blue collar worker, not them! We can only blame ourselves!

This company strangely kept most all of the truck drivers for about 90 days. They ran an add 52 weeks of the year, and had interviews every week. They always seemed to need drivers, between the fleet of about 20 dump trucks, and about 30 cement mixers. Almost on a daily basis somebody was let go, without any reason whatsoever. Half of the applicants were from South America, or Mexico, and didn't speak much English. Florida City, and Homestead are known for giant agricultural industries with fields of crops as far as the eye can see. Migrant farm workers are hired to man these fields. They come and live in the U.S. for the duration of the planting, and harvesting season. Then there were just a hand full of Americans, who have been displaced from the deregulation of the trucking industry. Only one old man had been with the company for 7 years, and he claimed he was the only one that lasted over 90 days. He had seen thousands of drivers come and go.

Jay T. Baldwin

This company took an hour out of our pay daily for a lunch break. Our rout led us into the Florida Keys daily, giving us a variety of fast food places to choose from for our lunch breaks. But all of the guys brought there lunches and Thermoses with them, since they never grabbed anything on the road. I figured they just didn't have the money to eat out. The first day I worked there, I decided to stop along US 1 in Key Largo, on my way back to the quarry,, to grab a bite to eat. I had noticed a couple of other trucks go by. When I got back to the yard to load up for another run, I was approached by the old American guy. He said he saw me parked along the road eating my lunch. He then explained to me, "You do not want to get caught stopped eating lunch, or stopping to use the restroom.!" I immediately replied, "Why not, they take an hour out of my pay daily, for me to stop and eat lunch!" He replied in a hush tone, "You will get fired that's why!" Well, I was still socially conditioned, to a degree, and needed the job, so I started taking my lunch, and gave them a free hour of my labor, by eating while driving, or waiting for the front end loader to load up our trucks. One day, I didn't have enough time to stop in Florida City to use the rest room, as I usually do on my way into the rock quarry. It was a 45 minute drive into Florida City from my home in Miami, and another ten minutes to the rock quarry from there. We had to be prompt to punch in at 6:00AM sharp. This particular morning, I figured, I would use the toilet after I loaded up the truck, and weighed out for the first trip of the day. I parked along side the entrance road by the maintenance shop, to use the bathrooms there. When I walked out. there was a supervisor standing there with his hands on his hips, and a stern look on his face. "What are you doing?" He asked. I replied, "I just had to use the bathroom!" He replied, "You can't stop, you must learn to control your bodily functions!" At those words, I felt as though the blood was boiling in my veins, at the same time, I thought it must be some kind of joke. I looked him square in the eye, and replied in an equally stern voice, "If I have to use the bathroom, I am going to use the bathroom!" "Every body has the right to use the bathroom if he has to!" He said, "We will see about that!" as he walked away. Later that day, when I came back from a late afternoon load, I went to the scale house to see if there were any other loads to be ran, or anything to be done in the quarry with the trucks. The scale master said for me to go and park my truck, turn in my paperwork, then to go and see the personnel manager. I had been employed for about 80 days. Well, I kind of knew what had already happened, so instead of parking the truck, I went in to see him, as it was closer to the weigh station. I wanted to face the music now. It was a long way back to where the trucks were parked about a ¼ of a mile back, and then I would have to fuel it up and wash it. Upon entering his room, he said to close the door behind me. He said in a calming, heavy British accent, "We have reviewed your file, and come to the conclusion that you are not going to work out for the best interests of the company." I immediately replied in as calm of a voice, "I guess this is because I stopped to use the bathroom this morning, Isn't it?" He replied, "I can not have my men stopping my trucks for anything, or I will not get any production done." I said, "You mean if I have to use the bathroom, I can not?" He said in a slightly cocky voice. "We are all adults, and we all have to learn to control our bodily functions!" As I attempted to counter reply, he said with a much more impatient voice, "I am a very busy man, and I do not have time to debate with you!"

With those words, the biggest changes in my life set sail. Knowing that my wife, and I had just moved once again, due to sky rocketing rents, and continual pay cuts for me, I then realized that life in the streets was closer than ever. At that time, my wife still hadn't found a job, since her battle with the flower distributing, company about Adriana's medical visits a couple of months earlier. With those thoughts, the deepest feeling of despair filled my head, as I thought back to all of the horrible experiences our entire family had with corporate America. I felt, as though we were nothing but an exploitable commodity, there for the sole use by businesses to make exorbitant profits. Nothing but animals to a farmer. David laid his head down for the last time, as I ingested a lethal dosage of sleeping pills, and had finally realized, I had been beaten by Goliath. Luckily, I had made a final call to my wife, at her mothers place, to wish Adriana all of my love. That must have been the call that saved my life, as my wife noticed something seriously wrong with the tone of my voice.

After several days of recovery at a local hospital, something powerful clicked in me. A sudden surge of energy and will came over me. Like a Phoenix rising out of the ashes, I suddenly realized a new purpose in life. I began my maiden voyage, on a new crusade with a determination that, had the force of a category 5 hurricane and burns like a super nova to this day. I made a secret promise to myself, and God, that a day will come when the working class, and middle class will never fall prey to corporate America again. This was the birth of my first book "Delight Of The Overclass, Demise Of The Middleclass." David will rise up again, by alerting the masses of the unethical turn American capitalism took somewhere between 1967 and the 1980s, and recruiting the common man on the most important battle, since the American Revolution, Civil War, and Dr. Martin Luther King's crusade against racism, America will ever see.

Corporate America's rap sheet reads like the Mafia Godfather "Teflon Don's". President Theodore Roosevelt quoted; "We demand that big business give people a square deal!" These are the words that somebody in power today needs to quote. Even J. P. Morgan, one of America's most successful entrepreneurs, stated that no CEO should earn more than 21 times his lowest paid worker. These men see the real role capitalism is meant to play in creating a prosperous America for all, not just a privileged few. For 20 years we have been getting a screw deal!

Here are the rap sheets. HMO's are not immune to the corrupting powers of corporate greed. As corporations themselves, they also play by most of the new greedy rules, that the rest of corporate America plays by. The Machiavellian rules, shine in all of their glory, in today's health maintenance organizations. These organizations literally put profits above the prime directive doctors, and all in the medical profession, take as medical morals to preserve human life, without regards to costs and financial hardships.

Jay T. Baldwin

Today's HMO's would rather pay continuous re-admittance of patients into hospitals, due to relapses of medical conditions, because these vary HMO's do not want to cover those patient's prescription medication bills for medications, to prevent the medical conditions. It's technically more expensive to put that practice into play, than to just pay the prescription bills for the medicine to prevent expensive hospital emergency room visits. In 2000, a local South Florida man kept ending up in the emergency room, because his medical insurance provider would not cover his heart medication. Yet, this HMO, so concerned about saving money to maximize profits, would spend thousands more in the man's continual hospital visits, than if it just gave the man his heart medication. Talk about being near sighted, these corporations cannot see their nose to spite their faces! It would be the same as neglecting to change the oil in a car to save on repair expenses, but having no problem replacing the engine on a continual basis. Some private corporations that produce disposable medical equipment sold to hospitals and medical centers, have been caught reconditioning, or reprocessing this equipment. Then they resell it to save themselves, their hospital, and medical center customers money.

These policies are harming our health. It is apparent that the greed factor is more important than the human life factor, and the logic factor. But who said corporate greed is logical?

Just wanted to throw a sidewinder to contemplate. Did you know that there is no laws, what-so-ever, in the federal, or state labor law books to make corporations give employees the freedom to eat lunch. They can literally tell their employees that lunch is not allowed, and anybody caught eating lunch will be fired on the spot. That's how much freedom today's corporations have to be as inhumane as possible, if they wish to. I guarantee the day will come, sooner than later, when some corporations will prohibit lunch eating. Apparently, they can tell their workers they do not have the right to use the toilet, as my Mom, and I found out first hand. And the state, and federal governments give these freedoms to corporations.

The law of the jungle, survival of the fittest sure seems to be king here! It definitely matters how much your net worth is, to determine how vulnerable you are. The poorer you are, the more likely you are to be scammed. A very eye opening article showing the pure evil in some of America's home mortgage lending institutions. The lending institutions that do give credit to those with too low of incomes, bad credit, or no credit are known in the industry as subprime lenders. "How unscrupulous lenders scam low-income homeowners" by John Stamper in The Herald Sunday, February 22, 1998, pgs. 1F, 7F 62 year old Geraldine Daniels a school crossing guard, re-financed the mortgage on her Washington D.C. home five times since 1988, in an attempt to lower her monthly payments. She originally took out a home equity loan to pay her bills since her husband died, and one of her sons has had brain damage. Well, she did everything, but lower her payments! "All I wanted to do was get the loan and pay my bills," Daniels said. "I said, 'give me the money.' I wasn't thinking about anything else." Consumer advocates, and regulators say she has fallen pray to a rapidly growing trend of lending money at very high interest rates to those who would not qualify for standard loans. "The profits that can be extracted from borrowers like Daniels are so large that lending to them more than justifies the financial risks involved. And, the customers-called subprime borrowers in the industry-are so unsophisticated that they make attractive targets for unscrupulous lenders." Just like a weak Zebra on the plains of Africa, people who are not fortunate enough to understand complex financial matters, are taken down, and devoured up before they know what hit them. I can sympathize with Mrs. Daniels, as I may be capable of writing this book, but when it comes to numbers, the stock market, or financial matters of any kind, I am totally out of my element too. I guess that makes me an easy target for some brainiac to pull the wool over my eyes too! My wife and I fall into the same category as Mrs. Daniels. We are considered low income, due to the very high cost to income levels living in South Florida, even though we make much more than Geraldine. We have little or no credit since our bankruptcy due to declining wages. We just do not know that much about money matters! But God help, the low life corporate scum sucker, that try's to scam either of us, he just might bite off more than he can chew! What we are lacking in the knowledge of all of the world's financial subjects, we more than make up in social self defense tactics, perseverance, defiance, patience, justice, patriotism, pride, and self-esteem. **Go ahead, make our day!!!**

One of the tactics practiced by subprime lenders is called "equity skimming". This involves luring unsuspecting lower income individuals, the elderly, and the naïve with valuable homes, and deceiving them into more credit than they would ever be capable of repaying. These loans have an interest rate of 12 to 24 percent, when the standard loan rates are around 7 to 8 percent. The ending result, more Americans are loosing their homes in record numbers. Patricia Sturdevant, a general council for the National Association of Consumer Advocates, quotes; "It leads to abuses of trust, poverty, foreclosure and homelessness." Just the heartless fleecing of America!

Sturdevant says predatory mortgage lenders are using high pressure tactics, charging outlandish fees with outrageous interest rates, to swindle low income people, and those who do not understand financial subjects. Daniels said in her attempt to save her home, they went without food, and clothing at times. These subprime lenders had used what's called the "dirty double dozen deeds" on Geraldine.

Consumer advocate groups also warn us of mortgage 'flipping'. These creeps, repeatedly refinance the homes mortgage over and over until all of the home's equity is wrung out. Then the company can legally foreclose on the home. Can you imagine the wealth gained by these companies by foreclosing, then reselling the same home again to another unsuspecting victim, then repeating the same process over and over again? It could literally be an endless cash cow! Now you can see why the plutocracy is creating more and more low income people. This is like a farmer planting more crops in the field to guarantee a larger, and more prosperous harvest in the future. By lowering the standard of average American wages, and raising the prices of American homes, this sets up the stage for further fleecing, and larger profit gains in the future. Daniels with the assistance of an attorney from the American Association of Retired Persons, won a law suit and lowered her mortgage by $28,000. She then re-financed her home at market value with out any closing costs. I think it's time to turn the tables on these corporate jack a _ _ _ s!!!

The next section really hits home. On August 24, 1992, the most costly natural disaster to hit the continental United States. Hurricane Andrew struck with a vengeance.

It was a usual sunny South Florida summers day, August 23, however it seemed hotter, and very still. I had been watching the hurricane looming off our coast, but the forecast was it would get swept up in upper level winds, and blow up the coast away from us. It's winds at that point were 150 mph sustained. I had taken a trip to Home Depot to purchase a few needed hurricane items. The store was packed with people buying plywood. Well, I got my few items, since we lived in an apartment building, there was not much to board up. As evening came, the bright white billowy puffy Cumulus clouds changed to a dark overcast Nimbo Stratus, and Cumulonimbus. The storm had not taken it's projected northerly turn. But they still insisted it will curve before midnight. By 9:00 PM, the final awaited forecast was broadcasted on all TV stations, and radio stations. "The storm is not going to take the expected turn." "Hurricane Andrew is making a direct hit on Miami Dade County." My wife was 6 months pregnant with Adriana. We stayed huddled around the TV as long as the power stayed on.

REVOLT AGAINST THE PLUTOCRACY

By midnight the winds started an eerie haunted howl. The view outside, between spooky aqua and purple flashes of lightning, showed trees bowing in the 80 mph steady wind. By 2:00 AM the power started to flicker, as the famous Bryan Norcross Meteorologist raved; "This hurricane is striking Metro Dade, and if you haven't hunkered down, now is definitely the time!" At the same time between the flickering power, the doors and windows started a methodical chatter. The noise outside, now sounded like a Boeing 747 had backed up to the building, and let all four engines rip! Then something weird started to happen, we started to hear popping and buckling sounds. Our ears started to pop as every airtight container, can, soda bottle, jug of water, even the Tupper Ware started to blow their lids. A flash light on the dining room table suddenly shot it's cap off, sending the batteries across the floor. Winds now were 150+mph outside. By 2:30 AM, the power flickered it's last surge of life. I now put my wife and Mother on the couch, with their backs against the wall, as the roaring wind now sounded like a million locomotives screaming. Every few seconds you would hear deep loud thumps, and cracks, as giant Malleluca trees came crashing down. I emerged from behind the couch, and went toward the front window to take a peek outside. The sight made very hair on my head stand on end. Between those purple and aqua flashes, rivaling a giant strobe light, I witness 60 foot trees pole-vaulting through the air, and roof pieces, airplane wings, storm shutters hurling horizontally, some slamming against the building. It looked like those pictures of nuclear bomb tests, as the shock wave struck test villages, trees and telephone poles bowing horizontally. We lived on the second floor, in a corner, since the building was L shaped. We also had a concrete overhang, over the cat walk to protect the windows. Now the roof and walls started to creek and groan, like an old wooden sailing vessel on a high sea.

After, a sleepless night, the winds calmed by sun up. We emerged to a totally different world, similar to the aftermath of a nuclear Armageddon. We lived right next to the airport, but an eerie quietness fell, no bird songs, no summer Cicadas with there summer chatter, no crickets, not even the usual sound of aircraft taking off and landing. you could only here the low grumble of people walking about holding hands in disbelief. Every thing seemed brighter than usual, as not a single leaf remained on the trees that survived the onslaught. Every street had tree carcasses, and debris crisscrossing them. Not a car roamed the empty main streets.

The nights after the storm were dark and hot. Since the electricity was out all over Dade, and most of Southern Broward, the nights were so unusual. You felt as though you were twenty miles out in the country, as every star, meteors, and the milkyway shined so bright it almost cast a shadow. Something never imagined in a city of this size of Miami. There was an unusual drone of frogs, with a spooky tone and rhythm of a space creature invasion never heard before, almost as though we were out in the middle of the everglades.

The next several years, South Florida became the nerve center of every insurance company known. Residents spent weeks, months, even years waiting for their insurance companies. to come through with settlements. They paid there bills as requested, but when they needed the insurance companies to do there job, it was like pulling teeth out of a jackass. Every excuse under the South Florida sun was given so the insurance companies didn't have to pay. Every fraudulent company, shined in all of it's glory. Anarchy was the word of the day! Price gouging, not just from individuals, but from supposedly reputable companies began. Greed descended upon the land like a giant vulture. There were a lot of sympathetic corporations obviously led by civilized leaders concerned with the well-being of mankind. We, and every apartment, got free hamburger roles from a Burger King down the street. They came in a van passing out boxes and bags of roles throughout neighborhood streets. Crystal Water came out passing free bottled water from their trucks. Local grocers, allowed people free rations. Some gas stations gave free gas. Some Dept. stores gave free clothing. But for every good deed done by wonderful kind and caring corporations, there were several bad greedy deeds done by other corporations. Some charged way over the going rate for their goods and services. The ones getting away with bloody murder were the roofing, and construction contractors. They canvassed entire neighborhoods getting supposedly, refundable down payments, from bewildered homeowners to proceed with repairs. Some claimed to be with insurance companies. Then once they got your down payments, they flew away the next night. Even landlords of apartment buildings no longer standing, demanded rent from tenants, and threatened them with legal action. Insurance companies demanded extra deductibles never mentioned in the contracts, or they would just plain drop the customer, and refuse blatantly not to honor their contracts. Others, immediately raised there rates five hundred percent. Even under court orders, some openly defied the law. We are not talking about run of the mill, never heard of insurance companies. These are the country's, largest, and supposedly best insurance firms. Eventually, to prevent mass exodus of insurance companies, the federal government under federal order, came in and ordered the companies to honor contracts. The order also stated if they packed up, and abandoned the state, their business licenses would be suspended. For one gleaming moment the federal government did the right thing, without messing it up. Due to the rapid increase of homeowner's insurance rates, more people could no longer afford insurance. The federal government ended up creating it's own federally funded insurance program for South Florida residents. The Hurricane Andrew situation brought out the worst in a lot of corporations. It proved that greed is even more powerful than a historical natural disaster, and corporations financially only look out for themselves. What happened to the old saying "The customer is king???" It's apparent, that all the king's men took off with all of the king's horses. Yet, the ethical corporations showed their best in community assistance.

while I am grilling the insurance companies, a little up date. In the spring of 2000, the federal regulators regulating the insurance industry, caught them using unsafe, and unqualified auto parts when repairing your car. A lot of the parts are critical in the safe performance of the vehicles. The hell with the safety of the paying customer, expecting quality services, profit is all that counts.

Here is yet another example of corporate America not keeping it's word. An article by Diane E. Lewis, The Herald, Sunday, October 19, 1997, pg. 1G, shows America's distrust of big business. "Bosses haven't kept their part of the new 'deal,' workers say". A study of 2,500 American workers by the International management consulting firm, Towers Perrin, "found employees are increasingly skeptical their efforts are being recognized and fairly rewarded." "But what troubles workers is that some employers are not honoring the deal. In April 1996 report, for example, Business Week reported executive pay jumped 27 percent while white-collar gains averaged 1.2 percent and factory employees' pay declined 2 percent." "Employees … have been working harder than ever," "Now with corporate profits up, they expect their employers to make good on these implicit promises and share the fruits of the success." Towers Perrin then stated; "If employers want workers to remain motivated," "they must share monetary rewards and benefits and offer growth opportunities."

Just some more proof that corporate America doesn't give a damn about you or I, but yet they expect us to give the world for them. I've heard of a one way street, but this is ridiculous. "Don't Count on That Merit Raise This Year', in The Wall Street Journal Tuesday, January 7, 1997. Joan S. Lublin says; "Routine salary increases are headed for extinction," "And the pay raises that are left-which will show up in paychecks in coming weeks-seems to be losing their punch. Average increases for salaried employees sank to 3.9% in 1996 from 5% in 1990." "Fears of a rank-and-file backlash recently persuaded one major insurer to drop its planned abolition of merit raises-even though it had paid a consultant more than $50,000 to design a substitute variable-pay plan." I want you to think deeply about that last sentence! This sentence couldn't have stated the deepest, darkest secret, that corporate America fears, any clearer than it did! This is unwavering proof that corporate America, and the power structure of this country are not stupid, and knows who really has the power. It also proves, even the mighty capitalist greed mongers, have a fear that is even more powerful than greed itself. Let this be a hint to every living breathing citizen of this country, that united, we are a very powerful force to be reckoned with. You and I, a people united against a common cause, form the most powerful force in the universe. Like kryptonite to Superman, or a crucifix to an evil force, we have the power to make corporate American do anything we want! We have just forgotten how! In the same article we have been reminded that the wheels in the mind of corporate American are still turning, as is said by a vice president of compensation and benefits of an American airline. "We are working very hard to get our employees not to expect a base-pay increase every year," "It's difficult to break the expectations people have developed over many years." **Ah Ha! Gotcha!** This is what I have been saying in my other book, when I said one of the most powerful weapons that corporate psychology has is **social conditioning**. Chapter 5 goes into detail on how to counter this powerful evil force. I can not figure how people, who spend their entire lives looking for stealthy, sneaky brain washing methods, to screw their fellow man, can sleep at night! Hypocrites, they are, because every year they sure want their pay raises on time, along with the other executive gluttons. Practice what you preach you corporate slime balls, we are on to you!

Here are many more instances that corporations are more concerned about the company's profits, and the CEO's pay check, than the well-being of society. On May 11, 1996 ValuJet's DC 9 took a nose dive into the Florida Everglades, killing 110 people. This opened up a full scale investigation of the airline industry by the National Transportation Safety Board (N.T.S.B.) and the Federal Aviation Administration (F.A.A.) This opened up a Pandora's box of lies, cover ups, and destruction of crucial records by airline executives. Those famed oxygen canisters, being shipped under another name to save shipping charges, were to blame, however, the investigators thought it was the plane itself. To spite the fact that ValuJet still has not been charged in connection with the crash; "Several witnesses testified Tuesday that the Valujet DC-9 was fraught with electrical problems and ripe for disaster." "ValuJet executives fretted over the company's stock prices after the crash, a Sprint telephone operator, who monitored a company conference, call testified Tuesday." This is just some of the allegations and ilk uncovered by John Holland staff writer of the Sun sentinel Wednesday December 1, 1999, "ValluJet cover-up allegation blocked" pg. B1. U.S. District Judge James Lawrence King felt that accusations of top company officials, meeting just days after the crash, to discuss keeping critical information from falling into the hands of the federal investigators, were to shocking to present in trial. He eventually threw out 8 of the 11 charges against the company, and it's sidekick maintenance contractor SabreTech. Federal prosecution attorneys also had testimonies that the DC 9's air-conditioners, lights, and speaker system failed three times on it's last flight. A warning light called a "go-no-go" had remained lit, even when the flight crew had closed the doors before takeoff. In the previous flights before the crash, a passenger had also reported the lights flickering on and off several times, and a technician working on the floor and wall panels. "Kathleen Wheaton, who worked as a telephone conference call operator for Sprint, testified to the judge that she arranged and then monitored a call among ValuJet executives, company lawyers and an insurance company. Wheaton testified that she heard Vice President Gil Morgan worry that investigators would find out that employees on Flight 592 violated regulations and opened doors on the plane during a fire." "Wheaton quoted Morgan as saying: "I hope the people or the FAA never find out we did not follow McDonnell-Douglas recommendations to keep those doors shut. If those doors were closed. that would have contained the fire." The judge kept the evidence out of the hearing because of the possibility of it not being true, and possibly a rumor heard by Morgan that he was just repeating. Jane Moskowitz an attorney quoted; "They're trying to keep it quiet, and you don't have to keep something quiet if you didn't do anything wrong,"

You know what pisses me off the most of all, is how this company was more concerned about it's Wall

Street stock standing than those 110 living breathing human-beings who died on that plane, and how they dodged 8 out of 11 allegations. If that were you or I, we would be so far in the slammer, it would take a whole day to walk to our cell block!

Three years later we had another airplane crash. Fine Air Flight 101A crashed into an empty field, and slammed into a warehouse district after sliding across a perimeter road. The accident occurred just west of the Miami International Airport on August 7, 1997. This is the same road I take to work every day. Three flight crew, a security guard, and a motorist in his car on the road were killed. It happened in the early afternoon when the road wasn't jammed with rush hour traffic. According to witnesses, the plane lifted off of the run way in a usual manner, and ascended to a few hundred feet off the ground. Then one man stated hearing a loud thumping pounding sound, and looked up to see the plane in a nose high, tail low configuration with puffs of smoke popping out of the engines in rhythm with the thumping sounds. The plane was falling like a diver, spread eagle, attempting to do a belly flop with his legs low, and head high. The plane then belly flopped into an empty field along a perimeter road. Then bouncing up with little forward momentum, and slowly slid across the six lane road in a ball of fire striking parked cars, and the storefronts of the corporate business district. They later found out the popping thumps were caused by turbine stalls. This is because the plane, in such a nose high configuration but falling almost vertically, prevented proper airflow into the air hungry, racing engines, creating backfires. But what would cause an airplane in perfect running order with four powerful engines "peddle to the metal" as one might say or "balls to the wall" as pilots say, to fall like a leaf, and pancake into the ground. They found out that the load, 44 tones of linens, and cargo shifted rear-ward throwing the DC 8's center of gravity too far aft. As a child, I used to build model airplanes and fly them. If I didn't put enough clay or pennies into the nose of the models, they would upon liftoff, nose up, and almost come to a stop in mid air, and belly flop into the ground with engines screaming. In the Sun Sentinel on Tuesday, March 28, 2000, Ken Kaye's article, "Airline, cargo company guilty in cover-up" pgs. 1A, 12A, spells it out. "Two and a half years after a fiery cargo plane crash killed five people, Fine Air and it's freight-loading company, Aeromar Airlines, pleaded guilty on Monday to attempting to destroy or cover up evidence of cargo-loading errors." "Under a plea agreement, the two companies were convicted of five counts of obstructing justice and making false statements." "Among the government's assertions: Fine Air supervisor ordered cargo documents destroyed while Aeromar erased a damning surveillance videotape and doctored the cargo manifest to understate the jet's weight by 6,000 pounds." Fine Air admitted shortly after the crash, a supervisor had all of the documents located and destroyed. Aeromar said it adjusted the paperwork by 1,000 pounds, but the government figures state 6,000 pounds. Aeromar also destroyed the pallet weight sheets after the investigation began. The feds were on the company's front door step within 45 minutes of the crash, but all requests for the proper paperwork were refused. Also employees taped over the videotape of the loading of the jet.

No single person was ever charged, but Fine Air had two felony counts with a $3.5 million dollar fine. Aeromar, was fined $1.5 million, and had three felony counts. Fine Air took responsibility for it's employees conduct. Aeromar fired some of the employees responsible for altering documents. Both of them were put on four years probation. Just a slap on the back of the hand. William Tompkins, a special agent in charge with the Inspector General's office of the Dept. of Transportation quoted; "These illegal actions undermine the strength of the entire safety chain,"

My fellow Americans, let me ask you a question. What do you think would happen if you, or I were found guilty of reckless conduct that resulted in five deaths, and millions of dollars of property damage? Then what if we were blatantly, caught destroying evidence at the crime scene? Then we lied to the police, and refused to obey the officers? **WE WOULD BE ARRESTED**, quicker than one could say "freeze pal!" There is a two sided justice system, one for the wealthy corporations and individuals, and one for everybody else. All of you Republicans out there, what do you have to say about that? You claim you are for the best interests of a free democratic society, it's more like a free democratic corporate society to democratically pillage, plunder, rape, and destroy society in the name of profit!! And then you have the guts to look America in the eyes, and claim you are doing this according to constitutional law!!! Unlike lying deceitful Democrats, I do give you credit for your arrogance, and openly supporting your beliefs with out lying, or cover ups. You said you would free corporate America from regulations, and you did. You, vowed to make the rich richer, and you did. Well, like Rush Limbaugh said, true Republicans are truthful, God faring, men of their word. Thank God for small miracles!

To bring children into the world is one of the most sacred journeys a loving couple can embark on. This is a time when there is enough changes, and stress in the lives of these young parents. For the first time they are now parents, in charge of a frail life-form They will make decisions that will shape a new human-being from a crying, weak, helpless, and hungry kitten sized creature. This is definitely not the time for these young parents to be concerned with anything else. However, the greed factor has even violated these sacred grounds.

President Clinton passed The Family Leave Act, in the early 1990s to protect workers, who want to take time off for maternity, paternity, and medical reasons, from corporate retaliation. To spite, The Family Leave Act being law, corporations, and even some state, and city departments are choosing to deny employees the freedom to take off for maternity leave, or medical leave. If they do not outright deny them this constitutional right, they make the lives of the employees impossible. They seem to be getting away with it too, as the system to enforce this right is getting bogged down with complaints. As you already know what my wife and I went through, with our first attempts to exercise this sacred right. The Wall Street Journal, Wednesday, October 30, 1996 had an article by Sue Shellenbarger, pg. B1, "Family Leave Is Law, But Climate Is Poor For Actually Taking It" "For more than a year, Kevin Knussman has been a poster dad for working parents." "When Mr. Knussman sued his employer, the Maryland State Police, over his unsuccessful attempt to win a 30 day paid child-birth leave, he became to many a symbol of men's struggle to balance jobs with father hood." During a staff meeting Mr. Knussman a paramedic was embarrassingly humiliated in front of his coworkers by a commander. The commander said that a local news paper had run an article on the Knussman case, and stated he should keep all dirty laundry at home. Then shortly after, he was transferred to a location tripling his drive to and from work. All of this, after being promised that transfers were out of the question. "Now, Mr. Knussman believes he is paying a price." "I can understand," Mr. Knussman quotes; "Why most people won't make an issue of these things." Dee Soder of a New York executive-advisory organization, the CEO Perspective Group says, "Employees are more at risk than they've ever been,". "Fear of retaliation, coupled with the exhaustion brought on by family stress, keeps many from asserting their rights," says Ellen Bravo of 9to5, National Association of Working Woman, a woman's advocacy group. She also adds; "To avoid hassles, workers who need family time off must find savvy ways to assert what for many is not only a right, but a deeply felt value." It is plainly apparent that most corporate leaders would rather have this constitutional amendment revoked. These creeps do not have a shred of human decency!

Jay T. Baldwin

On my pest control rout, I ran into a retired official of a political civil servant office. He let me in on a horrible, dirty little secret of today's federal enforcement administrations regarding these laws, and other constitutional rights. There is a certain quota of violation cases that can be resolved in a particular period of time. Once they exceed this, they must not resolve anymore cases, no matter how serious the violations against the victims are. He explained, it is all politics, and the government can not get too cozy with enforcement of laws, rights, and constitutional amendments. He said this would directly effect the political contributions from powerful corporate lobbyist groups, and Political Action Committees (P.A.C.s). He also added, it didn't matter if there was a liberal Democratic or a conservative Republican administration at the helm. Only high profile, large class action cases are usually resolved. The American people are the sacrificial lamb for the benefit of corporate America. It's the price of doing business in America, and big money gets it's way most of the time.

Now you see the kind of evil we are up against, and the need to counter social conditioning! Corporate strategists must calculate into their equations, that most people give in without so much as a peep. This is because they are already overwhelmed with extra family stress brought on by the arrival of the new infant, or the grief brought on by a sick member of the family. If this little secret is really out there, how the hell can these heartless creeps sleep with themselves at night?

I serviced a customer for a bad ant problem, that happened to be the owner of a large real-estate contractor firm in Broward County. He had forgotten about an earlier appointment with me that week. While I was servicing his house, the usual occurred. I became, the always smiling and listening, bug killing psychiatrist, that people unload their burdens on for a brief few minutes. He said he was sorry for standing me up earlier in the week, but he has been in and out of court all week. He said he is being sued by a couple of employees, because he fired them when they got pregnant, and needed maternity leave. He openly believed that employees, who decide to start a family, do not deserve the right to work. It's a burden to businesses across the country, and the family leave laws were crippling American businesses. He angrily grunted, that he would not settle out of court, even if it would be more cost effective to do so. He claimed, he was now on a personal crusade against these employees, and The Family Leave Act, and wanted to obliterate the both of them. Guess what my friends? He was also a father of several daughters! I wonder how he would feel, if he were in the employees shoes?

But little to his surprise, he didn't realize who he was divulging all of his dirty little secrets to. I felt like the fly that accidentally strayed into the spider's parlor! I kept listening very intently with the sound of my blood boiling, and the overwhelming desire to start a counter argument. I just played stupid, and prodded him for even more of his little secrets. I then realized I had an opportunity of a lifetime to see into the mind of one of these corporate monsters, and see what makes them tick. He followed me around the whole house, spilling his guts. I was very careful not to spook the spider, or rattle his web, because this little fly was dawning a spider suit and was going to dance with the Tarantula. I found out he does not hire employees who plan to start families, or who already have them. He made it clear to his current workers, if they ever decide to start families, he would have to let them go. I even found out his feelings regarding need for employees to take time off for medical reasons or sick members of the family. He was basically as Machiavellian about that, as he was about maternity leave. They're out-a-here! If they get sick, that's their tuff luck! It's survival of the fittest! He wished for the day when corporations had no federal laws, or worker's rights to contend with.

After an hour of servicing his country mansion, I was almost ready to break out laughing, just knowing he had no idea, he just brushed eyebrows with one of the largest worker, and consumer advocates this side of Ralph Nader. See how my job has given me, not just an accurate account of the suffrage of the working American, but a view from within the lives of the enemy. My experiences give me more reliable information than all of the government surveys and poles combined. I can rest assured my observations are a depiction of reality regardless of what anybody says! You will have a hell of a time proving me wrong!

Here is just one article I found, about this very problem. The Herald, Sunday 12, 1999, pg. 3B, by Jasmine Kripalani, "Woman discuss life, work, 'solutions to situations'. A special program, Women for Human Rights International (W.H.R.I.) at Florida International University, educates women on tactics to protect them from inhumane employers. They were founded in 1988, and have helped thousands of women, as well as men fight unfair, and discriminating actions by big business.

How to contact W.H.R.I.
Woman for Human Rights International
1550 Madruga Ave., Suite 200
Coral Gables, Florida 33146
phone (305) 662-7117
e-mail womhumrts@aol.com

Marcos Regalado, director of the Miami-Dade County Equal Opportunity Board says; "We get a lot of cases dealing with sexual discrimination," "You have to know what to look for. Many people may have been discriminated and do not know it." One red flag is an employer that asks a potential employee if she plans to have children. Regalado says the question can be used in the selection process.

I was asked at several places of employment if I was married, and how many children I have, when filling out their applications. One was a truck position I mentioned in my first book. The one that would not have hired me, because I was a family man, and could not support my family on the peanut wages he offered. He wanted to keep turn over to a minimum. I have also been asked what my hobbies, and interests are, and what kind of car I drive. There is even a question on whether I rent or own a home. I was even asked to sign credit release forms, so the company can look at my credit history. I am not there for a loan! That's non of there damn business! I later asked one of my managers that trusted me, after I got hired, why all of the questions. He was straight forward with me and stated, "The company wanted to know if your lifestyle was compatible with the wages they were offering." "They didn't want to hire somebody owning a large house, and driving an expensive car, with too expensive of hobbies." They seem to be very concerned about how many children I plan to have. I thought these questions were just familiarization questions. But these corporate wizards are probably assessing if I am a high maintenance employee, with adult financial responsibilities. Just the type they prefer not to have.

I have now seen the trends in both the trucking industry, marine carpentry industry, and the pest control industry first handed. I have also noticed these trends in many other industries. They are also simplifying the tasks so as not to require any thought, decisions, or experience on behalf of the employees. They create check lists with protocol procedures in numerical order, so all tasks at hand are treated the same way, regardless if each individual situation requires a different approach to properly complete the task. Even if the outcome is successful or not, they do not want employees making judgment calls out on the field. These corporate wonders don't seem to want people to use their brains. They no longer look for veterans, who have been in the industry for too many years. They seem to favor younger, inexperienced, single employees, minorities, and in some cases seniors on a pension income. Some employers no longer require experience, when in the past they only hired experienced. Maybe, they are afraid of somebody who knows the trade inside and out.

Do you want to hear my take? I believe there is something more to it than the usual excuses. They do not want to hire somebody that will get board with the

REVOLT AGAINST THE PLUTOCRACY

job and quit, or somebody that knows to much, and can not be tailor trained for that individual company, as old habits are hard to break, or they are attempting to standardize all procedures, etc. These typical excuses are just a front. Our company had been running adds for experienced pest control technicians for some time. They interviewed many people, but none of them ever accepted the new lower wages. The company was desperate for workers, and was falling behind in production, because of a shortage of help. It was also hesitant to allow the few of us left, after reorganization, to put in overtime. Then they changed the add to say inexperienced, will train. I believe they are really afraid of experience, because they will have to pay more for it. My company told me, after they reorganized, that experience no longer determines wage levels. This was the same week I was given a $2 an hour pay cut. Before the reorganization, I as hired at $11 an hour because of my extensive experience. Now, if I had 14 years of experience, I would start at the same rate as a rooky. They have also told me not to use my infinite experience on the field, if it breaks company protocol. Ironically, if the protocol treatments fail, as they do some of the time, the technician is labeled negligent in his duties. No two homes can be treated in the same manner. It depends on the pest, it's location, the shape the design of the house, the occupants, their ages, if any pets are free to roam the home. I feel all of my experience, and all that I have learned is now useless, even if it would greatly improve their service to the customers, and create a better quality service or product. I think they may greatly fear a knowledgeable workers, as he is more of

Jay T. Baldwin

a threat to those already in positions of power. He just might take their job! He could be experienced enough to identify injustices, discriminations as

Illustration 6

"Not paid to think on your own." With more companies centralizing, de-professionalizing and de-valuing American labor, so they do not have to pay Americans functional salaries, most tasks are now standardized in a procedures manual. This now allows companies to hire anybody that can read, and minimizes training time. Hence they do not have to pay professionals a high salary, and can slowly lower our salaries to keep corporate profits growing. However, quality and personal attention to the customer is sacrificed. Flexibility in dealing with variable consumer and employee circumstances is highly forbidden, unless it is clearly written in the company's procedure manual. Last but not least, individualities of employees of the firm are vigorously eliminated, and the consumers must adapt to the fact they exist purely for the company's benefit and profit.

defined by employee regulations, laws, constitutional acts, or improper procedures as defined by government rules, and see through all of the executive mind games. He can not be conditioned! He is too smart for his own good in the eyes of big business!

Yes! You corporate big shots, the American worker is on to you, and your psychological mind games!

Have you ever heard the saying, "Big money has no soul!" It definitely has no respect for human feelings either. I have been constantly reminded not to express any human emotions at the work place. It has been pounded in at all of the employment preparation courses. It is discrediting to be human in front of supervisors. We have to literally be automatons, machines with no emotions. Have you ever heard of such a thing? Humans by nature are emotional animals. It is also unhealthy to keep emotions penned-up, according to leading psychologists. In The Herald, Sunday, October10, 1999, pg. 1F by David Tarrant, "Tears at work reduce stress... and credibility" "Crying-by women or men-has been viewed as a sign of weakness and an undesirable reaction in the marketplace that values intellect over emotion." "However, crying is also the body's natural way to vent stress. Emotional repression can lead to a range of health problems from eating disorders to chemical dependency."

Thomas Anastasi, a specialist in controversial workplace behaviors, and a Boston University School of Management instructor, says if you are looking for a warm, emotionally understanding workplace, better think again! "If anything, things have become worse. Any type of emotional display-joy, sorrow, laughing-is frowned upon. People are expected to be even-keeled."

Yet, we wonder why more people are going postal at the work place. We have become an emotionally oppressed society, and we are now just beginning to see the side effects. This probably has repercussions throughout our entire lives, not just at the work place. It could be the root cause to many of society's ills. There has been an increase in road rage, air rage, desk rage, domestic abuse, child abuse, and emotional problems throughout society. It has no racial, sexual, or religious boundaries. This inhuman, unethical, expectation to be what we are not at all times, thrust upon society by corporate America must

REVOLT AGAINST THE PLUTOCRACY

be challenged at all costs. It is another battlefront we will face, in our revolution against the psychological warriors of big business.

Illustration 7

"The emotionless Vulcan an ideal employee." Self expression is the enemy of the business mind.

Jay T. Baldwin

Do you take medications? Most every person at one time or another has had to take that trip to the pharmacy. You feel as though you are taking a trip to the IRS, or taking your car in for repair work. You are scared to hear what the bill is going to be. Medication costs have skyrocketed over the past 10 years. In fact the United States leads the entire industrialized world as having the most expensive prescriptions. In democratic industrialized nations where the government controls the costs of medications, the prescription costs have been reduced by ¼ to ½ that of the United States. Less than ½ of all prescriptions in the U.S. are ever filled. The reason is not that Americans hate taking medications, but they just can not afford it. They, all too many times, have to make a choice between medications, food, and a roof over their head. Even with my wife's medical insurance, the deductibles for our monthly prescriptions are a financial burden. I, many times, have to choose the most important prescriptions first, and if there is money left over, fill the remaining ones. Imagine those without medical insurance, as we were just a couple of years ago. We had to choose not to pay something just to swing medication costs.

Then there are cheaper generic drugs, which we get whenever possible. However, the greed mongers at the world's 3 largest prescription medication producers, were found cornering the market on cheaper generic drug manufacturers. They pay the manufacturers of cheaper generic drugs not to market their generic equivalents. Many heart patients in America were denied cheaper generic drugs because of this practice. Some of these patients were put into a life or death situation because of corporate greed. I have also lost access to cheaper generic versions because of this corporate extortion, and black mail. This resulted in me forgoing the needed medication, because of the difference in cost. It seems capitalism is not in the best interest of human well-being, except for those privileged few wealthy executives leading the pharmaceutical industry. What is more important, human life or corporate profits? I thought we were in the 21st century, but it seems more like the Dark Ages. What the hell happened to civility? Are we regressing culturally, for the benefit of the elites? Must we continue to allow people to die because of the lack of money? Shall we allow a handful of greedy, wealthy, fat cats expose the masses of America, and the world to this form of decadence just for their financial well-being?

The rap sheet just keeps going on! It seems wherever there is big money, there is corporate, and political crime. Even drug dealing, with it's easy road to riches for those who know how to ride the intricate bronco of luck and reward, turns into a very lucrative venture. But, what is to be said, when big powerful supposedly reputable corporations, begin to dip their hands into the quagmire of dirty money? Now we raise the universal question, that nobody has been able to answer, through out time. *Is money the root of all that is evil?* No matter how tempting it is, for those being oppressed by big money, to label it as pure unadulterated evil, common sense dictates likewise. I am even guilty of thinking that money is pure evil, almost on a daily basis, but I have been very observant.

Jay T. Baldwin

My common sense continually keeps me down to earth. I have learned throughout history, that anything of value can be linked to evil deeds. In the past, salt, spices, incense, furs, silk, precious stones, gold, silver, and even food became the obsessions man waged wars, killed, cheated, and deceived all that is honorable to gain. Another common denominator, is the desire of man to have more than his rightful share. It seems that no matter how much any person gains or achieves, he is never satisfied. This results in a spiraling effect, the more one gains, the more one wants, the more one wants, the more the desire to gain. This can go on indefinitely until man destroys himself, and all around him in his quest to have more than his neighbor. This is similar to drugs, alcohol, or food to a substance abuser. Observation also teaches us that anything can be used for evil purposes, even things used to create. Example; guns, a tool originally used to hunt for food, used for protection, or for recreational sports. But guns can also be used for pure evil, in robbery, murder, intimidation, and destruction. This is a good one for gun supporters, and the anti-gun supporters. A car can be used for transportation, or it can be used for death, and destruction. A hammer can be used to build a home, a civilization, or it can be used to bash somebody's head in. All of you gun critics out there, what would you do if suddenly hammers were used in place of guns in all crimes, and murders? Would you change your crusade to illegalize all hammers? Would there be hammer control. Think about it!

This now leaves us with the last denominator, **MAN!** It is not the tool that is evil, but man himself! Money is nothing but a tool. Money is intended to expand prosperity, civilization, technology, and standards of living. The problem begins when the wrong people are given control of money, and it's distribution. In Chapter 4 we will discuss man's inability to control himself, and if we have de-evolved sufficiently enough to no longer deserve the right to such a wonderful tool as money, or capitalism. We may no longer be responsible enough to handle money, and capitalism!

In The Herald Tuesday, June 22, 1999 an article by Mimi Whitefield, "Companies warned not to launder money" pg. C1, says it all. "The Treasury Department warned Monday that it intends to crack down on U.S. companies that help Colombian drug traffickers clean billions of illicit drug dollars through black-market money exchanges." These drug lords have laundered an estimated $5 billion a year using prestigious American corporations, and the Colombian black market peso exchange market. The Treasury Department has vowed to crack down on this activity. Drug lords have to deal with pesos to run their daily operations. However, drugs bought in the U.S. are paid for with American dollars. Where American corporations get involved, is legitimate Colombian businesses need American dollars to purchase foreign goods. To change the dollars for pesos, the Colombian businesses contract the black market money exchangers who have access to the drug lord's drug money. The drug lords usually pay a 20% to 25% service fee for the exchange. The American businesses then gratefully accept the former drug dollars to be deposited in their accounts. "One witness, a Colombian black-market money changer identified only as Carlos, told lawmakers Monday how he helped launder drug money through purchases of products from major corporations, including Sony, Whirlpool, Kodak and General Electric."

The environment is the last vestige of nature. The environment has been stressed enough by man's conquering hand. Now to have corporations in the name of reducing expenses, and raising more profits, openly polluting it, is totally unacceptable. I can hear all of the conservative Republicans saying, "The environment can easily absorb anything man throws at her!". "Please keep government control out of corporations faces!" That may be partially true, as the environment has proven it's resiliency in the past to recover from devastating catastrophes. Man is not the only animal that pollutes the environment. Life forms in general emit waste products amounting to or exceeding any wastes put out by man alone. Attending many entomological seminars in the pest control industry, I have learned that something as small as an ant can have a devastating impact on the O-zone layer. Ants, in mass quantities, dump thousands of tons of formic acid into the air every year. For every person on earth, there are several million ants. This formic acid is used in trail marking, so other ants can follow a worker ant, that has had a good day at the grocery store, to the food source. It is an invisible dotted line, that ants follow with their sensitive antennas. Formic acid is not just a green house gas, but it deteriorates the O-zone layer as rapidly as CFC's. The environment has been dealing with ants a lot longer than she has wrestled with man. Animals are releasing by-products in their act of living and functioning. But to purposely try

Mother Nature's patience in the name of profits! I am not willing to take that chance. So it costs a company some of it's profits to be environmentally friendly. Maybe, it's time for the greed at the highest reaches of the corporate machine to do with a little less! What will be the straw to break the camel's back? Are you willing to gamble?

"Slick JUSTICE", in The Herald, Sunday, September 26, 1999, pgs. 1L, 2L, by Gregg Fields is a prime example of deliberate dumping in the name of profits. "A Cost Guard tracking plane was following the world's largest cruise ship, Royal Caribbean's Sovereign of the Seas, as it chugged toward San Juan on the morning of Oct. 25, 1994. It was a routine observation flight; the Coast Guard is charged with keeping an eye out for a wide variety of things from drug smuggling to refugees on rafts." "The crew dropped to a lower altitude, and this time saw the slicks with their naked eyes. The Sovereign was the only ship in the area."

Coast Guard personnel were dispatched from San Juan to collect sea water samples at the sight of the oil slick. Then they went back to port to wait for the cruise ship to dock. When the ship pulled into port, "The crewmen aboard the Coast Guard boat gathering the oil spill sample knew they were onto something when they saw oil being discharged directly into San Juan harbor."

These giant ships are basically cities afloat, and they produce different kinds of waste products. They also have a variety of methods of dealing with this waste. Gray water, the water from sinks, showers, and laundry, can be safely discharged at sea. Black water, or sewage from toilets, can be treated at sea and safely discharged, or can be stored until arrival at a port where it is pumped out for treatment. Bilge water, free water in the bowels of ships, can and usually is laden with oil, and fuel must be treated thoroughly before discharge. Chemical wastes are never to be dumped overboard!

Once in port, the Coast guard investigators boarded, and met with the Captain of the cruise ship. He insisted they were mistaken, as all of the ship's pollution control systems were fully operational. There is a filter called an oil/water separator that scrubs bilge water clean before it's discharged. The investigators were still skeptical, and wanted to meet with the ships chief engineer. After meeting with the engineer, who's story coincided with the Captain's, they insisted on seeing the equipment actually work. When down in the engine room, the investigators found some giant tanks full of oily water in the discharge bins. Now they were really suspicious. The Coast Guard denied the departure of the ship. It posted a $500,000 fine to be paid before it would grant departure of the ship. By evening, a second crew more experienced in these giant ships boarded, asking for diagrams of the boat's waste system, and copies of the Oil Record Book. This book is a log of all oil discharges. These investigators also took a little tour of the engine room, and found remnants of pure oil, not water, leaking out of the discharge pipes. Oil coated rags were also found inside a bilge tank meant for water only. It seemed the crew was trying to hide the mess before the inspectors had arrived, but were not able to finish. They then ordered the crew to operate the oil/water filters. The engineer said he couldn't because there wasn't enough water in it. Then they insisted the valves, that should only contain water, be opened. Pure oil flowed out! Either the filter system was malfunctioning, or it had been deliberately bypassed.

Twelve hours after the initial violation, it was now, almost midnight, and the investigators were met by the cruise line's attorney. He accompanied them the rest of the investigation. The crew was once again ordered to demonstrate the filtration system. The system failed miserably, and didn't clean the water. Even the sensors that detected oil in the water were not working, and didn't return improperly filtered water back into the system to be cleaned again. Ironically, the ships logs showed that the machine hadn't been operated in almost a month. The investigators finally found proof through pictures taken at two different times, that there was indeed a bypass installed to dump waste directly into the sea. The crew had removed the pipe, and cut it up into small pieces to hide it more easily. Later they disposed of the pipe scraps when they returned to Miami. The Coast Guard later learned that the Oil Record Book was also called the eventyrbook (fairy tale book) in Norwegian. Basically a lie book, only designed to fool authorities.

The big question is why the crew was not using the pollution equipment? "Partly, money. The oil is cleaned from water by running it through expensive membranes-that cost $10,000 a set, and they needed to be changed up to 10 times a year. Furthermore, the cost of removing the oily sludge that remained has been estimated at several hundred thousand dollars a year, depending on the amount."

"It was cheaper just to pump it overboard." The membrane technology for the oil/water filter has not been perfected, and is a pain in the a _ _ to operate.

This resulted in the FBI, the Environmental Protection Agency, grand juries in New York, Alaska, California, and the Virgin Islands also getting involved. After some investigating they all found 8 other ships from the same company had been doing the same violations, falsifying records, and lying to the authorities. Other wastes such as solvents, dry cleaning fluids, photo processing fluids, etc. were dumped into the ocean. "On one sailing in 1994, the Song of America discharged 5,000 gallons of oily bilge between new York and Bermuda. Such discharges were routine on the ship, which had doctored sensors so that polluted water would actually read as clean enough to discharge."

"In Miami, Royal Caribbean's home port, it regularly dumped pollutants into the Port of Miami, including silver used in photo labs and a compound known as perchloroethylene used in dry cleaning. Other toxic wastes it simply stored at the port, without permits."

"In Alaska in 1994 and 1995, its Nordic Prince routinely discharged oil-contaminated waste, and in fact didn't use the oil/water separator at all. The waste was typically discharged around midnight to avoid detection."

"In St. Croix in the Virgin Islands, the Song of America, Song of Norway and Sovereign of the Seas dumped dirty water directly into the sea on a weekly basis."

"In California, the Nordic Prince rarely used its oil/water separator, instead dumping its bilge waste into the sea. As with other instances, it would later present fictitious Oil Record Books to the Coast Guard."

"In January 1995, the Coast Guard videotaped an oil slick trailing the company's Monarch of the Seas. The slick was 22 miles long." According to the article, the president of the company quoted; "'The investigation clearly revealed we had some shortcomings in our oversight of waste disposal programs. I haven't distanced myself from what happened in the early '90s, but the fact is I wasn't here.'"

On December 19, 1996, the cruise company was served a 10-count indictment in San Juan Puerto Rico. However, the indictment only charged the chief engineer, and the first engineer for the actual crime. It never made it clear if the company's top brass knew anything about the dumping. The employees following corporate directives ended up taking the fall for the corporation! This ended up being just a slap on the back of the hand for the executives, with a promise to inflict more serious punishment to any cruise line that dares to pollute our oceans.

Jay T. Baldwin

Illustration 8

"How many times do I have to tell you?" Like children, corporations must have constant supervision from regulators. The moment you turn your back on them, they are back to their mischief.

From the seven seas to the wild frontier, the corporate greedmonger is still king of the jungle. You will need a giant, safe, sports utility vehicle to explore the wild frontier. The SUV is one of the safest vehicles to ever be mass produced for public use, providing you operate it in a civilized manner. They are roomy, luxurious, and carry many more passengers than a family sedan. It's mad max on the exterior, and the Ritz/Carlton on the interior. The SUV has replaced the station wagon as an all purpose family vehicle. But the problem begins when something totally unpredictable comes into play as a new variable in the design equation figured by the designers. An SUV is only as safe as the giant tires it is riding on. Being inherently top heavy, they were not designed for catastrophic tire failure, but for the average flat tire. The problem is the tire manufacturer has let down the auto industry, and has not played by it's reputation. One of our nation's, supposedly most reputable tire manufacturers, has lived up to capitalism's new more greedy and heartless attitude geared only toward the bottom line. "Firestone plant cut corners, ex-workers say" in The Herald August 13, 2000 by James V. Grimaldi rakes, yet another cold hearted firm, over the coals for crimes against the society. "Bridgestone/Firestone, a subsidiary of the Japan-based Bridgestone Corp., recalled an estimated 6½ million ATX, ATXII and Wilderness tires, many that came as standard equipment on top-selling Ford Explorer sport-utility vehicles, after the federal government began investigating tires in accidents that killed 46 people and injured 80." 14 lawsuits have been recently filed against the corporation. Retired and former workers about to testify allege that;

"Decature workers engaged in practices such as puncturing bubbles on tires to cover up flaws on products that should have been scrapped."

"Conditions in the plant, particularly high humidity from lack of air conditioning in some areas, made it more likely that corrosion would occur on the brass-coated steel in the steel-belted radial tires"

"Employees had powerful financial incentives to release botched tires to the motoring public"

Bruce Kaster, an Ocala based attorney assisting some of the victims of the faulty tires, subpoenaed some former employees. The employees stated, they were paid on the basis, if they met or passed their production quotas, forced upon them under oppressive, stressful conditions. "It is not the fault of the workers," Kaster said. "They are doing the best they can under adverse working conditions."

"Clarence wood, who worked at the plant until 1996, said in a signed statement that workers, who were paid on a piecework salary program, protested – to no avail – that quality was being sacrificed for quantity."

"When inspectors complained about tires not being right, the response from management would be, "'You don't understand the tire business,'" "Wood said. "We knew the tires were bad."

Whether these practices were just a localized problem, or they were practices dictated by the highest ranks in the company, one will never know! The same motive, get away with it as long as they can, until they get caught, then use the employees as scape-goats.

Think about it for one moment! Number one, if you or I were to get caught doing this same crime on a private level, we would be arrested on sight, sent to jail, slapped with an unimaginable bond amount, fined to the extent we could never pay. We would then have our day in court, and since we have no money to cover the fines, we would end up back in jail for a very long time. Number two, if we happened to have a house, and dependents, the kids would end up in state custody, and in foster homes. The house would be foreclosed, and all of the furnishings would be auctioned off. Proceeds from all of this would be gobbled up like pieces of carrion by the vultures. Like sharks in a feeding frenzy over fish heads and chum, our entire lives would end up being obliterated. Do you see this happening to those big rich fellows heading America's corporations?

This surely reminds me of my dealings with the trucking companies. The companies refused to correct unsafe equipment or some other criminal violation, but when the employees brought it to the attention of management, they would be ordered to ignore the problem, and continue with their duties. God forbid the companies got caught, they would lie to authorities, blaming the employees. They would claim total ignorance about the violations, turning the bewildered workers over to the authorities for punishment. Or the companies would put on a big show for the inspectors by firing the employees, and reassuring them the remaining personnel would receive safety procedure protocol briefings so it would not happen again. Just use the American workers like a piece of toilet paper to clean their a _ _! Is this what America is all about?? Is this just another example of a duel justice system, one for the wealthy corporate elites, and one for everybody else? Must the few remaining morally, and socially responsible corporations left out there wear the bad name along with the immoral majority? Why the Sam hell are we just sitting back, and taking this, when we have the power to change this?

Every time I here the statistics of the civility of our capitalistic system, and it's supposed milestone improvements over the past twenty years, I writhe. From the view point of a blue collar worker, these statistics couldn't be any farther from the truth. I feel as though we have traversed some time warp, and arrived at some late 1800 uncivilized job site. We are de-evolving back to some simian, pre-homosapien age when it comes to humane treatment of our work force. Capitalism is tarnishing it's image with this Darwinian survival of the fittest ideology. In a literal sense, mankind has only evolved in his methods, and efficiency in exploitation. He is using modern tools, and ideas coupled with prehistoric territorial, and domination traits over his fellow man. With these dark forces at work, will capitalism ever re-evolve back to a more humane civilized state? Is capitalism just a modern expression of primitive animal instincts, and are we only fooling ourselves when we claim to be intelligent, civilized beings?

Chapter 4 Designed by greed. New world economic & political order.

plu.toc.ra.cy 1. the rule or power of wealth or of the wealthy. **2.** a class or group ruling or exercising power by virtue of it's wealth.

de.moc.ra.cy 1. government by the people; a form of government in which the supreme power is vested in the people, and exercised directly by them, or by their elected agents under a free electoral system. **2.** a state having such a form of government. **3.** political or social equality; democratic spirit. **4.** the common people with respect to their political power.

Which one of these definitions looks most like the United States of America today? ***Remember***

Jay T. Baldwin

campaign finance reform, soft money, and big money interests! If you can not figure this one out, then chalk another point up for social conditioning!!

After the election of 2000, we have seen what "soft money", and big money has done to our government. Party affiliation makes no difference, when it comes to "soft money", they are all big money interest whores. The Democrats claim they want to eliminate soft money, at the same time they are also using soft money to keep up with the Republicans. They admit soft money is wrong, but they will also continue to use it as long as nobody is willing to promote campaign finance reform. The Republicans openly support soft money, claiming it is democracy at work. I hardly believe it is the type of democracy, I would want to be a part of. One with survival of the fittest, law of the jungle philosophy. One with those, who have the most amount of money, winning over those with the least amount of money. I guess you could say it is a democracy, if dollar bills are counted as voters instead of American citizens. Then it would be the call of the majority! This type of Democracy is, which ever candidate can sell himself for the most amount of money, gets elected. I thought a democracy elected candidates for president based on which candidates can bring the most benefit to the most number of people, not the privileged few, who give the most money, get their candidate elected to watch out for their own greedy interests. Even after 8 years of Bill Clinton, the Democratic Party has still allowed most

Illustration 9

"Down for the count" What is constitutional? Big money interests or the less funded majority? Once again campaign finance reform has taken a back seat and probably will not be addressed for some time. The American voters have been pounded by the big money of a scant few. Is allowing big money in the hands of a wealthy minority to overrule the vote of a mass majority an expression of freedom of speech? Is this democracy? Is this what our founding fathers intended in the first amendment? It doesn't take a rocket scientist to figure this one out!

Illustration 10

"**Addicted to sweets**" If the government deregulates corporate America the flow of sweet campaign contributions is never ending. If it clamps down on corporations, the flow of contributions can dry up. Can our government ever wean itself from the complete influence of big money? Is democracy in it's literal form become a myth?

of the Republican policies to continue to function unchallenged. They have done a little to help by raising the minimum wage, and adding the Family Leave Act to the Constitution. However, in 8 years, they have only tapped the brakes on this run-away locomotive, and have not reversed it to raise the standard of living of the working masses, by a milestone. In the face of an economic hayday for the corporate elites, still millions of American workers are taking pay, and benefit cuts from corporations with record exploding profits, and stock margins. To spite a supposed booming economy, millions of people across the nation are still slowly loosing their grip on the American Dream. Regardless of the reports of American work hours declining, millions of workers are working harder, and longer hours, some more than one job, to compensate for leaner paychecks. Even with reports of inflation being almost stagnant, prices of houses, rents, cars, gasoline, health care, college, and all kinds of insurances are skyrocketing, and Millions of families are loosing their health insurance. Every year more middleclass children fall into the ravages of poverty, and more poor children are getting poorer.

Jay T. Baldwin

Joe Lieberman quoted; "When the Republicans want to feed the birds, they feed more oats to the horse." That basically describes both parties as far as the working class is concerned. They are both wolves! One is a little more compassionate, and is wearing sheep's clothing. The other arrogantly flaunts his wolfness, in an extreme Darwinian fashion. With both of these ideas in mind, maybe we should change the definition of our country, and it's political system! The definition would read somewhat like this.

Illustration 11

"Trickle down theory" In a horse's a _ _! The conservative idea of workers pay raises is to feed more oats to the horse to feed the birds.

REVOLT AGAINST THE PLUTOCRACY

United States, 1. a large North American republicratic plutocracy, comprising 48 conterminous states, the District of Columbia, and Alaska in North America, and Hawaii in the N. Pacific. **2.** once a thriving democracy ruled by a prosperous, powerful, free middleclass majority, now ruled by a powerful, wealthy, corporate elite minority. **3.** a nation with a social/economic system, with an absolute free capitalist economy, that prides itself with an oppressive Machiavellian/Darwinian ideology, that preserves the current status quo in favor of corporate/commercial prosperity at the expense of an ignorant, socially conditioned, oppressed majority. **4.** a country with a population consistent of a 5% wealthy elite and a declining 90% middleclass merging with a 5% underclass poor as a proletariat servant class. **5.** a nation where freedom of choice, constitutional rights, human rights, and legal/social justices are mostly enjoyed by citizens with financial resources able to purchase or access such privileges. **6.** U..S. Also called United States of America, America.

Re.pub.lic.rat.ic par.ty 1. the combination of two U.S. political parties with like ideals, and oppressive objectives, and goals, only differing as follows; Democratic Party ideals favor a large centralized, corporate sponsored, un-compassionate, government oppressing the society, citizens, and the economy with socialistic/Darwinian tactics to keep them dependant. Republican Party ideals favor a small corporate sponsored government with a hands off, let capitalism, the free market, and corporations with their wealthy leaders oppress the society, citizens, and the economy with un-compassionate Fascist/Darwinian tactics. **2.** a corporate sponsored party that gracefully, and deceitfully rules a country, society, economy, and a people through economic/social oppression, of ignorant unconcerned masses with Fascist/Leninist tactics that favors a wealthy, elite, oligarchical power structure. **3.** a politico/corporate party with centralized power concentrated in a wealthy few sponsored by corporate contributions. **4.** a governmental party that is known to utilizes press control, propaganda, and social conditioning to maintain status quo, and reserves most freedoms, privileges, and justices for an upper-class minority with large financial resources. **5.** a political party that strongly opposes power vested in the majority, but hypocritically preaches democratic principles. **6.** a party indigenous to the United States of America.

If you lean to the liberal left, or to the conservative right doesn't matter much, because it's open season on democracy, freedom, financial security, the American Dream. My role models Donald L. Barlett and James B. Steele Pulitzer Prize-Winning Investigative Reporters for the Philadelphia inquirer writers of "America: Who Stole the Dream?" had this quoted in their book; "Who Revoked the Dream? Let's suppose for a moment, there was a country where the people in charge charted a course that eliminated millions of good paying jobs. Suppose they gave away several million more jobs to other nations. Finally, imagine that the people running this country implemented economic policies that enabled those at the very top to grow ever richer while most others grew poorer."

"You wouldn't want to live in such a place, would you?"

"Too bad."

"You already do."

"These are some of the consequences of failed U.S. government policies that have been building over the last three decades-the same policies that people in Washington today are intent on keeping and expanding. Under them, 100 million Americans, mostly working families and individuals-blue-collar, white-collar and professional-are being treated as though they were expendable."

"Most significant of all, the American dream of the last half-century has been revoked for millions of people-a dream rooted in a secure job, a home in the suburbs, the option for families to live on one income rather than two, a better life than your parents had and a still-better life for your children."

"As a result, the United States is about to enter the 21st century much the same way it left the 19th century: with a two-class society."

"Both government and big business are encouraging the shift-dividing America into have-mores and have-lesses. While the nation's richest 1 percent is accumulating wealth not seen since the robber-baron era of the last century, the middle class is shrinking."

"Who is to blame?"

"In a word: Washington."

"Or more specifically, members of Congress and presidents of the last three decades, Democrats and Republicans alike. Of course, they've had a lot of help-from lobbyists, special-interest groups, executives of multinational corporations, bankers, economists, think-tank strategists and the wheelers and dealers of Wall Street."

"The losers? Working Americans who have been forced to live in fear-fear of loosing their jobs and benefits, fear of the inability to pay for their children's education, fear of what will happen to their aging parents, fear of losing everything they've struggled to achieve."

"The winners say if you're not a part of this new America, you have no one to blame but yourself." "They say you have failed to retrain yourselves for the new emerging economy. That you don't have enough education. That you're not working smarter. That you failed to grasp the fact that companies aren't in the business of providing lifetime employment. And they say, it's all inevitable anyway."

"It's inevitable that factories and offices will close, that jobs will move overseas or be taken by newly arriving immigrants, that people's living standards will fall, that you may have to work two or three part-time jobs instead of one full-time job. These things are inevitable, they say, because they are the products of a market economy, and thus beyond the control of government."

"Don't believe it."

This is one of the most direct references to social conditioning I have come across, with the best yet to come. It is abhorrent that supporters of this new world order have blamed the people of this country for their own middle-class demise, for a horrible new economy they forced down our throats. This is the example, I mentioned earlier in previous chapters, about the thief arrogantly blaming his victims for the pain, and suffering he is inflicting on them. So it is our fault for once having the financial security, and the American Dream of the past. It is our fault because some greedy financial corporate thinkers decided to take it from us, because they want more for themselves.

These two authors should be publicized on international talk shows across the globe. They should assist other authors, with the same message, to join forces to urge the American citizens vested with the ability to change this using the Constitution, to rise up, and revolt. These wonderful guys have also written another book called "America: What Went Wrong?" These two books are at the end of this book under the Other required readings section. Please read them, and add them to your library! These will become good tools in your quest to unite against this plutocracy. They are your weapons, and ammunition for our war!

These authors also insist that all of this is basically planned by those in power to create a strong plutocracy. I can guarantee that pure Darwinian greed is the life blood of this terrible abomination.

Texas Agriculture Commissioner Jim Hightower in 1987 quoted; "The economic agenda of the past seven years produced one of the quickest and most regressive redistribution of wealth in U.S. history. For all of it's impassionate rhetoric about removing government as a force in our financial affairs, the Reagan government injected itself more enthusiastically into the economy than any administration since Lyndon Johnson's Great Society. Indeed Reagan's administration took so much money from the pockets of the middle and lower-income Americans and shoved it up to the wealthiest 10 percent in our society that a top-heavy structure now threatens to come crashing down on us."

Is this a plot that goes all the way up to the highest levels of Washington? Is this the most horrible secret in the history of mankind?

This current abomination of an economic system seems to self propagate. We have a serious problem in America's capitalist free market economy today. Socially destructive economic policies practiced by today's mega corporations are now considered admirable in the eyes of corporate America. The more a firm fleeces society, and boosts it's profitability, the more attractive it is to Wall Street, and investors.

REVOLT AGAINST THE PLUTOCRACY

Illustration 12

"Like moths flying into a fire" Today's business tycoons are literally hypnotized into appeasing the stock market, even if it means their own doom and the destruction of their employees' quality of life.

Jay T. Baldwin

What used to be considered bad, unethical business practices, now is admired and striven for. The chivalry of the old ethical capitalism is now considered a sign of weakness in the eyes of investors, business leaders, corporate, and economic think-tanks.

Apparently, I am not the only one that recognizes how unethical modern American capitalism has become. We have an educational radio station at the lower end of the FM dial here in South Florida. Every day I listen to WLRN 91.3 FM to the political, scientific, social, and economic talk shows. These educational talk shows give me some food for thought, all day, while I drive to my pest control clients. One day they had a small program, first thing in the morning, about the Orient's impression of American capitalism's ethics. The old British protectorate Hong Kong in China, as well as Japan, in the light of being commercial industrial giants in world economics, are very concerned about America's new business morals. They are afraid to have a totally freemarket economy. They have chosen to have regulated capitalism, fearing to model their systems after ours. They fear that American capitalist business qualities, and the greed of our business owners, would disrupt, and destroy their entrenched set of business virtues. In their society, providers, as they call their style of corporate leaders are looked upon as honorable leaders. These leaders look at their workers as the life blood of the company. Therefore, they are compensated well, and honored by the corporate leaders. They are not looked at as pesky corporate expenses.

Japan is now ahead of the U.S. in the standard of living of it's poor, and middleclass. Japan, just recently viewed in the past decade, as the workaholics of the world, has been eclipsed by the United States in the numbers of hours worked by their employees.

I have talked to many foreigners, with vacation homes here in Florida, on my pest control routs over the years. Europeans especially, have less respect toward our country's business ethics, and manners. They view us as ruthless, self centered, untrustworthy, dishonorable, and greedy when it comes to the way our corporate leaders conduct themselves. They can not even figure out how our corporations treat employees the way they do. A lot of German, Dutch, Swedish, and Norwegian immigrants are moving back to their countries, after they got a taste of our "in your face capitalism." They feel betrayed because of the supposed image of the U.S. having the best standard of living, and the best society to make home. We have changed so much in such a short 15 years or so, that our reputation now outlives us. One customer from Norway, asked me if we raise our children to be so greedy, and Machiavellian. I had no other comment to say, unfortunately, but YES!

I have listened to a program on WLRN about how our lives are becoming faster, and faster. We instill more, and more greed, and self centered aspects in our children. We start at a young age with sports, hobbies and as they get into later years in school we keep drilling this supposed winning attitude into them. We create monsters, by telling them not to accept anything but winning at all costs. And that free time is time wasted. It's good to teach them to strive for excellence, but not for perfection. We stress competitiveness to the max. We are creating a generation of ruthless, competitive, greedmongers for our future corporate, and national political leaders. We have created probably one of the most ruthless, heartless, selfish, and spoiled generation of future leaders. Everything our older generation grandparents taught us not to be. In some cases, even parents have taught older generation Xers not to be so greedy. But now, we look at this competitive quality as an excellent quality to instill in our children. The greedier the better. Go for it, and don't let anything, whatsoever, stand in your way. This addiction to competitiveness can be seen at the after school ball practices. These parents hammer home the idea, that to win, is the only alternative, and no other choice is acceptable. Parents literally getting into fist fights with other children, other parents, as well as the coaches. The kids see competitiveness as the only viable way to survive the game. Now we have little-league ballpark rage! We have coaches pushing our children beyond their capabilities. Children see their parents running around, in a competitive manner, like chickens with their heads cut off, rushing all day between work, and every day chores. Parents plan every minute of their kid's day, and do not let their children just have plain old un-regulated, unplanned fun! Our children do not know how to just stop and smell the roses. Life is one big competitive rush! What are our children going to learn??? They are going to learn that in order to survive, they are going to have to become competitive, greedy, self-indulged, cheating, heartless, rushed, perfectionist, workaholics! Then we pass it down from generation to generation! I can hear some of the parents out there saying; "But we have to prepare our children for life, and reality!" Life and reality may now be the epitome of pure animalistic, competitive greed, but we are not going to incite societal change by turning our children into greedy, survival orientated animals. Man ascended from the ways of the animal by daring to change in the face of adversity, creating modern civility. One thing is for certain, you will be preparing them to pass the new Darwinian self destructive, law of the jungle, me, myself, and I qualities on to the next generation. As a parent myself, I am educating my children about all of the socially-destructive qualities in today's society. They are learning about uncontrolled greed, unethical capitalism, and the importance of changing the plutocratic nature of our current system. They are learning the importance of sharing, equality, fairness, courtesy, and concern for the less fortunate. The Europeans, and the Asians may have something worth fearing in American style capitalism, and societal culture! Being the socio/economic bully on the block is not an admirable trait! I will fight to stop this trend!!

Oh Dear! I can hear all of the conservatives out their! These are pure socialist ideas. That boy must be a commie!! I am sick and tired of hearing anything relating to fairness, justice, social, economic, and societal equality being compared to communism. Sarcastically speaking, I guess Jesus Christ was a Communist then! And the Bible is the Communist Manifesto! I guess Allah is a commie-pinko! And the Koran is nothing but Communist propaganda! Maybe Buddha is nothing but a Communist sympathizer! And anybody who cares for the well-being of the majority is a red spy! Oh no! There is another paradox! Democracy, the needs, and the desires of the masses, outweigh the needs of the powerful elite few, is the definition of pure Communist Doctrine! Then our founding fathers were Communist plotters. Then the question is, are Communists really concerned about the well-being, and equality of all? It doesn't take a rocket scientist to figure that one out! If I recall my history properly, it seemed all of the Communist leaders were really concerned about maintaining power for themselves, the privileged wealthy few, and retaining status quo. Look at the fat, wealthy Communist pig, Fidel Castro, and his cronies living in luxury, while his countrymen are living in squalor. Greed is denounced in all religions. Whether it is The Bible, The Koran, or any other religion's Bible, greed is the enemy of man. Greed has three partners in crime. The three corrupters of man, Money, Power and Sex. It seems there is greed in all three of these corrupters. And it seems greed is in constant competition with time. Then the true definition of greed, is to get as much of the three corrupters as one can, in as little time as possible. Then back to the rushed society of pure greed. Animalistic, man has become!!

Living in such a rush-hush, hustle-bustle society, chasing the ever elusive dollar, in our quest for more time to chase more elusive dollars, could be why, rage-o-mania is taking over our society. Road rage, air rage, ballpark rage, and now the latest, construction zone rage. Man has reached maximum efficiency in satisfying greed, now he is frustrated, because he can no longer continue to appease greed in an ever faster means. This then creates pure uncontrollable rage. In his rush to have more, and more, or his rush to please his boss, or superiors, man is becoming more frustrated, less courteous, and less human. His RPMs are maxed-out.

I have found myself falling into the grasps of some of these rages. I am most vulnerable to road rage, especially when I am given impossible quotas to meet at work. Also being overworked, frustrated, and underpaid, or just stressed out by our too fast paced of a lifestyle. I developed my impatience, not only to traffic situations, but to life itself because of the years of being rushed, and expected to perform more, and more efficiently by the supervisors at the various jobs I have had. As the years went by, I found myself getting a shorter, and shorter temper. I would be running my pest control rout as fast as I can, and still be criticized by the boss, that I am not as productive as I should be. They would give me more service calls, and one day they would add still more to my rout, and expect me to complete them in the same time as before. Then if I had rushed, hurried as fast as I could, had a smooth day, and was able to finish in time, this was now my new quota. The variables such as weather, traffic, distance to service calls, or unseen problems at the calls were not acceptable as excused, in the eyes of corporate bosses. Then in the not to distant future, they would add even more to my rout, and expect the same. This scenario would be repeated, indefinitely, until the employee would burn out, quit, be fired, or an accident would occur, and the employee is blamed for not taking the time to be careful. Then he/she ends up being fired anyway! A catch 22 situation every-time! The only one winning here is the boss!

When I used to drive eighteen wheelers, I faced the same set of circumstances. I was given twenty deliveries to run over to Naples Ft. Meyers. I was also given petty cash to eat dinner, and spend the night, if I was held up, and couldn't return at a decent hour. Then they started to add one more stop at a time, and said I still had to complete the deliveries before the shops closed. Eventually, they added so much to the rout, that I could not get to all of the deliveries in time, and not just ended up spending the night, but finishing the deliveries in the morning. Now the boss started to get mad, lecturing me each time. He claimed I was not improving my efficiency. Good God man! I literally had the pedal floored all the way across Alligator Alley, over the Everglades. The truck would wind out it's RPM,s at 70 mph. The speed limit then was 55 mph. At 70 mph it would take 2 and a half hours to 2 hours, and 45 minutes to reach Ft. Meyers from Ft. Lauderdale. I would leave at 4:45am to be at the first customer, before they even arrived. I could then get the load out, and stacked up by the delivery door, then when they arrived, I could have a load on the hand-truck ready to roll in. When I finally sat the boss down, and explained to him that I am risking a speeding ticket, his only remark was; "You have to do whatever needs to be done to get the deliveries done, in the same time frame as before, no questions!" Since I had reached saturation point long ago, he made it so, I would have no choice but to get back in time. He stopped providing the petty cash to spend the night, and eat dinner. He said if, I ended up stuck over there, it was on my tab! The next run, I had 25 deliveries to be done, from Ft, Meyers all the way down to MacGreggor Florida, South of Naples. This was up from 18 or 19 deliveries when I first started with the company. As expected, I never completed the deliveries before the customers closed their doors for the night. I didn't stop to eat breakfast or lunch, and only used the bathroom once all day. The driver, I replaced, was barely completing the old quota. I ended up staying all night, and finishing the remaining 3 deliveries in the morning. When the boss came in the next morning, and didn't see my truck there, he was furious. He called the last few stops to locate me. He sarcastically said on the phone; "Boy, you are slow, I could run that rout, and complete that rout myself!" "I am over fifty too!" "Bring that truck back right now!!!!"

I came back around 11:45 am. When I turned my paper work over to the boss, he shut his office door, and lectured me. He said, I will be replaced if this happens again. I took a glaring look at him, and commented; "I would need the Concorde to complete that rout as it is!"

Jay T. Baldwin

Illustration 13

"Beyond the limits of machine and man"
Faster! Faster! Faster! Never satisfied regardless of how fast you perform! America's RPMs are maxed-out and red-lined. Corporate pressures to perform better and better, more and more in a given amount of time is tearing our society apart. It's creating an entire population of careless, impatient, trigger-haired nervous wrecks ready to fly of the handle at the smallest thing. Road rage! Ball-park rage! Office rage! Air rage!, etc. Take your choice. Forget about quality of goods and services!

I tried to reason with him, explaining that men, and machines have their limits. I would have to encounter no traffic, no weather, no delays at the customers, such as rotating the stock for the customers as our job responsibilities dictate, and a truck that goes faster than 70 mph. Then, I just might finish on time! He replied; "Those are just excuses!" At that I saw red. I handed him the keys, and said; "If that is the case, you can now run that rout!" "I quit!!!!"

As I worked at more jobs, from pest control to Truck driving, and the various odd jobs in between, the same scenario would pop up it's ugly head. And my patience with traffic, people, and life grew ever thinner. I found myself punching the steering wheel, the dash, and cursing out loud at traffic, as I screeched around corners on two wheels, taking risks, taking stop signs, and running lights in a vain effort to please the boss. This behavior slowly crept into other facets of my life. I ended up being cranky, and short fused around my wife, daughter, and other people. I felt compelled to rush at everything. I gave up things like model airplane construction, not just because I no longer earned the spare money, but because I no longer had the patience. I started having insomnia at night, sleeping through nightmares of time urgency, and deadly deadlines. Even in the grocery store waiting at the check out, I found myself becoming enraged at the clerk, or another customer because they are taking too long. I am now on a prescription sedative, twice a day, for the rest of my life, since my suicide attempt. My doctor has explained to me the serious toll our society is taking on the human mind. She said we must change or the consequences would be unimaginable. Career stress is the leading direct cause of spouse, and child abuse, and ultimately, suicide! Followed by drugs, and alcohol abuse. More people are seeking psychiatric treatments, and are now on sedatives than at any other time in US history. Nervous breakdowns are on the increase amongst working Americans. I could almost bet that most of the cases, of employees going postal, are a direct result of this societal ill.

As a society, we are killing ourselves, all in the name of time, and money. And what is most alarming, we kill ourselves for what, so our boss gets more bonuses, fatter pay checks, more free time, and we end up exhausted, and poorer? Yet as a people, we refuse to recognize this problem, much less declare it as a problem! We mark it off as the inevitable. That takes us back to the big question. Is money, in it's current form, pure, unadulterated evil??

If the Republicans had their way, we would all be working seven days a week, 18 hours a day, with no benefits, no employee's rights, no lunch, no breaks, no holidays, no vacations all the while earning minimum wage regardless of trade. If the Democrats had their way, we would all be dependent on social services, and taxed to oblivion, making it impossible to support ourselves. Greed for power, and money no matter how we look at it! The Conservatives use money, and big capitalism to yield power, and dominance. The Liberals use the power of welfare, dependence, and big government to yield power, and dominance. Both rob prosperity, and power from the people. Both are headed by the wealthy political, or corporate elite.

REVOLT AGAINST THE PLUTOCRACY

Illustration 14

"Sink or swim" Conservatives whole-heartily believe in the Darwinian theory of the survival of the fittest. Conquer society by the shear power of corporate financial brawn. The strongest survive at the expense of the weakest. In the animal kingdom the physically strongest animal got all of the food, all of the females, the best territories, and the best shelters. Therefore, money has taken the place of physical brawn in modern man. The corporate man with the most money survives at the cost of twenty men with little or no money. Freedom and liberty is reserved for those corporate elites and their families with the most money, and out of reach for those masses with little or no money. Not very democratic, oppressive and definitely not very civilized.

Illustration 15

In need of a helping hand" Your wish is my command! Strings attached is an under statement! Caution! Read the fine print first! Liberals, like a genie in a bottle, cater to our every desire making us dependent on them. What better way to conquer a society than to tax them into poverty, and make all of it's population totally dependent on them. Hence, freedom, liberty and money is suppressed from the masses and reserved for a few wealthy government political elites and their families. The servant is not master and ruler of the house! Not very democratic, oppressive and not very civilized. Liberal or conservative doesn't make much difference to the working masses. They both bolster plutocratic ideals and direct freedoms, liberty and money from the masses to the elite few. Greed is king in both accounts.

Therefore, it is in both party's interest to keep America leaning to the far left or the far right.
Ahhh! Haaaa!!! Now the American people are on to all of you!!! Liberalism is nothing but big government gone awry, resulting in oppression of the masses socially, and economically. Conservatism is nothing but big capitalism gone awry, resulting in oppression of the masses socially, and economically. ***Communism is nothing but big government by wealthy political leaders, and big capitalism by wealthy oligarchs gone awry!***

ol.i.gar.chy 1. a form of government in which the power is vested in a few persons. **2.** a state or organization so ruled. **3.** the persons or class so ruling.

Maybe, this is why both parties are adamantly against the independent parties. Independents are for the people, not the privileged wealthy few. America is most free on the freedometer, when she is directly in the middle, farthest from the left, or the right. And all along, you liberals thought this book was all about bashing the right. **Surprise!!!**
In The Herald Wednesday, July 30, 1997, by David Hess and Jodi A. Enda. "Budget pact on fast track for approval" quotes; "Congressional leaders put a bipartisan budget agreement on the fast track for approval Tuesday before too many questions arose about the trade-offs that had to be made to seal the deal."

"Republicans and Democrats predicted that the agreement would be adopted in tact."

The article explains that the liberals were complaining the tax cut provisions of the package gave too much relief to the wealthy. The conservatives were complaining about the minimum wage increases would mean welfare recipients would have to pay Social Security, and Medicare taxes. The story again backs my suspicions. This quote is the key; "But visibly absent from the celebration was House Minority Leader Richard Gephardt, D-Mo., who argued that the budget pack disproportionately rewards wealthy tax payers."

Gephardt said the tax package would "deliver a whopping 36 percent (of the benefits) to the 1 percent of income earners….Only a quarter of the tax relief goes to people making less than $100,000 a year."

"A separate preliminary assessment released Tuesday by Citizens for Tax Justice, a liberal group, estimated that the richest 20 percent of Americans would get more than 70 percent of the tax plan's benefits."

What does this tell you? Whatever consequences of domestic affairs decisions must be shouldered by those least able to shoulder them! Other words, "Delight of the overclass" at all costs, and "Demise of the middleclass" as an acceptable sacrifice for the cost of doing business in America! The shark of greed, and oppression is circling ever closer!

The fact our government, and corporate America are not in the business of seeing to the well-being of the masses becomes ever clearer, if you do not have the cloak of social conditioning over your head.

And the likelihood of some kind of central plot, of biblical proportions, being designed by those in power, to eventually destroy freedom, and democracy for the majority, more believable. This would then guarantee the absolute power, and reign of the elites for America, and the world forever. I have a quote from the leader of our nation's Federal Reserve, Fed Chairman Alan Greenspan who has served under both Republican, and Democratic administrations; "We must keep inflationary pressures down such as wages. Twice we have had to lower America's workers wage expectations in the early 1980s and again in the early 1990s. Now it is going to be even harder with a robust economy but it must be done to ensure continued economic growth and not cut into corporate profits resulting in inflation."

If there are elected officials with such abominable goals, the plans for America, and we do not call it treason, then we do not know what the definition of treason is! This is literally destroying America!!

This is a prime example of greed of biblical proportions, and the American people refuse to fathom such an evil travesty. They can not even believe such a thing could ever happen in America. American leaders would never allow such a thing, and America is too powerful to be destroyed. In our minds it's too "far out" and conspiracy theorist to believe. Only a certified wacko could believe such nonsense! This is our Achilles heel! Our enemies know this. My training in Taido, a Japanese three dimensional martial art founded by Grand Master Dr. Shukumine (Sh.ku.min.ney). It was carried to the United States by

7th degree black belt Mits Uchida, and teaches one to use an enemies strengths, goals, and desires against him. Tai means "the physical body" and "the spiritual being", do means "way of life". Combined they mean "the way of life that combines the spiritual and physical self." Through BUSHIDO (Bu.shi.do) directly translated; Military-Knight-Ways a form of fighting which follows a strict code of ethics, and morals a knight is required to observe. "The loftiest of moral standards were adopted from every source over the generations to form this unwritten code."

"Today's fast-moving, high tech society is, of course, quit different from the samurai society of centuries ago. But the high code of ethics employed in that day should not change regardless of how highly developed society becomes. Often the human being tends to chase the materialistic things, newer cars or, bigger and better homes. They frequently choose the easiest and fastest means to an end, pushing ethics aside. As a result society's problems, greed, corporate crime, street crime, substance abuse, etc., are growing as rapidly as society itself."

In the Spring of 2000 a new ordinance passed with overwhelming assistance from the Republicans. This ordinance makes it impossible for patients to sue their HMOs for any kind of malpractice whatsoever. Literally, HMOs are immune to any form of justice by the American people. The fox is in charge of the hen house! Will our next leader dare to reverse this ruling?

We seem to be seeing a pattern here. It seems that the wealthy, powerful corporate, and political elites are slowly, openly, and inconspicuously building an iron wall around themselves. Are they up to no good, and are currently setting the stage for their benefit in the future? There are already provisions in place, that protect the government from law suits by individuals, that have had injustices, malpractices, etc., done to them by government, or any of it's departments. One cannot sue the sovereign! Most likely backed, and designed by Democrats! Now there are provisions slowly being snuck in, by fraud, or force, by the Republicans, that make suing a private corporation, such as an HMO impossible. HMOs, with the blessings of government, and the Republicans, are circumventing democracy. In the Spring of 2000, the patients bill of rights suffered a defeat with overwhelming assistance from the Republicans, and the HMO's lobbyists. Now it's impossible for patients to sue their HMOs for malpractice. One patient, that wishes to remain anonymous, complained of a stomach ache. Her HMO put off medical treatment for a week. Before they authorized her medical treatment, she ended up in the hospital, and found out that her appendix had ruptured. A further investigation uncovered HMOs were paying doctors not to refer patients to specialists. Yes, you can bet, all to save money, and keep profits to a maximum. The hell with human life, money is more important! The bean counters, with no medical knowledge whatsoever, are playing doctor, specialist, and God with our lives. They are only concerned with the health of the overhead expense margin, and if it doesn't impact the profits too much, they will offer some medical treatment. This is a crime worthy of treason against the human race, much less complete negligence, with attempted first degree murder! No questions, they should be shut down, tried, and prosecuted to the full extent of the law. If Republicans have their way, we will no longer have the right to sue any private corporations for employee rights violations to consumer protection violations. We would not even be able to sue for defective merchandise, that resulted in death or injury, if we allow the current course of our domestic affairs to continue. I try, on a daily basis, to dismiss the possibility of some sort of elitist plot against our society, but the evidence is too clear, and undeniable. One grain of sand at a time, we are slowly loosing democracy to the elites!!

The need for campaign finance reform is now undeniable in light of our current state of domestic affairs. These undemocratic, plutocratic campaign actions are just another piece of the puzzle fitting into place to form some larger picture. It is apparent that special interest groups, backed by wealthy individuals, and organizations are attempting to head democracy off at the pass. Example; The American people using democratic processes, overwhelmingly voted for the Patient Bill of Rights. However, their vote was in vain. The HMOs still got their way! Their vote, even in landslide numbers, didn't deflect the power of big money. This way HMOs have unchallenged access to the rights, and privileges offered by the founding fathers before the mass majority of the American people do. ***The perfect description of an autocracy!*** Now we have politicians, financially obligated to look out for the policies of a privileged few with most of the money. You can almost bet that most of these policies do not benefit the majority. They only benefit the wealthy, and powerful that have donated the largest sums of money.

Here in South Florida, the tolls have gone up three times in about 10 years. Each and every time they had a vote. The people overwhelmingly voted against the increases, but their votes were overridden. The last time a vote was held for raising the tolls again, Democracy, the will of the majority, was cornered in totalitarian style blackmail. They knew that the people would once again vote against the toll hikes, so they gave us two choices. One choice was to vote for the toll hikes up front, openly supporting the Turnpike authorities. The second choice was to vote for a penny increase in sales taxes. The money from the sales taxes would then be given to the Turnpike authorities.

Jay T. Baldwin

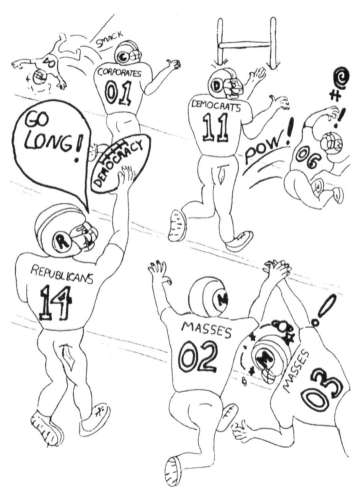

Illustration 16

"At the bottom of the fourth, 10 seconds left on the clock." Plutocrats 20, American masses 0. The entire plutocratic system is slowly attempting to monopolize on democracy by playing the "keep the ball from the other team" game. This way democracy, liberty and freedom can be utilized mainly by an elite few. This leaves the masses less America, less liberty, and less freedoms of choice, unless some of them happen to be lucky with a business venture, in the right place at the right time, or win the lottery. Hard work and loyalty, the standard acceptable method of prosperity, are today much less likely to result in the American Dream than any time since the Great Depression. This is slowly resulting in a two class society, everything America is supposed to be against.

Either way the state got it's way! A prime example of treason against the democratic process. The Florida Dept. of Transportation is committing treason! One who can't see this is really socially conditioned!

Who ever has been overriding the democratic process should be held in treason court. A catch 22 situation. We could just as well be in the former Soviet Union, because they will continue to get away with it!

We are seeing most domestic affairs policies of the United States being influenced by a minority political, and corporate elite. From neutralizing democracy, to channeling most of the national income to themselves, the wealthiest few are converting our wonderful nation into some form of quasi-Communist, Pluto-autocracy. It seems survival of the elites at the expense of the mass-majority. The classic rob the poor, and powerless to feed the wealthy, and powerful. Must we continue to shoulder the negative fallout from biased domestic affairs decisions?

You are probably so frustrated by now, and are thinking that we should just give up, and let them have their way. That is exactly what they are betting on!!!

Jay T. Baldwin

They are thinking, "Let's just run the confidence in democracy into the ground." "Then we will have our way indefinitely, because the people will stop voting!" If we do not vote, we will not have the right to choose for ourselves. You will learn in following chapters how to make life impossible for the plutocrats, by making it not a lucrative, profitable venture to cross the will of the people.

In Newsweek magazine February 26, 1996 an article by Robert J. Samuelson pg. 50 explains our current state of affairs. "The Politics Of Self-Pity" "Government can't erase job insecurity. Pretending it can may win votes now and cause cynicism later."

As we enter another election year in 2000, we see the same hollow promises from candidates. "We are now witnessing another outbreak of one of the most destructive tendencies in American politics-the practice of our leaders to promise phantom solutions for all our economic problems. The latest object of this compulsion is job insecurity. "Yo, America. Government can't suppress it, and trying too hard could cripple the economy's job-creating capacity. This perpetual pandering to Americans' every anxiety is a political disease that ultimately feeds popular cynicism." Therefore, nothing ever changes, and status-quo is unchallenged.

"Voter Anxiety; A Chronic Condition" pg. 58, Time magazine April 22, 1996, by Jeff Greenfield continues it's cynical view of current domestic affairs. "Fear of the future is nothing new in America. Maybe it's time to start addressing it." "It is finally dawning on us that we may have made a Faustian bargain a half-century ago, swapping community and neighborhood and roots for the expectation of material abundance for ourselves and our kids, only to find stagnant living standards and overworked two-and three-career families making that promise more and more dubious for more and more of us."

"If we are going to have an honest political debate about the most dicey and un-American of ideas-that the American dream is floundering-then we are going to have to have concrete, specific ideas on the table: Retrain workers? Limit corporate power to downsize or to move abroad? Lower taxes across the board? Stop promising an ever brighter tomorrow for everyone?" Basically, to halt ideological social control in it's tracks!

"The Hit Men", a mind blowing article so large and controversially spoken that segments are in my first book. It's first debut was in Newsweek magazine pg.s 44-48, February 26, 1996, by Allan Sloan. "Will my boss ruin my life to make another cent of profit on her stock options? Cheer up, you're serving the greater good by being blown away by what economist Joseph Schumpeter christened "the gale of creative destruction." This is just another example of the urgency, on our behalf, to unilaterally stop this type of exploitation by as many methods as we can. Again, anybody openly supporting, or sitting back, and allowing these types of abominations to wreck havoc upon American society, must be prosecuted for treason. For all practical purposes, a bloody class war has been waged by the plutocrats against the masses. The need for immediate, and swift retaliation by the people is warranted. ***Wake-up America!!!***

The same article goes on; "What really matters is that although unemployment is relatively low and the economy is still cranking out new jobs, millions of Americans believe they're being screwed by corporate America and Wall Street." "Then to recoup, they offer up employees as human sacrifices to Mammon, god of Wall Street, hoping to get their stock prices up. When the price rises, it's like Wall Street spitting on the victims' bodies. And the CEO gets a raise. How many CEOs of big down-sizing companies sacrificed some of their pay, and perks to encourage a sense of community? Did they apologize publicly to the people they fired? Did they take any personal responsibility for the mistakes that helped cause the problems they're solving with layoffs? No way, that's not macho."

"Now let's look at the behavior that convinced Stephan Roach, chief economist at Morgan Stanley, that business is carving itself a disproportionate piece of a pie that's supposed to be shared with workers. Roach is hardly anti-business-he loved downsizing in the early 1990s. Yet a few years ago he realized something was wrong: workers' output was rising, but their incomes weren't keeping pace. "This isn't the way economics is supposed to work," he says. "It contradicted everything I was taught to believe." When he warned companies to do something before a political backlash struck, they giggled on Wall Street. "I don't think they're giggling now." At least one educated gentleman, has finally seen beyond his own nose, and has realized the Frankenstein that has been created is no longer doing what it was intended to do! This man from Morgan Stanley has got all of my forgiveness, even though he may have had a hand in creating this Frankenstein. It's people like him that can assist me, and the people of America to right a societal wrong. They are a valuable ally, as they created, and understand their beasts the best of all, a lot better than we can.

This takes me back to the book "Politics of Rich and Poor", by Kevin Philips. As I read the book, I found out that even Ronald Reagan realized the monster he created, has turned into one of the most lifestyle destructive enemies of American history. Pg. 168; Even the republicans seem to have guilt for the terrible destruction of middleclass prosperity they unleashed. Kevin Philips chief political analyst for the 1968 Republican Presidential Campaign quoted in his book; "Many of the last manufacturing jobs had been high paying tickets to middle-class status for two generations of postwar blue-collar workers, a process that limited socioeconomic disparity. In 1968 or 1972 hundreds of unionized plants across the North employed large numbers of $20,000-a-year workers in industries where Fortune 500 company CEOs were making $200,000 or $300,000 a year. As service industries took over, with education and talent counting for more and unions for less, much wider cleavages would be the rule-a bottom stratum of low-paid $4.50-and $6.26-an-hour employees supporting an upper echelon of senior executives and professionals making forty, fifty or sixty times as much."

"This started other salaried and hourly incomes, like a domino effect, to plummet, as corporations of all kinds not just services saw that the income standards of all Americans were being slowly lowered. Hey all of the stable blue collared high paying manufacturing jobs were shipped off overseas, where employees would work for $1 a day."

This is capitalism at it's worst greediest extreme! The information technology age has picked up where the service industry left off. Now the income disparity is just beginning to go into overdrive, with the nitro and the turbos kicking in. We will see the finalization of the grand plan the elites have planned for all of us! This could very well be the final pieces of the grand puzzle falling into place, unless we can throw a wrench into the works, and halt this supercharged dragster of disparity!

In USA TODAY, "House bill links minimum-wage hike to tax cut", by Owen Ullmann. "The House of Representatives voted Thursday to link a $1 an hour increase in the minimum wage with a $123 billion tax cut targeted toward business and the affluent, setting up an election year confrontation with President Clinton." "Nearly two-thirds of the $123 billion in GOP's 10 year tax cut would cover a reduction in estate taxes, paid by less than 2% of the USA's families. The tax hits assets exceeding $650,000." "Although Clinton supports the pay raise, he vowed to veto the bill, complaining that the GOP linked the minimum wage with "risky tax cuts that threaten our prosperity and the future of Social Security and Medicare." Although the minimum wage and tax provisions were voted on separately, they will be combined into one piece of legislation."

"Gop leaders let members who face tough races vote with the democrats, so they wouldn't be seen as blocking a raise for up to 13 million workers."

Democrats complain that the Republicans only care about the wealthy. "Their minimum-wage proposal is a meal ticket for their fat-cat friends," House Minority Whip David Bonior, D-Mich., charged."

The tug of war between the Democratic, and Republicans continues. The only losers here are the American workers. The Republicans attach a leach proposal to decrease estate taxes for the richest of the rich to the Democrat's proposal to raise the minimum wage. They are sly as a fox, knowing darn well that President Clinton would have no choice but to veto the bill, minimum wage increase and all, because of the tax break for the elites. That way the republicans have their way anyway, because their original goal, and more important order of business, is to prevent raises in the minimum wage at all costs. So they float the tax idea as a sacrificial lamb to stamp out minimum wage increases, because the minimum wage increase would ultimately effect larger numbers of corporate elites than the estate taxes would. Give another point to the psychological prowess of the political think tanks. We've sure been fooled!

One thinks that Republicans are the only ones guilty of crimes against the people, the Constitution, and the United States of America. We all are aware of President Clinton's cut backs on welfare, and the welfare to work program. This is raising the requirements of welfare recipients, and taking millions off the welfare roster. This is wonderful if full-time wages are high enough, however, the welfare recipients are much worse off, and end up on other forms of local welfare to survive. This is because most full-time labor, and service jobs pay below the living wage levels. The current poverty level is decades out of touch with reality. Mind you, the living wage is the real poverty level, not the one the government constitutes as the poverty level. The idea of the government's out of date poverty level more indicative of the late 70s to early 80s, is just an attempt to smooth over the facts. The government is in the business of propaganda, and social conditioning also! ***Spin-doctors!!***

In The Herald, Sunday June 6, 1999 "Feeding program may lose $45,000" an article by Shari Rudavsky pg. 1BR, 13BR, shows the impact the Clinton welfare reform is having on local charities.

"The proposed change comes at a difficult time. With the government putting limits on welfare assistance, more people are turning to organizations such as the feeding program of Fort Lauderdale.

Even with growing numbers, the Cooperative Feeding Program's pantry-handing out bags of groceries to between 20 and 50 families a day, many of them former welfare recipients or working poor-has not turned away a hungry person since it opened in 1985."

"Organizers worry that without food assistance, many people may have to choose between paying their rent or buying food."

One recipient tells the facts of life and the order of her priorities. "I'll buy food; I'll feed my children before I pay my rent. My children come first," said Jamia Reddick, with four children, ages 8 months to 8 years old. Reddick was suddenly cut off from food stamps under Clinton's welfare reform. She is now dependent on the feeding program along with thousands of others. The kitchen now serves one meal a day for up to 250 recipients.

"We're definitely a gap-filler in this community, and an important one at that," says social worker Lisa Margulis. "Last year, it gave away 16,725 meals for the same period; the 1997 total was half that amount."

A special report in The Herald, "after welfare, **what now?**", by Lori Teresa Yearwood, pgs. 1L, 2L, 3L. "Although far fewer people are on the dole, many of those who left it for work say they are worse off. Far from being self-sufficient, they are relying on friends, family-even strangers-for survival."

Thousands earn so little, they can not afford a car or ride the public transportation to even get to work. Thousands can not afford child care while they are at work. Because of this, they are not hired or end up being fired, and can not keep steady work. Remember what I said in an earlier part of this book? Employers pay so little now days, yet they expect you to have a reliable fully functional automobile. I guess they think that people can get free cars, and free gas from the welfare system as well! It's the companies responsibility to pay living wages. That is not the government's duty to pay the difference for low wages so the companies profits can soar, and the CEO can own another Rolls Royce! Wake up government, you are being exploited as well as the American workers by corporate America!

"In the eyes of the federal government, Jackie Colon is a success story. She's off the public dole. She works now and then. Problem is, she's worse off than

Jay T. Baldwin

ever. She can't keep a job for more than a couple of months because she doesn't have a car or steady child care. Her job pays so little she can't afford a roof over their heads."

Things got so bad she ended up living with a complete stranger who was kind enough to take her and her kids in.

This is just one of the millions of untold stories that the government, and corporate America wish to sweep under the mat. Out of the 4.5 million people on the welfare tab, two out of every five that have left welfare for work, more than half have found work. Even with work,

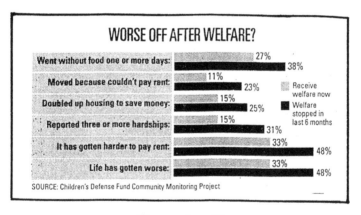

Illustration 17

"Welfare to worse-fare!" Thanks to Clinton's welfare to work plan, more Americans at the low end of the economic scale are left without a safety net. They are forced to double up with other friends and family just to survive. I thought democrats were for compassion? Not if they are plutocrats! The rule of thumb, democrats or republicans, might as well be thrown out the window when dealing with plutocrats.

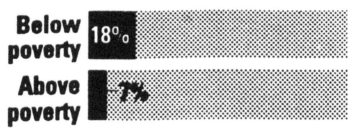

Illustration 18

"Fare as fare can be" Child care cost for the poor doesn't differ much from that of the rich. Therefore, a larger chunk of poverty salary is needed, leaving less for survival needs.

Jay T. Baldwin

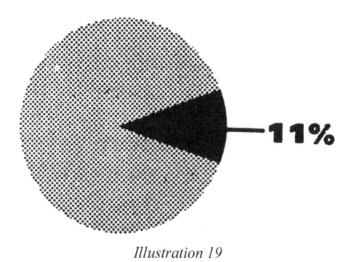

Illustration 19

"America's supposedly prosperous middleclass" 11% of the middleclass now without any health insurance.

over 40% couldn't even afford to put groceries on the table. 50% couldn't afford to put the lights on in their homes, or even pay for a home to make that decision. One third have to rely on friends, and family members for survival. "We've merely switched dependency from the government to a dependency on family and friends," says Broward's welfare reform head Mason Jackson.

Carla Taylor is another one of the supposed government's success stories. Carla had landed two full-time jobs, one telemarketer position and a child care provider. "The first employer fired Carla on her third day because she told him she had to go to the Department of Children and Family Services to sign papers to receive the temporary subsidized childcare benefit for former welfare recipients. The employer told her she had a choice: stay at work and keep her job. Or leave the office to sign the papers-and face immediate termination."

"The second job at Dade County's Cope Center North, a school for high school parents, lasted longer- about three months. The problems were basically the same."

"The scariest fact is, we may have a booming economy, pumping out jobs at a record level, but the jobs being created are far from the affluent blue collar jobs of the fifties, and sixties. "Still, obstacles remain- like raising the minimum wage, and providing benefits to part time workers. While the booming economy is churning out jobs at record levels, three of four new jobs don't pay enough to lift workers out of poverty, says Duffield, of the National Coalition for the homeless."

It's ironic that our government's branch office of the Federal Center on Budget Policy considers $8.56 an hour for a four member family a living wage, yet the government on the other hand has a minimum wage much less than that. They are hypocrites!

Only 12% of the people seeking assistance are officially homeless. Most are full, and part time employed workers. This should be a wake up call to our dear Democratic Party, that this welfare reform is not working as long as employers are willing to pay people un-livable wages. President Clinton, how can you sleep at night? Maybe Clinton should have raised the minimum wage $4 more an hour as part of the welfare to work proposal! I do not want to hear it, that those people are working low skilled, minimum wage jobs, and do not deserve anymore income than that! **That is a cop-out!!** With an economy supposedly doing so damn good, and corporate profits breaking all-time records, there is no excuse why even the damn toilet washer can't be paid a living wage! Why do three out of four jobs being created nowadays have sub-poverty incomes? If the companies are earning record profits, why are more of their jobs now catering to the sub-poverty class? Is this their other secret goal? Where is all of the money going? The CEO and his cronies! The upper management should be forced take a pay cut, so the company can pay the janitor a living wage. The next Democratic President should put a cap on corporate upper-management wages. Must government force civility out of corporate America? **WAKE UP PEOPLE! Is this what you want??**

Our corporate society has the tact of a King Cobra, and the patience of a Turkey vulture. It seems greed is still not enough for them! Not only do they exploit our work force, and pay them less, and less every year, but they have created new innovative ways to legally screw the American citizens again. This defines; "Screw them coming, and screw them going!" "Kick them when they are up, and kick them when they are down!" Yes, the government, hired by the people to do their bidding, is just sitting on it's thumb, and twirling around in circles.

This next article literally brings tears to my eyes! I can not imagine how any human-being can have the heart that some corporate whiz creeps have. They should be tried in Federal court for racketeering, and never be allowed to open a business again!!!

A Special Report "The High Cost of Being Broke", The Herald, Sunday August 8, 1999, by Steve Bousquet and Jacqueline Charles pgs. 1L-3L. "Jobless, penniless and desperate, Larry Moore walked into a store near his Miami apartment and used the spare key and title to his car as collateral to borrow $1,000, at a yearly interest rate of 264 percent."

"It was like stepping into quick sand. Unable to repay the loan, he had to take out a second loan at a higher rate of interest to begin paying off the first loan and keep his '95 Pontiac Grand Am from being repossessed. Moore ended up in a homeless shelter."

Another lady named Barbara Bryan took out a car title loan on her 1991 Acura in the amount of $3,000 to prevent foreclosure on her home. The car was wrecked in an accident, but she still had to struggle to make the $362 a month payments. The yearly interest rate charged by the title loan company turned out to be a staggering 144 %.

Mrs. Bryan quoted; "There are a lot of people like me." Low income people have little choice as to where to buy a car. They end up buying from buy-here, pay-here lots with ungodly interest rates as high as 29%.

They also end up unable to afford the high cost of maintaining a checking account. As most banks no longer cash pay checks with out a several day waiting period, if you do not have the same amount or more to draw from. I have switched banks at least 5 separate times as the banks stopped cashing my pay checks on Fridays. With out a savings account to draw from, I need my money now. I had groceries to buy, baby supplies, diapers, food, gasoline, or we would starve over the weekend. Monday would come, and there would be no gas in the car to go to work.

I entered the bank as usual to cash my check one day. Upon handing the check to the clerk, she would apologetically say, "sorry we can no longer cash your check without at least the same amount already in the account to cover it" I would reply, "I can not afford to keep that amount in there at all times as we live from pay-check to pay-check." She would again repeat her canned lecture. I finally ended up screaming at her, "I am the customer, and you do not have the right to keep me from my money!" "I am the one paying your pay!" "So give me my money right now!" By that time the manager was on the spot. I developed a method of humiliating them in front of dozens of customers, with a planned act. By the time I was finished, I would say in a loud stern voice, "You can just cancel my account right now!!" "I will take my business some where else!" By then, half of the people would be mumbling phrases of agreement, and hassling the manager, and clerks too. It is these moments of mass agreement, amongst so many people, at one time that would literally scare the pants off of those bankers. **This is how we can start a revolution to put a stop to these greedmongers once and for all!** More people should do these scenarios to incite mass anger, then things get attention. Maybe, one day I will start a riot in a bank.

As more blue collar working Americans slide into the ranks of the poor, there has been more predatory businesses such as payday advance stores, loan title shops, and pawn shops popping up like mushrooms in the Spring. All of this kind of capitalism has accelerated drastically in just the past few years.

"Although these "fringe banking" businesses will lend their money with few questions asked, their interest rates, when calculated on an annual basis, can top 300 percent. "in South Florida.

If you end up unable to repay your auto title loan, and the car is repossessed, the lender usually keeps all of the proceeds of the re-sale, as well as the amount you still owe. A practice Bob Butterworth Attorney General of Florida says is totally illegal. But is not enforced, Literally, becoming legalized robbery! You can thank the Florida Legislature, the same pod of, most likely Republicans, that created the Right to Work Laws in Florida, which guarantees corporate prosperity at the expense of the workers, and consumers.

"At the request of Don Tucker, a former Florida House speaker and now a Tallahassee lobbyist, lawmakers legalized the title loan industry, carving a loophole in the state's usery law in a hastily passed bill."

These type of borrowing practices further perpetuate poverty, by fanning the flames of debt by locking people into debt forever. People end up taking out more loans to pay off the first ones. One ends up in a financial death spiral tail-spin.

These loan stores boomed from just a handful only a few years back, to over 1000. They replaced traditional banks that fled the area to more affluent areas. "Plenty of customers" "South Florida is loaded with low-wage workers." Florida is like a giant magnet, drawing these type of entrepreneurs (raptors) who pray on desperate people. This defines the definition of "raptor". Our society is cannibalizing itself!

"The state is plagued with so many of these despicable, loathsome businesses because Florida has a rapidly increasing minimum wage work force, as wages plummet. The people are getting more desperate and need money in a hurry." Jean Ann Fox of the Consumer Federation of America quoted; "That's the market these high-cost lenders try to target."

Most likely due to some republican plan, Florida consumer protection laws are almost none-existent, leaving nobody to speak on behalf of the consumers. It's definitely a free market here, "the market is free to do anything it wants, legal or not, just so it makes a few people rich." "Years ago, Miami-Dade government had a consumer advocate, a politically ambitious man named Walter Dartland, but some commissioners viewed him as a pest and the job was eventually phased out." He was a pest to the plutocrats as he kept them in check. The people should petition the local government, in Miami, to force the position to be reopened for Mr. Dartland. Big money has no right what-so-ever to remove the last vestiges of democracy in Dade County. We live in a supposed democracy, REMEMBER!!

The title loan industry has successfully purchased democracy in South Florida society by making massive campaign contributions. This has bought out the Florida Legislature, and kept them from outlawing high-interest lending, or loan sharking as it is more commonly called. Chalk up another point for big money, and lack of campaign finance reform!

However, due to an avalanche of complaints recently against the loan sharks, the local government put it's foot down with a 30% max. cap on annual interest rates.

The loan sharking industry retaliated with a three pronged counter attack, suing the counties, changing their title loan stores to the un-regulated paycheck advance loan stores, and openly threatening the customer base. The loan sharks sent letters to each of their customers, threatening to close on all of their loans immediately, with no grace periods or any mercy at all, requesting complete repayment immediately, unless they could convince county commissioners to rescind the new laws. Each letter had the phone numbers, and addresses of all of the county commissioners. **Oppression? This is corporate fascism at it's best!!**

Under any other set of circumstances, these actions would be considered racketeering, blackmail, extortion and a felony! The CEOs should be arrested immediately, upon conviction, they would be locked up for a very long time! Why do these guys get away with just a slap on the back of the hand? Is it because they are entrepreneurs, who have fat juicy contributions come election year? Take another point from freedom and democracy, and the rich creeps gain a couple of points! If I had my way, each one of these brainiac creeps would be hauled out to the Everglades, tied to the nearest cypress tree, and left for the gators to do the rest! Mess with somebody your own size, **COME-ON JACK!! TRY ME!** Who would have ever imaged that it could be so expensive to be broke. When you are broke, everybody suddenly becomes a loan shark!

Our society has progressive punishment. The poorer one is, the more punishment is dished out! It rewards the wealthy, and brutally punishes the unlucky, down-trodden, and the working poor. Greed is the driving force blinding people from compassion.

Now this same greed has robbed each and every one of us in trade careers, and some white collar positions, of our American dream standard of living. "Economic segregation" "Where you live increasingly depends on what you're worth", by Richard Morin, Sunday January 25, 1998, The Herald.

"It was the great story of the American Century: the fusing, after World War II, of the broadest, and most prosperous middle class the world has ever seen. In it's ticky-tack ramblers and backyard barbecues and unbridled sense of confidence lay a historic reversal-the steady closing of physical and economic gaps between America's rich and poor."

"The postwar American middle class was capitalism's answer to socialism. As much as any nuclear-tipped missiles, its egalitarian ideals of comfort and social mobility-transmitted by movies and television around the world-helped win the Cold War. Richer and poorer Americans were moving so much closer together throughout the 1950s and 1960s that "Observers at the time thought class segregation was on the wane," says demographer Douglas Massey of the University of Pennsylvania."

Today, we are regressing back in time as economic lines are moving farther and faster apart than any other time in American history. Once a three class society, America now is beginning to look more like a third world plutocracy, with 5% of the population rising to socio/economic demigod status. The rest of the population has become an exploitable commodity, or natural resource abundantly ripe for harvesting. "We have entered a new age of inequality in which class lines will grow more rigid as they are amplified and reinforced by a powerful process of geographic concentration," quotes Douglas Massey.

"By the standards of demography, the resegregation of America along economic lines is occurring at dizzying speed." Paul Jargowsky, a professor of economics at Harvard University. Jargowsky quoted; "When I was growing up, my family was working-class," he says. "Back then, this was a kind of country where I could rise up from that and go to Princeton and Harvard. I wonder if that's going to be true in the future."

I can just hear most people, that agree with me one hundred percent, saying' "You can't return to the past." "Things change unfortunately!" "Good things don't last." "You can't change the world!", or a whole host of other looser proverbs. The plutocrats know this, expect this, and literally bank on this. We just keep handing democracy over to them without even a peep. That is what really gets my goat! I am sick and tired of all of you out there, speaking as though there is no more hope whatsoever. You all act as though this social problem is inevitable, and uncontrollable like some form of weather phenomenon. Anything man made is not uncontrollable. It can and will be undone just as it was created. The only thing that's stopping you, is **_YOU!!! ONLY YOU!_**

The choice is not the government's, it's not the president's, it's not Congress's, it's not even God's, it's yours! If this country is lost to the plutocrats forever, ***you have nobody to blame but yourselves!*** Then you will have to live with your conscience, and will deserve to become some proletarian work slaves with no liberties, freedoms or rights! I will have nothing to say but; "I told you so!"

Another dose of greed, my fellow Americans! "Phantom road work uncovered", by Tom Duboco and Rosa Townsend, pgs. 1A, 10A, 11A, The Herald Sunday, November 2, 1997. "Metro-Dade paid more than $1 million over the past year for roadway lane stripping work that was never done, according to a Herald investigation of a controversial paving contract."

They discovered the discrepancy by comparing the bills to the actual footage of lane stripping material that cost the tax payers $2 per foot. The equivalent of 97 miles of stripping could not be accounted for. "I am sick over this," said Anthoney Clemente Utilities director. "Whose department paid the bills?" "I just find it appalling that we could have received and paid invoices that were so overstated. How did it happen? It's going to take the power of the state attorney to find that out."

Many of the records had been falsified. Some had county inspector's signatures on them showing that the work had been completed. However, some had been paid without any signatures at all, completely violating regulations.

REVOLT AGAINST THE PLUTOCRACY

The most expensive cases, the county paid 10 times the amount of stripping than what could actually be found.

Palm Springs North, the county had six work orders showing $371,202 of stripping. Only $9,792 was verified, short some 34 miles of stripping.

El Portal had seven work orders totaling $318,722 worth of stripping. Only $19,358 worth was verified, short by twenty eight miles.

Little Havana had $277,536 over six work orders. Only $61,426 worth of stripping was verified, short by 20 miles.

Highland Lakes had two work orders totaling $109,400 for stripping. Only $6,068 was verified, short by 10 miles.

Downtown Miami had $53,672 total for work done. Only $594 could be accounted for.

Guess who is paying for this runaway greed, and crookery? You and I, the tax payers.

Here is a little food for thought instead of your stomach! This is enough to make you sick to your stomach. Ever wonder why food prices continue to slowly increase, to spite conservatives insisting food prices are not inflating? Yet farmers are being paid less, and less every year for their merchandise. It seems that mega food chain corporations are also conspiring to corner the food market, to prevent democracy, and the natural order of supply, and demand to take place. They try to prevent natural forces of the market to take place, so they can have all to themselves whether they have earned it or not. Pure, relentless GREED!

Jay T. Baldwin

These mega corporation food chains practice what is called slotting. They charge excessive fees to suppliers, as an access fee for the privilege of the big chain store to sell their goods to the public. This is an example of pure extortion, if this were any other situation. But this is a practice condoned by the government. The classic look the other way syndrome! This only allows the wealthiest of the suppliers access to the public guaranteeing their survival. It literally puts smaller suppliers out in the cold! Bada-Bing, elimination of competition. The farmers get screwed with lower purchasing prices, on behalf of the suppliers, which leaves them with less profits to make farming lucrative. You and I are footing the greed bill, paying more for our food for a handful of fat cats living the life of Riley. Once a handful of mega-grocers, and the last of the wealthiest suppliers bump off all competition, they will be able to raise prices through the roof. It's like a cooperative, symbiotic, monopolistic, facist plot.

I sat and thought about it for some time, and said to myself, if I were a bottom-line orientated, greedy corporate strategist, what would I do to guarantee profit growth, and wealth indefinitely? I would remove all competition. I would want to make sure the public would want to, or have no other choice, but to shop at my place. I would corner the suppliers, and set my own prices for supplies. I would want to pay my employees as little as possible, with as few benefits as I could get away with. The ultimate challenge would be to force all citizens to have no choice, or not to be able to shop anywhere else. Think deeply about this, my American readers, after I write the next paragraph.

Big chain corporations usually sell things cheaper than small corporations, or mom and pop shops. Financially stable, or well off middle-class citizens are more likely to buy, or utilize services from smaller companies, or mom and pop firms. They are less likely to buy from larger firms that can discount goods, and services, as they are not on such a tight budget as a lower income person. So the dilemma is to eliminate every small firm in the country, which is absolutely impossible. Or work in junction with the Federal Reserve, financial planners, and other mega world class corporations to slowly lower the income standards of all working Americans. As business owners, they had a lot to do with this step already, as they are paying their employees less, in all of their branches across the nation. This would force people to purchase their less expensive goods, and services, than to buy at smaller mom and pop firms, that can not discount as much. They would have no choice, as they will be on a tighter budget. Bye mom and pop! Problem solved!!

Well my reader friends, sounds too plotist, illogical or far out in left field, doesn't it? Not really, if you put logic aside, and think like a greedmeister with one goal to have your cake, and eat it too!

Corporate types have never been logical anyway. Greed clouds their perception of time, space, physical laws and limitations. They are penny wise and dollar foolish. I have learned that first hand at the many places I have worked.

Jay T. Baldwin

The greed factor of laissez-faire (un-regulated free-market capitalism) is also seen in the energy utilities of our nation. "The Nader Page" January 4 2000, by Ralph Nader website http://www.nadir.org/interest/1400.html, critiques the exploitative practices of our nation's electrical utilities. With the blessings of legislators both Democratic, and Republican, the deregulation of utilities was supposed to open the market to free market competition. Theoretically, on paper this deregulation is supposed to create lower prices, and a better service to American consumers, by virtue of free-market competition. However, remember where greed is concerned, our apple doesn't always follow the laws of gravity, and fall downward. Again our apple defied the laws of physics, and fell upward here too!

A study done by Moody's Investors Service in the Detroit area uncovered an overcharge by Detroit Edison exercising "stranded costs" for it's Fermi II nuclear power plant. These costs are added to customer's bills in anticipation of competition. The overcharges break down to $43 per year for residential consumers, $456 per year for commercial consumers, and a whopping $82,600 for industrial consumers.

Even corporations can become victims themselves to the other firm's greed factors. "The business group is demanding a rollback in electric rates for Edison's two million customers who already are paying among the highest prices in the Midwest."

"Michigan has not yet joined the nearly 2 dozen states that have passed so-called full electricity deregulation laws opening up markets to supposed competition. I say "supposed because in California, there has been very little competition to the erstwhile electric utility monopolies due to huge "strandedcost" subsidies and other advantages exacted from state legislature in return for giving up their monopolies." Enron, one of the competitor energy firms, had planned to compete with Pacific Gas & Electric and California Edison. Two years later, they bailed out due to the totally unfair playing practices. Now only 1.7% of Detroit's households have switched to competition. What little competition left!"

Nader quotes; "The looming question arising out of the Moody's report is: Are other electricity companies overcharging in other states under the non-watchful coziness of their state regulators? If so, then billions of dollars are being taken from customers under the accounting formulae applied to the "stranded costs" doctrine—i.e. making consumers pay again for the uneconomic investments in nuclear and other inefficient plants as a condition for open competition."

It just seems today's capitalism is as Darwinian as our animal friends on the open plains under Africa's Kilimanjaro.

"Judging Microsoft" by Ralph Nader and James Love http://www.nadir.org/releases/110999.html November 9, 1999. The Microsoft indictment was a devastating blow to the American monopoly. Nader quotes; "The judge found Microsoft responsible for a litany of anticompetitive and illegal practices that have harmed consumers." A 207 page guilty decision was a breakdown of monopoly powers in the U.S. "The court found that Microsoft strong-armed personal computer makers and software against competitors and sought to limit competition through collusive agreements with actual or would-be rivals." "Microsoft was seeking to control and monopolize key sectors of the PC software market." the judge quoted; "Microsoft has demonstrated that it will use its prodigious market power and immense profits to harm any firm that insists on pursuing initiatives that could intensify competition against one of Microsoft's core products."

Ironically, it was a Reagan-appointed judge that ultimately sided with the Dept. of Justice, and agreed to halt these anticompetitive actions. Hey, a smart conservative with some good old fashioned democratic virtues, as in democracy, not leftist! Miracles do occur!!

Technology is a tool to advance, and simplify our daily lives, but it can backfire on us. We can become slaves to this wonderful tool if we allow ourselves to serve it relentlessly, or the person at the other end of the line happens to be a boss.. What times we used to have to ourselves when we were in our cars, taking a walk in the park, a day at the beach, when nobody could bother us. If they wanted us, they would have to wait until we were finished with our stroll. Now we have cellular phones, laptop computers with E-mail, computers with E-mail at home, and beepers. I see people walking the dog with one hand, and a cell-phone in the other hand. Just about every car has a driver with one hand on the wheel, and the other with a cell-phone blabbing endlessly into space as though they are talking to themselves. I have been to the beach to see somebody laying in the hot South Florida sun, punching keys on a laptop. Somebody stop the world so I could get off!!! These things are excellent, so we have the discipline to know when to shut them off. A cell-phone is great as an emergency communication device, or that last resort if all directions fail to get us where we want to go. A lap top can be great, when aboard a plane flight or bus ride, instead of reading a book. But don't let it interfere with leisure time. Shut that boss out of your life, when you get home from a long day at work. Instead, surf the internet to some web-sites that cover some of your hobbies, or throw that favorite game program software in, and tear up some intergalactic spaceships with photon torpedoes, or fight some Rambo-Terminator character when you have kicked back for the night.

Under the new world order, greed even effects the mom and pop corporations. I went to work for a small pest control firm in the Broward area. They only had 2 routs for residential pest control, and 3 lawn spray routs. The immediate supervisor was also acting vise-president, and was the owner's son-in-law. He was rather small in stature, and had always been rather arrogant by nature to make up for his small size. One day, I had a customer in Weston, the elite enclave I mentioned earlier. I was to perform a normal household pest service. She insisted I remove my shoes before she would let me in. I mentioned that it is not advisable to apply pesticides without shoes. I also mentioned Dept. of Agriculture and O.S.H.A. laws about applying pesticides without shoes. The customer arrogantly said I would not be allowed in otherwise, and she was going to call my supervisor. I then commented that's fine, and walked away! Upon return to the office, I was confronted by this short supervisor, and basically raked over the coals about not removing

Jay T. Baldwin

my shoes to perform the service. I mentioned the laws, and the danger to me, but was told I was going to have a longer talk with him in the morning. By the look in his face, I knew tomorrow was going to be another day to remember for a lifetime. That night, I went to Office Depot, and purchased a small micro-cassette recorder to slip into my pocket. I remembered that whatever happened, I would be the last person to be credible in a confrontation with the corporation, in the eyes of the Dept. of Labor, or some other government regulatory agency. The proverbial guilty until proven innocent scenario, I had the honors of personally being a part of so many times before. This time I will get it all in indisputable fashion. I will play the part of Allan Fundt in Candid cassette!!

The morning came, and I was ready to click the recorder in an inconspicuous sweep of the hand, in and out of my pocket. I had spent at least a half hour practicing at home, in mock conversations, to see how clear the device operated closed inside a pants pocket. Well, as I entered his office, my hand did it's little sweep. He then quoted; "Yesterday you had no authority to refuse a customer's demands!" "You are going to go back to that house today, and you are going to remove your shoes, and service that customer!" I then sternly said; "No I will not remove my shoes, but I will be happy to service the home!" At that his eyes got big as saucers, and full of anger. "Jay!" "This is not Jay's pest control! If you do not cooperate, I will take you out there myself, and make you take your shoes, and make you service that house!" That was the wrong thing to say to me, as I again felt the blood boil, as I had when I was fired for stopping to use the toilet a few years earlier. I then remarked; "I will do no such thing, as I know my rights, and I will not do anything that is not safe, as I am a husband, and a father." At that he literally exploded; "Your fired!!!! I do not care what you think, or what the law says, this is my company, and you will do as I say!!!" He then asked for the keys to the truck, and promptly dismissed me. I then felt a feeling of confidence as, I knew I got the whole thing on tape! As soon as I got into my car, and started it up, I rewound the tape, and listened to the music! I will sue for a lot of money, and get them in trouble with the authorities. Sweet revenge!!! At last a victory for the little guy!

I then went home, and started a nice long letter to the Dept. of Labor, and O.S.H.A. I didn't fill them in on the tape immediately, as I knew what the usual process was. They'll just take forever in responding to the official complaint, then state there is nothing the Dept. of Labor can do as it's my word against theirs, and Florida is a right to work state blabb! blabb! @ # * and a whole host of other bull s _ _ t!

Well, several weeks went by, and I did finally get that letter. As I figured, it basically said that in a nut shell, with a whole section that the Dept. of Labor interviewed the owner, and the supervisor, and that my story didn't match theirs. The supervisor said you refused to perform your duties, and were very belligerent, and arrogant leaving them no choice but to let you go. They were also dismissing the case due to insufficient evidence. I said to myself, now you guys are going to see the wrath of your lives, as I unleash the nuclear missiles! I laughed as I wrote a letter basically stating the decline of the American worker's human rights, constitutional rights, and standard of living. I mentioned how so many corporations have been given the hen house on a silver platter, and a whole host of patriotic phrases. Then I let them have it! I wrote something of the like; "I am sick, and tired of not having any justice! It seems if you are a corporation, your word is God, and you would never tell a lie. What you say is believable beyond a reasonable doubt in the eyes of society, and the government, after all you are a corporation, and would never do anything illegal. Well, my friends, this little lying, un-believable, non-credible blue-collar worker for once is telling the truth! I do not mean to rain on your parade! Unfortunately, this time the lovable, respectable, truthful corporation was caught lying through it's teeth! You better re-evaluate your inspection procedures, and start doing your jobs. The taxpayers like me have hired you to protect us, and it's about time to start living up to your part of the bargain! You put this little tape into the nearest tape player, and listen to the truth! Then you re-think your strategy, and get back to me! Thank you for your cooperation!"

I must have waited over three months. I had called them on several occasions, and could not get a straight answer. Fate must have been on their side again. The letter I got back had the tape I sent them, and a very sarcastic, disciplinary response. It basically said; "Dear Mr. Baldwin, The Dept. of Labor has reviewed your case again, and listened to the tape. After a conference with our superiors in Washington, and Tallahassee, we have concluded you have violated individual privacy laws laid out to protect privacy." It then stated a whole bunch of legal jargon under this section, of this act, subtitle, @ # *! *. "You are in violation of these laws, and it is a felony. If you do not drop your charges against this corporation we, and the corporation's legal staff will be forced to take further legal action against you! Any questions please feel free to contact us! Thank you very much, The Dept of Labor." I felt as though I had been victimized twice. What is the job of the Dept. of Labor? Are they there to protect the American workers, or are their new orders from the plutocrats in government, to look out for the best interests of corporate America, and it's stooges?

    I called them, and said; "why can they violate the law, and get away with it, and if I violate the law I get punished?" They could not give me a full answer to that question, then I asked them another. "I hear of situations with corporations secretly recording their employees on the phones, reading the employee's E-mail, and video taping them un-knowingly." "What law gives them a one way street?" They answered that the laws do give corporations legal rights to record employee activity. This is to protect private commerce from theft, fraud, and non-productivity. But there is no right for employees to turn the tables on the corporations, even if they openly violate laws, the worker's human rights, civil rights, and constitutional rights. I replied; "We will see about that! "I will do whatever I have to do, to change this abomination of justice! I wonder if a Republican created this travesty of justice? Maybe, it is due to the right to work laws in Florida, as I found out when I went to purchase the small microphone for my recorder. I went to one of those stores, that sell counter-surveillance equipment to purchase this small microphone. This mic is to place through a collar or button hole, to get a clearer recording than in a pocket. I even showed the accessory guide for my recorder with part number. The clerk then explained that in Florida these types of surveillance items are not sold to the public. If I owned a business, he could order one for me, but not for an individual! Question answered! It seems the bad guys won again, and the victim was victimized twice! American justice??

Four years later, I would be tested again with outright violations of my legal rights, and liberties. At the international pest control company, I am still currently employed with as of the holiday season 2000, known for it's once a year pest control, I faced the capitalist greedmonger again. This company should be one of the best employee friendly, as it is associated with one of the nation's supposedly most reputable department stores. I started with them on November 5, 1999. This is the one, that I mentioned earlier in the book that hired me at $11 an hour, then re-structured cutting my pay back to $9 an hour.

When re-structuring was finalized on December 1, 1999, a large percentage of technicians, as well as supervisors gave their notice, and resigned shortly after. I guess they didn't like the company's Christmas present of pay cutbacks!! Our branch manager, a wonderful man, the one that hired me at $11 an hour, also packed it in, and resigned. Our service manager chose to relinquish his manager's position for a sales position. Now their was nobody at the helm!

The company scrambled to fill the void, by allowing the Pompano's branch manager to run both branches. Two of the employees, who have been with the company the longest, were promoted to service managers. I had enough on December 23, 1999, when we had to check our previous day's work in. On the new manager's first day, he scrutinized our service times at our customer's homes, and the times taken to travel to other clients. He literally made each of us deduct time from our time sheets, if he thought the drive time was too long between stops. Most of the deductions he made us take, happened around rush hours between 3:00 PM and 6:00 PM. This is because the traffic gets so bad at these times, that a usual 20 minute commute to another customer's home, can take an hour or more. I was forced to remove an hour from the travel time, from West Miramar out by Interstate 75, to NE Fort Lauderdale by the beach East of A1A, just South of Oakland Park Blvd. This is a 25 to 30 mile trek, add traffic, and one can see why it took over an hour in rush hour traffic to get to this other customer's home. Now I was seeing red! I went out back, and talked to some other employees. We mutually agreed this was way out of line. I calmly said to the other technicians, I would go by the Dept. of Labor, and find out if a company can force an employee to deduct driving time between stops.

I took my lunch time, and did what I promised, passing by Ft. Lauderdale's Dept. of Labor. As I guessed, the law was clearly violated. Regulations Part 785 Hours Worked Under the Fair Labor Standards Act. of 1938, as Amended, Reprint December 1986.

Subpart C-Applications of Principals Section 785.38- Travel That Is All In A Day's Work. States:

Time spent by an employee in travel as part of his principal activity, such as travel from job site to job site during the workday, must be counted as hours worked. Where an employee is required to report at a meeting place to receive instructions or to perform other work there, or to pick up and to carry tools, the travel from the designated place to the work place is part of a day's work, and must be counted as hours worked of contract, customs, or practice.

I made sure every employee had a copy of this booklet and a cover sheet I wrote (sample in last chapter). The Dept. of Labor also sent a copy to corporate headquarters and our branch. I also made sure a copy mysteriously appeared on both the manager's, and service manager's desk when they were not looking.

The next day, he had a complete change of heart, and did not question anybody on commute times. Nipped at the bud! We never had to worry about this again, so I thought!

Almost a year later, my truck's speedometer stopped working, and the brakes had been squealing for about a week. I took it to our repair shop, on a day I had some spare time between clients, contracted to do all of our mechanical repairs. We very rarely have free time to even think about taking our trucks in for repairs. Most of the younger naïve employees take the trucks in on their days off, because of this. They spend their free time (non-paid time!) tending the company's equipment. Since the re-organization, the supervisor tried once to get me to do the same. The company loves this, as they used to have to pay the older experienced employees, down time, before they all resigned. I asked the mechanic if he had one of our other trucks ready so I could finish my day, because I refuse to give them time, that must be paid, for free! The mechanic had one truck ready, but it was being picked up by another employee later. He said it would be at least three hours. I told him to go ahead and repair it.

The next day, I was ordered by the branch manager to remove the three hours for the down time, at the repair shop, from my time sheet. This happened in front of all the other employees. I said; "I will do no such thing! He again said; "You better do something, I do not pay people to just sit around waiting for repairs!" I again stood my ground; "I know the law, and waiting for repairs to ones equipment, is working time!" "I will not touch that!!!!" He said; "We will see about that!" I knew what I had to do! Another trip to the Dept. of Labor for lunch. Subpart C-Application Of Principles under Section 785.15-On Duty States:

A stenographer who reads a book while waiting for diction, a messenger who works a crossword puzzle while awaiting assignments, a fireman who plays checkers while waiting for alarms and a factory worker who talks to his fellow employees while waiting for machinery to be repaired are all working during their periods of inactivity.

I was informed by the investigator, that my situation fell into this category. The investigator elected to fax a copy, and mail a copy to corporate headquarters, and the same to the local branch. She promised I would not be mentioned in any correspondence.

    The next day came, and I got my folder with time sheet to check in, but the time-sheet was missing! The service manager stated the branch manager had my time-sheet, just to keep track of my time on a separate sheet. Again, I talked to the other employees, passing out the usual copies of the law, and what I heard made me furious, and sick. One guy had broken down on the road, and admitted he automatically deducted the 5 hours while waiting for a tow-truck from his time. One of the only two girl technicians, also broke down, but automatically deducted her time too. Two more stated they do not want to cause any trouble. They all looked at me, after reading the law, and stated they would continue to deduct the time in the future, and accept it as the cost of being employed in America. They said there is nothing that can be done, and they would openly accept it. I truly feel like a lone crusader, on a futile mission, against all odds, in a society invaded by the body snatchers! Employees, that do like these gullible fools did, are just digging their own graves, and making it more lucrative for corporate America to continue this blatant assault on the few responsible American workers, that wish to earn a half decent living for themselves, and their families! Yet, most of these same people would be very upset, if some guy dressed in a suit, walked into there homes, reached into their pockets, took the wallet out, and helped themselves to $50 or so! Then, he said to them it was perfectly customary, since he was a corporation! **There is not a lick of difference, and if you think differently, have pity on your soul, as you**

are the irresponsible fool wrecking this nation!! Chalk another point up for social conditioning!!

Maybe it's true, that our founding fathers may have done all they did in vain! Just to prove my point! The Consumer Product Safety Commission said, since corporations have basically been allowed to police themselves, 50% of them do not even bother to contact them to report unsafe or defective products! This includes products that are literally killing hundreds of Americans. All of this because it is no longer illegal to withhold this information from the public! Yeh, right! The Republicans want to allow private corporations to police themselves! A big, big, big mistake!! Let the crooks, burglars, and rapists set the laws that directly effect them!! We might as well give the keys to the hen house to the fox! Then we can ask him nicely to notify us if he gets tempted once in awhile, and gobbles up a few fat hens!!

In a book by the New York Times Special Report The Downsizing of America. It likens the current economy, to spite a record boom, to waves crashing against a wider beach front. "And those waves seemed to be crashing over an ever-widening spectrum of Americans-no longer strictly the much-battered blue-collar workers, but increasingly the once impervious highly educated middle-and upper-class managers and professionals, people who never thought they would face want." "Workers have always lost jobs in America to the churning cycles of the economy, and more jobs were being created than eliminated, but never before had layoffs persisted with such tenacity and in such magnitude in an expanding economy."

Jay T. Baldwin

The New York Times poles stated roughly 50% more Americans, around 3 million, are violently affected by layoffs than the 2 million that are victimized by violent crime. The problem is the replacement jobs pay no-where the same incomes of past years. "Labor Department numbers show that now only about 35 percent of laid-off, full-time workers end up in equally remunerative or better-paid jobs."

The Times Poles show roughly three quarters of all Americans have been effected by corporate layoffs. 20% have been actually effected. 38% have a friend that has been. 14% have somebody in their household. Total of 72% have been effected in some manner. "The result is the most acute job insecurity since the Depression. And this in turn has produced an unrelenting angst that is shattering people's notions of work and self and the very promise of tomorrow, even as President Clinton proclaims in his State of the Union Message that the economy is "the healthiest it has been in three decades" even as the stock market had rocketed to 81 new highs in the year ending March 1, 1996." "The job apprehension has intruded everywhere, diluting self-worth, splintering families, fragmenting communities, altering the chemistry of workplaces, roiling political agendas and rubbing salt on the very soul of the country."

The Times book also sheds light on rage-o-mania, as I have earlier in the chapter. "At the same time, the job insecurity is unleashing a "floating anger that is attaching itself to all sorts of targets as a form of scapegoating," said Danial Yankelovich, president of DYG Inc., a polling firm. Polls have shown this anger directed at targets as diverse as immigrants, blacks, women, government, corporations, welfare recipients, computers, the very rich, and capitalism itself."

I have now had a revelation as I read those words. I will come, and be frank with all of my readers. This relentless greed, and cutting back in corporate America, that has negatively effected every member of my family, cost me the American Dream, and the possibility of my children ever living as good of a life, as I had earlier in my life, has made all of my new crusades a reality. It has created me in this new image as an anti-corporate, anti-capitalist activist. It is also responsible for the mass majority of my pest control customers having the same sentiments as I do. Now you know the secret to this writer's source of overwhelming energies to write my first book Delight of the Overclass Demise of the Middleclass, this book and two other future works now on the drawing board, plus the formation of Americans to Preserve and American Dream and Democracy (A.P.A.D.D.) launched in the first book. I never planned to be a writer, a political cartoonist or even an activist, but too many times I had been stepped on, slapped around, and proverbial "screwed, blued, and tattooed" by corporate America. A human being can only tolerate so much before he snaps!!! Luckily, I am a man of morals, and chose a constructive method of venting the furious rage in me! I have already figured out why people go ballistic, and go postal. Corporate America, and the plutocrats have created people like me, the authors of similar books, anti-global trade nuts, and the crazys that take automatic pistols to their work-places, and vent lead and fury! People must eventually break under constant assault. Fate brings us to new challenges, and new horizons, and now this is all I live for!

This "floating anger" is also creeping up in other facets of our life besides our society. The Times book quotes in New York Times polls; "The floating anger is also influencing people's attitudes toward politics. Pollsters say it is making centrist politics harder to practice and making people less faithful to any one party, less likely to vote, and more willing to entertain the idea of a third party." The Times polls also go on to say that the majority of Americans that have had a taste of "in your face capitalism" are more likely to support bigger government, more social programs, and ultimately ***MORE SOCIALISM!*** I sure hope every Republican is listening to the sound of the winds these days!! By too much big capitalism, our country could very well go more socialist, or even Communist! Like a teen-ager that has abused his freedoms, corporate, and plutocratic America will be grounded, and loose all of it's freedoms if they are not careful. Now you know the other little secret to this author's relentless determination to save American capitalism, American democracy, and ultimately the American Dream through "creative destruction". "Too much of a good thing is a bad thing!" Our economy is very much like our physical bodies. If one system is sick, stressed-out, defective or even if it is functioning too good, it can have a negative effect on the whole being. As I said in my first book, I am anti-Communist and am very much an American patriot!

This next set of poll figures, from the Times book, re-enforces my belief, that we all have become spineless, gutless, defeatists unwilling to stand up to this terrible "deformed" capitalist monster.

If it would help them keep their jobs, 93% of Americans not already bit by the greed bug, would increase their training. 95% of those who have already tasted "in your face capitalism" would get more training. 82% of Americans, who have not tasted greed, would work longer hours. 87% of Americans, who got a bite, would work longer hours. 71% of Americans, not bit by the greed bug, would take fewer vacation days. 80% of them with welts all over their bodies, would part with more vacation days. 53%, not victimized, would accept smaller benefits. 69%, already chewed up, would gladly accept less benefits. 49% of unaffected Americans would not even consider challenging the boss. 66% who have already been bug food, would not even think of looking the bear in the face. The next one makes me want to vomit!! 44% of Americans, who have not had a taste of greed shark, would happily accept a pay cut! *A shocking 59% of those, who have had a butter basted fillet of poison greed stuffed down their throats, would more than happily part with their hard earned money!*

What do you think the CEO of a company thinks, if he knows all he has to do is look at you, and you would literally give up all of your liberties as well as your pay, work ten times as hard, and put in double the hours???? Boy we've been beaten into submission!! **Hello, Wake up America!!!!! All of the lights are on, but nobody is home!!!**

We are gladly giving up the keys to the hen house to the fox, just so he will not even consider biting us! What do you think the fox is thinking to himself? "Well look at those cowards!" "They are so afraid I will nip their little heels, they will do just about anything for me!" "Not only will they give me the hen house, but if I show my teeth, they will give me the keys to their house too!" "Hey, maybe if I let out a little growl, they will give me the whole damn country!"

Maybe this will slap some sense into you!!
When asked if companies are less loyal to employees, than in days gone by, a shocking 75% of Americans voted yes, less loyal. Only 6% were brainwashed into believing the companies were more loyal. 70% of workers feel that they have become more competitive toward their co-workers. Only 20% were tricked into thinking that there is less competitiveness and more cooperation. When asked if they feel more hostility, and anger at work, 53% said yes! A mere 8% were conditioned into believing that there is less hostility, and anger. Maybe, not all hope is lost! Now we are taking one little step in the right direction! Americans, who were asked if they were more or less loyal to their bosses, some 64% claimed they were less loyal. Only 9% were sucking up to the boss. America use your common sense, add up the numbers! Just maybe, with a lot of patience and counter brain washing techniques, we can get this revolt off the ground after all!!

I started listening to socio-political radio talk shows a lot more, after I had been run through the meat grinder of capitalist America. When asked if they listened to political radio call in shows, 24% of Americans that have never been grinched by the greedmeister, listened to them. The ones that have been visited by the greedmeister Grinch, amounted to

36%. When asked if they would like more socialism, more and bigger government, Americans that have suffered at the hands of greed, and think government should intervene amounts of a whopping 63% polled. Out of those same jilted Americans, only 29% thought that government should keep out. those with better luck or are a member of the top 5%, believe that government should take a hike, account for 47% of those polled. Out of the other lucky or elite who, to spite their financial prosperity, still believe government should still get involved amount to 42%.

Even though formerly a Republican, I am now leaning heavily Reformist. Not only do I listen to the Ralph Nader and other reform radio programs, but I also listen to the biggest right wing conservative this side of Moscow, Rush Limbaugh ("Maha Rushie"). We both hate commies, and Clinton! I believe in only about 25% of what this wonderful bastion of the First Amendment says, and disagree with the other 75%. I am 25% "ditto head" and 75% Nader noggin! I still respect the man for the "balls" to stick to what he believes in, even though it isn't always in agreement with Ralph's or my viewpoints. In a twisted way he is still one of my other role models, besides Ralph Nader, Ross Perot, John McCain, and Patrick Buchannon.

You also have to listen to your enemies viewpoint, so you can make an educated assumption based on all facts, from both sides of the coin! If Rush or Ralph were ever silenced for their political viewpoints, I would absolutely go ballistic, and petition to get them both back!!!

I now realize why so many married couples are ending in divorce! The New York Times pole states that if asked, where would Americans place themselves on a chart consisting of various economic classes? All Americans in general would look something like this. 6% consider themselves in the ranks of the lower-class. 55% think of themselves as working class. 36% feel they represent the middle-class. Only 2% represent the upper-class or elites. Of those Americans polled, and asked about their current marital status, 11% are divorced or separated, and 62% were still locked into their vows. of those who have been in the downwardly mobile middle, and working-classes, due to corporate greed, 17% have lost their spouses, and 65% remained married.

As I have personally experienced the gradual loss of the American Dream, it is hell on a family! Even though, one could go out, and get hired the same day, due to the fact now we have more jobs than workers, he/she will most likely to earn less money with less benefits. Usually if the laws of market are true, and the forces play out, without the intervention of greed, the American workers should be paid a lot more than they are. I guess the forces of social conditioning are resisting the laws of supply and demand. A handful of powerful people somewhere, have decided that working America's income standards are too high. Therefore, in order to remain competitive in the new global economy, our living standards must be lowered to that of a third world country. This all in order to continue to rake in record profits, to pay the fat cats at the top, ever increasing salaries. Millions of Americans, even those with college educations, who used to live a decent standard of living, now must settle for more minimum wage jobs in retail or service industries!

The Times polls also ask Americans how they feel about their economic prosperity in these supposedly fantastic economic times. If asked if they are better of today as they were in days gone by, 53% said *NO!* Of those already fed through the corporate meat grinder, 71% **claimed to be worse off!** If asked, are you getting ahead?, 28% said they are falling behind, 51% claimed to have stayed the same, and only 20% feel they are excelling. Americans asked if there is a possibility of loosing the middle-class standard of living, 35% overall say yes! 23% feel the loss of the status could occur, belonged to the few lucky ones unaffected by corporate greed. 53% feel that somebody, as well as themselves, may feel corporate downsizing sooner or later.

This greed is tearing away at community, and civic pride. I was at my child's school PTA meeting the other night. It was the first meeting this year, and it was time to elect new board members. At the announcement of the need for volunteers, a death silence fell in a room of about 200 parents. The assistant principle asked multiple times, if anybody would volunteer for the position of PTA president. Not a soul answered! She then asked if the audience thought of anybody in that room would fit the bill. People started mentioning names, and those called out by hidden voices in the crowd, were asked to stand up. People started acting like a bunch of children in a class room, upon being propositioned to fill in for the teacher. They were passing the proverbial hot potato around like, it was a pocket sized nuclear bomb. Each prospective embarrassingly standing up and saying; "I do not have the time!" "I work two jobs now!" "I work odd hours and do not know if the schedules would clash." "I have nobody to take care of my children!", or some other version of "I do not want to be bothered, just leave me alone!!!!" My wife nudged me and said; "How about me? I could sneak it in after I finish at my school!" I immediately said; "You are already maxed out with your teaching position at another school, and the time you spend helping at your mother's flower shop! Then the 1 hour to 1½ commute, for a distance that should take only 20 minutes, in bumper to bumper, dead stop traffic, from your other school. Besides, you always complain you never have time to do your lesson plans for the next day!" I knew if she wanted it she was going to take the position. Later she may regret it, but I hope she can pack that one into an already swamped schedule. She has always been full of energy, bordering on hyper, but with the patience of Jobe. I just prey it will leave enough time for family. She raised her hand, and announced her desire. The audience looked as though there was a small relief, then they democratically approved with a hand count. My hand went up as well, I always support her in her undertakings. Landslide vote!! Now they needed Vice President, and a few other positions from spokesman to chair-people. You can guess the audiences reaction! Cheers, and applause! **NOT!!!!**

My wife has a fairly manageable schedule, if all she did was teach, and come home to finish the lesson plan. She teaches from 8:00 am to 2:15 pm, then allow another 30 minutes to straighten up the class. I can imagine those Americans who put in an 11 to 13 hour day. They would never have time for extracurricular civic duties. The problem is the neighborhood volunteer positions like girl and boy scout volunteers, PTA, and the church, to name a few, are running out of volunteers. People that are overworked, and underpaid enough to worry where the next pay check is coming from, tend to not have the will-power, or patience for more responsibility. Does every facet of our lives have to be negatively effected as the price to pay for a booming corporate economy? Maybe I shouldn't say every! We do have computers that can do things unimaginable even 5 years ago. We have an excess of bizarre low paying jobs in service, and retail positions. We have automobiles that look like something from Star Trek, with technology embedded in them that makes the Apollo 11 space craft of the 60s look like a tin horse and buggy! We have watches that have more computer guts, and brains, with more megabytes than five Apollo missions. We have miscellaneous gadgets and thingamajigs that rival any episode of Star Trek's Voyager. Some with definite purposes, and others that defy the imagination if you have one, if you don't then they are as useless as a warts on a hog! We can get money from just about anywhere there is an ATM. Convenience abounds, if one has the money to access these technological wonders. I was watching our channel 2 a learning channel on NASA's first fledgling steps to harness warp lightspeed star drive for future starships. It is based on intense blinding lasers of all colors emitted out of the bottom of a small test model UFO style flying-saucer. As it is cranked up, it makes a deep hum with popping sounds, and levitates on a cushion of light, so blinding, that it resembles the stories told by victims of close encounters of the second – fourth kinds. In the November 2000 Popular Mechanics Magazine, the Air Force is playing around with mankind's first real UFO style flying saucer, complete with nuclear drive, and everything that even Gene Rodenberry would marvel at, if he were still with us! We have black, bat shaped airplanes, with liquid crystal display, and holographic instruments with armrest mounted joysticks (the stick or steering wheel looking thing in older airplanes that comes up between the legs), that look like something Batman or Darth Vader would fly. The Europeans have created an Airbus Industries commercial airliner resembling, and about as large as two 747s on top of each other, with all of the luxuries of an ocean liner. The US government, and it's subcontracted aircraft companies with an army of scientists, are playing with smart metal. This metal can morph into any shape the computer tells it to, then it hardens into it's new shape until it is given a new command. Eerily similar to the liquid metal man, resembling a cop, in Terminator Judgment Day. They claim in the future to make airplanes, and spaceships that can change shape in flight to accommodate new speeds, or control commands. Spooky, that back in the 80s there was a movie called The Navigator. It was about this boy, who finds a dart shaped UFO, and befriends the ships computer. He ends up taking it for a flight as the host navigator, and flies into space, and back into the earth's atmosphere. The ship turns to a semi-liquid state, and actually poly-morphs to accommodate any flying speed. The Japanese are playing around with a boat that can form an electro-magnetic field around it's hull, and can propel itself with out any propellers or mechanical interaction with it's environment. Just about any science fiction pipe dream will soon be a reality.

But what good are all of these technological wonders, bordering on the power of gods, if the average working masses will be unable to enjoy them. Will they be only for the wealthiest privileged few? Will they look as impressive, intimidating, and as alien as a king's chrome clad knight, with a chrome lance, on the back of a chrome clad horse, to the peasants bound to endless servitude, to the tenth century castles? Will the future proletarian masses peer out from their concrete, outdated, cold, dark, stinky, cramped, and dilapidated, corporate issued housing projects, at spooky, blinding, sleek, gleaming, UFOs of every shape, whirring by at mind-boggling speeds, to and from distant glistening, force-field encased, Wizard of Oz style emerald cities of the elites stretching to the stratosphere?

Here are a few other less noticeable impacts, the new greed culture has on our society. Being interested in model airplanes as I am, I have noticed a change of culture, less interested in pure play, hobbies or any other recreational activity. I have seen hobby shops close by the dozens.

When asked why they are closing, these small business men, tell stories of dwindling sales as fewer people have the time, patience, or money to spend on these unnecessary luxuries. Only a few board retires, or elites, that have made their millions in the stock market and have retired early while young enough to play, make up their most common customers. The specialty hobby shop, and the serious modeler may be headed for extinction. They will end up buying expensive but cheaply made, less detailed, less intricate, less quality, styrene plastic replicas of quality models of the past, in large chain toy stores.

Here in Miami, public transportation is becoming the only way to get around, as traffic gridlock has become intolerable. It can be faster to walk in some instances. The local government is toying around with the idea to ban personal automobiles for those residing in the city limits. It will literally be illegal to have a car, or any other mode of transportation, that requires use of the public streets. They envision the day when there will be a Metro Rail, People Mover, or tram at every intersection. People will get around like they do at Walt Disney in Orlando. Just catch the next tram, train or trolley to the destination of your choice. Eerily, similar to the song, I grew up with, by Rush called Red Barchetta. It is a rock song that also tells a story of a future teen at his uncle's rural farm. He stows aboard a turbine freighter out to his uncle's farm, and in the barn, he removes a dusty debris encrusted cover from a gleaming red muscle car. He starts it up with a roar, and with spinning tires, he races out of the barn with the surging power from a more free era. As he is racing through the one lane country roads, he encounters two police aircars, hell-bent on enforcing a motor law in the future, preventing citizens from owning their personal modes of transportation. He engages these two lane wide, Hovercraft patrol ships, and runs for his dear life, straining machine and man. He finally leaves them stranded at a one lane bridge, over a canyon, as the aircars need to maintain a cushion of air near the ground. He races back to the farm to tell stories with his uncle by the fireside.

Until then, we have to rely on our cars, if we do not wish to use public transportation. However, there is corporate greed in this infrastructure as well. The Port of Miami employs hundreds of people in the cruise line, and shipping industry. A lot of the jobs are minimum wage labor type jobs, and the employees do not earn enough money to own a car. They depend on the public transportation system to get there. But there is a problem! Somewhere along the way, a private jitney service staked claim to the port, but charges outlandish fees. They commute passengers from the entrance of the port, over a massive bridge at least ½ mile long to the gates. The public bus would be much cheaper. The city tried to start service into the port, but the private company threatened with a lawsuit. They claim the competition with the public transit system would threaten their profitability. Since the city took a corporate friendly stance with the state of Florida, it had no choice but to back off. Case dismissed! Now hundreds of workers are dropped off at the entrance by the metro buses, then they either have to pay the high fees of the jitney, thumb a ride with somebody else, or walk. It seems another greedy corporation, refuses to allow the laws of the market to operate freely! A classic case of a monopoly! Yet, those in favor of allowing the free market to operate freely (laissez-faire), seem to be hypocrites, if it turns against them. Then they wish to interfere with the market in all sorts of ways, until it turns in their favor again. God forbid, if the government were to attempt the same, then every right wing, conservative Republican will be spazing out and crying foul!

March 2000, there were charges made against asbestos removal companies. They were found, in record number of incidents, violating asbestos removal laws. The reason is **GREED!** Workers were not informed on the risks of the job. The companies were cutting corners to reduce expenses, by not providing the proper safety gear for the employees, to not disposing of the asbestos in accordance with the regulations. in their pursuit of the almighty dollar, and to save money, these companies are needlessly exposing employees, and the public to a toxic substance. Never satisfied with current profits, corporate America is constantly attempting to rake in more, and more profits, to pay the owners, upper management, and stock market, bigger, and bigger incomes. This further tarnishes the image of the free market in the eyes of Americans, and the world.

Corporations that profit on others debt, are seeding their future profits now for an even more bountiful future. These are the legitimate credit card companies, and loan lending institutions. They are turning up at college campuses across the nation, to snare young adults naïve enough to spend themselves into a hole. Most of these students have never had a credit card before and are lured with free gifts, into the world of dept. Right off the get-go, these young adults are guaranteeing a future of booming profits for these corporations. Or is this a plot on behalf of the wealthy corporate plutocrats, not only to rule, and dictate the standards of living of the future generations, but to create credit junkies out of them? Pure human exploitation!

I was cleaning out some old boxes the other day, and came across some old magazines at least 15 years old. It was like looking into a time capsule of 1985. There was an advertisement about a 1985 Dodge Omni fully loaded at $6,879. Today, this same compact car would run about $12,000. Then I found a magazine with an ad on a 1986 Mazda B2000 pick-up truck with a full sized bed. Brand new off the assembly line, it cost $6,995. Today, it would cost at least $15,000. It also made me remember where I was working back then. I was making $3+ more an hour, as a rookie bugman, back then, than I am now as a well seasoned veteran with 14 years experience. I remember the car I bought then. I remember the boat I used to go out in every weekend.

Early in 1998, my wife and I tried desperately to purchase a Volkswagen Jetta. After, several attempt, we didn't have enough income to swing the payments. Our credit was still tarnished, due to financial turmoil caused by my wife's battle with corporate America, back when my daughter was born. In this magazine there was an ad about a 4 door turbo Jetta, fully loaded off the assembly line at $7,995. I literally felt sick, as when I was attempting to purchase one in 98, they cost $26,000 stripped with no turbo. Ironically, I was earning more money then, and the rental rates near the beach were half of what they are today living far inland in Miami. It re-ignites my anger toward the aborted American Dream for a mass majority of working Americans. Why does greed have to destroy millions of lives, all to allow a few to live the life of

Riley? Even with my wife now working full-time as a school teacher, and my fulltime job, we still cannot live the quality of life we had in the 80s. Will I ever have another boat to enjoy what the Florida living is meant to be like? Will I, again, ever have the joy of buying a new car? Will I even be able to purchase a home? Will my children ever live as good as we had once? I ask myself, is this all there is to life? I am now getting older with the possibility of retiring on social security, with no money to do anything but sit around listening to the radio, sipping Metamucel, while waiting for the early bird specials.

While on this note, I found an article by Michelle Singletary in the Sun Sentinel August 14, 2000, pg. 20 of the Your Business section. Due to the continual rising cost of automobile ownership, and the fact a large number of American's incomes have not kept pace with the cost of living, a new method of car ownership has emerged. It's based on the principles of time-sharing.

"Car-sharing is like time-sharing. But instead of buying a week's use of a vacation condominium, consumers pay an hourly fee for the privilege of using a car when they need it, avoiding the ownership, insurance and maintenance headaches. Essentially, it allows a group of individuals to share access to vehicles that are parked close to their homes or offices."

It is just another sign of the times. I think it is a good idea, as it allows, those who would not be able to swing auto expenses and payments, an opportunity to use a car. What I am criticizing, is the fact, that because the declining standard of living of a lot of

Americans, society has to change to accommodate this lower standard of living. Just like auto title loans, home equity loans, now life insurance equity loans, who knows whats next. Maybe there will be jewelry-sharing, cloths-sharing, appliance-sharing, pet-sharing, or some other unheard of until now, form of services. All of this to make us more dependent on a corporation, and less independent. We are just adapting to the inevitable, it seems. Instead of fighting for what America is all about, we just tuck tail and make due! Most people who read this article, as well as I, the author, probably due not see the other real reason this new service has popped up. They just think; "What a wonderful idea!" They cannot see through the cloak of social conditioning, in it's attempt to lower standard of living, and income expectations of Americans. This could be intentional, or coincidental as an adaptation of society.

Not even our children are safe from human exploitation. In the Good Housekeeping magazine April 2000, pgs. 114-210, an alarming article by Patrick Kiger, "Risky Business When teens do adult work." sheds light on a most unimaginable dilemma. A teen-ager named Brian Schwartz took a job washing windows on an office buildings. He was saving for a first car. He was a healthy, six-foot, strapping youth eager to prove his worth to his boss. After washing ground floor windows, he elected to go into the tethered chair, and tackle some high work down the side of the building. He had only been with the firm for a couple of weeks, and only earned $8 an hour, a real bargain, as professional high-rise window washers get paid a hell of a lot more.

Jay T. Baldwin

The boy attached his safety line to the metal rig mounted to the building. Little to his surprise, even a safety harness wouldn't be able to save his life. As he mounted in the chair, with a snap, the metal mounting rig, Brian, his assistant, the safety harness, and all came tumbling to the ground. After the fifty foot fall, Brian suffered serious head trauma and died at the scene. His partner suffered a broken leg. The reason for this accident was youthful confidence, a desire to prove worth, and job ignorance. The morning crew had disconnected the counterweights, and laid them a few feet from the rig, when they left for lunch. Without the weights, the rig was un-balanced, and would never stay attached to the building.

"What went wrong? Everything. Brian's employer had violated state child-labor laws by assigning him to a task that requires training in the proper use of safety equipment. It also requires the sort of informed judgment that comes with adulthood. A trained adult worker might have noticed what Brian didn't: The morning crew had unhooked the rig's counterweights before taking off for lunch; they lay unattached, 30 feet away. He also might have known to strap his safety harness to the building, and not to the movable rig that pulled Brian to his death."

"Kids just don't have the maturity and the experience to look for things like that," says Greg Mowat, who leads Washington State's child-labor regulation program. "That's why we don't want employers putting them in dangerous situations."

When asked why Brian was on the roof, his uncle said it was money! His employer was getting a real bargain as an adult worker would have cost the company much more. The uncle quotes; "The bottom line for some businesses is going to be, if you can get a kid for eight dollars, why pay twelve or fourteen?"

In New Orleans, a teen-age construction worker was digging in a trench under a concrete slab to reach a pipe. The concrete slab came down on top of the youth. He died later because of his injuries. The employer had violated age limits for that type of work, and was fined $3,000 for various safety violations.

A Wisconsin teen-ager cut two finger tips off in a meat grinder machine. It is illegal to allow under-aged employees to operate power equipment, and the supermarket was given a $22,100 fine for two finger tips. In 1938 The Fair Labor Standards Act was passed to protect these young workers. Under this law, teen-agers cannot perform jobs that require driving, operating saws, excavating, roofing, power meat saws, dough mixers, bailers, and woodworking equipment. "Research by Rutgers University economists indicates at any given time, 150,000 teenagers across the nation are working in ways that are illegal under the federal labor laws."

Due to de-regulation, the Dept. of Labor's Wage and Hour Division only has 1,000 inspectors left to enforce regulations for the entire United States. Most labor law violations slip through the cracks, until somebody gets hurt or killed. This is what corporate America wants!

"For those willing to risk federal fines if they're caught, the economic incentive to break the law is powerful: U.S. businesses save an estimated $155 million annually by using young laborers instead of adults."

Jay T. Baldwin

Democratic Congressman Tom Lantos of California proposed the Young American Workers Bill of Rights Act. It prevents employers from working 14 and 15 year old kids more than 15 hours per week, during the school year. 16 and 17 year old kids would be scaled back to 20 hours or less during the school wear. The proposal also puts teeth back into labor laws. Corporations that are caught violating these labor laws, the executives responsible, would face a five year prison sentence, if a young worker is injured. If a youth is killed, the responsible executive would face 10 years in the slammer. Congressman Lantos quotes; "We pay a horrendous price when young people work under dangerous conditions, and when their work detracts from their education." In spite of violent opposition from corporate America, Congressman Lantos has gathered 58 cosponsors. The bill will end up in front of congress in the 2000 sessions.

As for Brian this will be too late for him. He never got the chance to even cash his first paycheck.

God bless the Democrats on this one subject. So help me God, if there are any politicians, in D.C., who want to shoot this bill down in favor of corporate profits, each one should be impeached and banished from this country! It is F _ _ _ _ _ g (excuse my French!) amassing, that there are people in our society, who would rather let corporations continue this human exploitation all in the name of the bottom line. If there are any conservatives, or liberals, out there, who do not support this bill, along with the Congressman, they should be investigated for treason!!! **Good God man!!!** What is it going to take????

If you are a parent, and passionately support Congressman Lantos, I want you to go to your table and write a letter of support. Make it out to:

> The Honorable Tom Lantos
> United States House of Representatives
> Washington D.C. 20515

Then write another to the president of the United States.

President _____
_____
> 1600 Pennsylvania Avenue
> Washington D.C. 20599-0001

America having the best economy in decades, has paid a hefty price for this prosperity. We have paid the fox with the largest number of chickens, to keep him from nipping our little heels! In three decades, our country has gone from the most prosperous nation with the strongest middle-class in the entire world, to the richest nation in the world with the largest income disparity in the world, and in recorded human history. To a nation that ranks fifteenth, half way down the scale of all industrialized nations, in life expectancy of it's citizens due to the lack of proper affordable healthcare. To a nation that pays $700 billion out of pocket expenses toward healthcare, the largest chunk of household out of pocket spending, in the entire industrialized world. to a nation that has the most highly priced healthcare in the industrialized world. To a nation that has the lowest percentage, at 21% of the population, with healthcare insurance. To a nation last on the list, to spite the fact it is a democracy with 7 out of ten citizens, supporting a national maternity leave program. To a nation that is number one in the industrialized world in infant mortality. To a nation that is number one in the industrialized world in percentages of low birth weight of infants. To a nation that is number one, out of the industrialized world, in pre-schoolers not fully immunized against polio and other deadly diseases. To a nation ranking number one, out of the industrialized world, in death of children younger than five. To a nation that ranks number 18 behind other industrialized nations, that provides compulsory education that meets the demand of modern civilization. To a nation that ranks last in **rewarding our teachers.** To a nation that ranks number one in billionaires. To a nation ranking number one, out of the industrialized world, in children and elderly living in poverty. To a nation number one in the homeless out of the industrialized world. To a nation last on spending on the poor, the elderly, and the disabled. To a nation last in giving to developing nations. To a nation number one in Fortune 500 international corporations. to a nation ranking number one in Fortune 500 corporations loosing money. To a nation first in poor bank customer satisfaction. To a nation number one in S and L, and bank failures and bailouts. To a nation number one in number of supervisors and managers. To a nation first in largest executive salaries. To a nation last in paid vacation days. To a nation last on the list in voter turnout. To a nation ranking 17 out of the industrialized nations in efficient use of natural resources by government. To a nation number one in not ratifying international human rights treaties. To a nation first in citizens victimized by crime. To a nation number one in murder. To a nation ranking first in murdered children. To a nation number one, out of the industrialized world, in emission of greenhouse gases. To a nation first in forest clearing.

Last but not least. Out of the entire industrialized world, the
United States is last in book titles
published per capita!

We are making the bed!
Well, my wonderful readers!
Pull back the covers and have a good night!!!!

Jay T. Baldwin

Chapter 5 The paradox. Big, plutocratic, capitalism, the new communism.

When one mentions communism, chills race up and down the spine. It brings back memories of Adolf Hitler, Joseph Stalin, the Soviet Union (Union of Soviet Socialist Republics), North Vietnam, North Korea, Fidel Castro, and Red China (Peoples Republic of China). It also brings visions of radical oppression of a people. Visions of government oppression, where people can not live life as they choose. They aren't allowed to own their own property, start their own businesses, or voice their own opinions. The state will decide the job you will have the rest of your life. It decides where you are going to live, and how many children you will have or not have. It creates paranoia in it's populations. If you break their laws, you will probably be executed by firing squad. The state becomes your new mother from hell. Human life is meaningless to Communists. You are just another expendable bee in the hive, another worker ant placed into servitude for the elite state, another termite of the colony under direct oppression of the queen.

If you have watched Star Trek, you are probably familiar with the Borg. They are a mixed race of various humans and aliens from all reaches of the galaxy. However, they are under complete cyborg control from one queen, Their bodies are possessed by nano-technology, turning them into half carbon based humanoid and half machine creatures. This makes them all plugged into one consciousness, the queen, all other Borg outpost, and cube shaped ships, that resemble a plumber's worst nightmare, and an electrician's combined into one. The thing is, they have no individuality or freedom to be independent in being or thought. If one is accidentally disconnected from the hive mind, his valuable equipment is stripped from him, and the organic parts are vaporized.

Sounds shockingly similar to communism doesn't it? All for the benefit of the few, or the one! As Jeff Goldblum, in the modern movie version of The Fly, said; "Insect politics!" "There are no insect politics!". Insects do not reason, they just do, out of instinct, genetically bred into them." If one bee deviates from the orders passed on through chemical pheromones, he/she is swiftly eliminated. Maybe, as we still do not know if insects have self awareness, for all we know, they may also be controlled by shear terror. **Communism! Total lack of desire to, or**

ability to question authority! Pure unchallenged authority. Maybe, that is what the Communists were trying to perfect, a population of people that do not question authority, and perform for the well-being of the privileged few or the one. They were attempting to recreate hive society for humans. Another bee in the hive!

When one thinks back to the days of Kings, Queens and castles, for all practical purposes, these social models represented hive society or a form of communism. It seems our whole history is echoing hive mentality. The ancient Egyptians, the ancient Romans, the Messopotamians, and just about every other culture worked on the basis of unquestionable control of the many by the powerful, usually wealthy and privileged few. Maybe, take a trip to the library one day and look up some of our past, history, and form your own opinion!

The big question is, why do particular humans constantly attempt to rule over other larger clicks of humans? For all practical purposes, democracy is a very young ideology. Maybe, democracy conflicts with human nature! This puts democracy in a very precarious position. We could either be this way by choice, or by genetics. Now we are getting into sociology. Now we are back to the three corrupters of man. Power, money and sex. Any one never comes without the other two, forming **GREED!.** If you may, a three for one bargain! These same corrupters are very primal, by their very nature, and can be observed in the insect and animal kingdom. Because democracy is not found in the world of wildlife, man in his assent to become more civil, puts democracy in a power struggle against man's nature. If democracy were a person, he/she would have a love-hate relationship with man. Some thoughts would be mutual, and others would clash. The trick is to make sure the constructive thoughts, civility, and logic are not overridden by these primal forces. So far the battle has been going in the right way, when the entire history of man is laid out on the table. If not, we would still be sailing around in fleets of Viking like ships, bashing in everybody's skull with a club, who didn't get out of our way. Hence modern civilization. However, like two teams pulling on a rope in a tug of war, the course waves back and forth. The times, communism, and any of it's brethren such as autocracy, totalitarianism, plutocracy, and dictatorships, have raised their ugly heads is another ebb. We take two steps forward, then one back, two more forward, and one back. So communism or any of it's relatives are echoes of our less civilized past, in it's attempt to once again gain the upper hand. It's the primal half of humans reminding us **it's still there!**

Now we have an idea, based on my hypothesis or educated guess, where the roots of oppression come from. Let's take a look at the particular person, persons, or institutions that make oppression (Communist like) ebbs occur in our history, like the plutocratization of the Untied States today.

au.thor.i.tar.i.an **1.** favoring complete subjection to authority. **2.** domineering autocrat. **3.** of or pertaining to a governmental or political system, principle, or practice in which individual freedom is completely subordinate to the power or authority of the state, centered either in one person or a small group that is not constitutionally accountable to the people. **4.** a person who favors or acts according to authoritarian principles.

An authoritarian, is a person who tends to be over domineering, pushy, bossy, demanding or even very self centered, with no consideration.

An authoritarian can also be a person completely loyal to authority. You know the one we have probably all heard say, "rules are rules, you can't go breaking the rules!" "rules are laid out for your best interest!" "you have to do what they say, no matter what!" "Don't question authority!"

An authoritarian, can also be very deceiving to the casual observer. Now that we have passed another election year, I have observed a majority of everyday Americans, mostly from the middleclass and poor, that strongly condemn the influence of big money, and special interest groups. They adamantly declare the autocratic, un-democratic, totalitarian effect of big money altering our democracy, absolutely un-constitutional and un-American. Then in the next breath they say, "there is nothing we can do about it!", or "we have to learn to put up with it!". "Even though, we demand change, Democrats as well as Republicans circumnavigate any question about finance reform. It seems, the current status-quo is violently resisting any attempts by the constitutionally endowed masses, to institute change. The proof is in the campaigning administration of both parties to lock out any third parties. They aren't allowed to debate. They aren't allowed to have T.V. advertisements. Why do you think not much is ever known about these third party candidates? All of this is absolutely un-democratic according to the constitution. It is also very apparent to the casual observers, such as the thousands of people, I have interviewed, that declare the locking out of third party members inhumane. This is how our current aberration of a supposed democracy has taken on communistic qualities. This has led up to my final definition of an authoritarian. These evasive authoritarians most likely do not even consider themselves authoritarians. They are the American majority by count, that I have seen in my decade and a half of serving the public as a pest technician. They are the people, that seem at first glance, to want to institute change for the better, but as you talk to them, you find out they have literally given in. They are the two gentleman, I met at the car dealer, the day we were all screwed with the fraudulent charges, that bitched, ranting and raving, that the dealership was crooked. At the same time, they were reaching into their wallets, and paying those very fraudulent charges. When asked, "why didn't you threaten to report them to the better business authorities, or Channel 7 News Real Deal, that responded with, "It isn't going to make any difference, they will still screw the public!", "Who knows how many people they have done this to?", "We have to learn to live with it!" They are the thousands of people of all races, and religions, I have spoken to personally, that agree with my philosophy, and writings, but on the other hand say; "There is nothing we can do!" "That's the way the cookie crumbles!" "One voice is not going to make any difference!" "America is going to hell in a handbag!" "Unless you are wealthy and powerful, nobody gives a damn!", etc..

These are the most common, and destructive authoritarians in our society. They are the final product of decades of social conditioning, or as called in sociological circles, Ideological social control. If there were this many of them, back in 1776, the American Revolution would never have occurred!!!!

These are the same p _ _ sy whipped, hen pecked, citizens that take a beating at the hands of corporate America, and not so much as a peep is heard, or do not even voice there discontent. They are the same individuals to gladly give in to un-democratic, un-ethical and inhumane treatment at the hands of their employers. Worst of all, these same beaten citizens are just like the ones that gave in to Hitler's wrath, Fidel Castro's tyranny, and communism. They propagate oppression!

Democracy has only been tried on a grand scale with the birth of the United States of America. Now the very institutions that supposedly guards democracy, have been corrupted by the mighty power of big capitalism. Unlike, for instance, Soviet style communism, in America, we can still travel abroad, choose our mates, select a trade, etc…But our communism really takes hold at the economic end of society, then it appears disguised, like a chameleon, all the way to the political end. Everything in this free market economy comes at a price, not just material things, but including a lot of rights, privileges, also some constitutional rights, and even human rights. Even your health. It works basically like this, the homeless man has absolutely no rights, the poor man basically has very few rights, a working middleclass man has limited rights, the upper middleclass has most rights, an upper class elite such as a millionaire, even a billionaire, the sky is the limit then some.

A homeless man doesn't even have the right to walk the streets freely. He can not even lay his head down to sleep. He basically doesn't have a right to eat, unless he can find some money to buy food or lucks out at a shelter. He doesn't even have the right to medical attention, since it to comes with a monetary price. Technically, he is worse of than if he were in the Soviet Union. Even at the height of the Soviet communism, the citizens still had healthcare, however, it may have been primitive and outdated.

The poor man may be lucky to get foodstamps and Medicaid. But due to long hours, low paying jobs, he doesn't have the financial resources to live where he wants. He doesn't have the time or energies to get involved much in civic affairs. He probably, is less inclined to vote in election years. He probably doesn't even have the funds to purchase a home of his own, and ends up a renter, where he has no say in the property, living under the rules set by somebody else. He can not have as many children as he would like to have. His financial position, in society, limits his travels because of automobile expenses, if he can afford a car, along with the facilities of society, such as beaches, parks, transits, schools and medical care. Parks and beaches may be un-accessible due to their location from his neighborhood, or they require the use of his limited, precious funds for parking or entrance fees. Medically, he cannot afford medical insurance, but may earn enough to disqualify him from welfare programs. Food amounts fluctuate according to his paychecks, extra side jobs, bills, and are very limited.

If he is working full-time, he is exploited by his employer, and is not respected at the work place. He is expected to be there like a piece of equipment, also he doesn't have any rights, freedoms, and has little human rights. His children probably will never see college education. His freedom of choice is very limited. He doesn't experience much recreation, other than TV time, due to the fact of limited funds, fatigue and no spare time. Mostly votes Democratic, if he votes at all!. Unlike the homeless man who lives an existence like an animal, living from minute to minute, he still lives a life of pure survival. He is probably about as free as a citizen of the late Soviet Union, unless tomorrow he won the lottery.

The working middleclass (lower middleclass) man is better off, but still is strapped for cash. He is usually a loyal, diligent, hard worker, but is still at the mercy of his employer. He earns pay at $2 to $4 dollars above the minimum wage. There is a good chance, he used to make much more money in the past, with his trade and experience. He has had the American Dream in his hands, then watched it slip away, regardless of how hard he works to hang on to it! He is also treated like a machine at his job, is worked very hard, and exploited by his employer. He has a little respect at work, depending on trade. Human rights, and his constitutional rights at the work place are very limited, depending on his ability to stick up from them or not. He is somewhat limited to his travels, depending if he budgeted for them. He can have a car, or two in the family, if he is very thrifty. They would be very used too! If he had a higher salary in the past, he should own his own home. If not, he had owned a home, but was forced to sell it, due to declining wages, and increasing property values. Taxes also added to his property loss. Access to facilities of society are limited, depending if he budgeted for parking, and entrance fees. Beaches and parks can get his goat, as he will have to dip into some of his lunch money or grocery money for the funds to access them. Medically speaking, he has a fifty-fifty chance of having any medical insurance. It depends on his job offered benefits. His freedom of choice is limited. He also cannot be bothered by civic duties, volunteering, or church activities, unless motivated, due to the fact he works long hours with the possibility of a second job. His wife usually works full-time too, if he is married. If he has not given up in democracy, he has a good chance of voting. If he has, he will say, "what's the use, it isn't going to due any good!". Recreation outside of TV, is fleeting and too expensive. He has to do a lot of budgeting, and sacrificing, to sneak in an occasional trip, party, or a night of dinner on the town. All of this depending on paycheck size minus the bills. In the past, this American may have had it better, with more trips, vacations, and maybe a small boat, or classic restored automobile. He will not starve, but most of his pay now goes for groceries. He was the classic image of the prosperous American middleclass in days gone by. The Leave It To Beaver style. Once having the American Dream, he is now very disgruntled, displaced, searching for the meaning to life, and may be very depressed. He is probably a renter now, and has lost the pride of owning a piece of America. His kids have a fair chance at college, depending if his area has any sort of scholarships, grants or gifts. It is harder to once have had, than to never have had! He is better off than in the Soviet Union. But he doesn't enjoy the America he had learned to enjoy. He lives from paycheck to paycheck now. He and some of his peers my be knocking on poverty's door, as the working poor, even with two full-time jobs in the family. Mostly Democratic. He is smart enough to know democracy is slowly slipping away with his life's savings. In his mind, America has made it to the half way point of being Communist!

The upper middleclass man has it much better. He is either headed upward or downward. His class is the dividing point, the chasm, like two continental divides, at which America is splitting into a two class society. If not already a small business man, his job is more likely to be an executive style. He works out of an office, has great respect and a lot more freedom at work. He has a more democratic atmosphere at the work place, if he plays his cards right. He may be a work-a-holic, or chills out and enjoys the fruits of life. Access to the facilities of society is not much of a problem, that is if he is the chill out type! He has a nice car, most likely new or a year old. If married, two nice cars. He usually has a release, such as a nice boat, classic car, or small airplane to fiddle with on the weekends. The wife has a good chance of being a stay home spouse taking care of the kids. She may assist husband by performing computer duties out of the house, or have a little hobby like business operated out of the home. The kids are going to college if they choose! He has a nice nest egg, maybe some good stocks and options. His house is probably located in an enclave gated style community, or have some water in the backyard. He and his neighbors combined, have some political clout in local civic matters. He or his wife are more likely to be involved in volunteer, civic duties, such as coaching little league sports, Boy and Girl scout leaders, and church duties. Recreation is no problem, vacations are much longer, and more numerous than his lower counterpart. Nights out on the town are guaranteed, and regular. Politics are a big part of his life, as the decisions may move him upward, or downward. But he still doesn't make enough money to donate a significant amount to any political parties, if any, to make government cater to his desires. He can almost taste, complete self sufficiency, as it's just out of his reach! Like a frustrated dog jumping at a steak, dangling from a pole, so he may very well be depressed. He is at the level of the working middleclass back in the good-ole-days. Mostly Republican. No need to even mention the Soviet Union here! He is living the life of the Soviet politicians and oligarchs (Russian entrepreneurs, and private businessmen that had the graces of the Communist party).

Last but definitely not least, the elite class. The top 5% wage earners. Individuals with incomes starting at half $ million, to the sky is the limit. The level of corporate, and political plutocrats. Most own international corporations, chain stores, or are very savvy in the stock market. Also the inheriting class, born with silver spoons in their mouths. Mansion given to them when most in their age group are still in college. Some may never have to work a day in their lives. A good day's work is spent on the golf course, or in their private yacht. As for some, they toiled their way up from the bottom, by luck or grace of god. They live in exclusive communities, like the best parts of Weston in Broward, or right on the intercoastal waterways. This is most likely one of several homes scattered through out the world. Their yachts look like miniature cruise ships, resembling some Italian style future starship. We will not even mention access to society's facilities, as he probably sponsors some of them, if he is civic minded. Again he could be a very prudent work-a-holic never taking a day to himself, but most likely he only works a few days a week, or in some extremes a few hours. Hobbies, recreations abound, golf, tennis, race boats and cars, classic car collections, expensive model airplanes, real airplanes as in Lear Jets. A Rolls or two in the garage, with a Ferrari side kick. Vacations! World tours on bi-monthly schedules! Sometimes mixed with corporate boardroom appearances along the way. Stays in luxury resorts and hotels. $1000 dinners! Politics! Did you say politics? This is the motherlode. If not a politician! Mostly Republican! Our whole economy, and half of the world's is decided here. Massive campaign contributions, most through soft money loopholes. Every single American's quality of life is decided here, and for the next 120 generations. American society supports these lavish standards of living, fraudulently or faithfully! The incomes that are equal to most third world nation's entire national reserves. Who knows how many families are homeless, have gone to bed without a bite, have lost there entire life's savings, how many divorces, how many destroyed towns, how many trampled rights, how many suicides, how many murders, how many lost hopes, how many Communist style laws imposed, how many third world nations, not given a chance at prosperity to allow this fantasy to become a reality for some of these elites.

These are our adversaries! The ones that have taken America from the average Americans. These are the ones that will make America a middleclass bastion again, or will turn it into an oppressive, two class, Communist style plutocracy. This is the colossal apple tree, we must shake, with this revolution, all the way to the roots, to jar out all of the rotten, worm filled apples, in our search for a few, glistening, shiny, gems with glittering diamonds inside, like Mr. Thompson in the first chapters. Those with more concerns, than just themselves. Those who sacrifice a lot of their pay, to enable them to pay their employees above average wages.

Big capitalism mostly caters to the forces of greed! Greed by all inherent qualities, when at the hand of a few powerful, wealthy, political and corporate plutocrats, is as oppressive as pure communism. However, if you happen to be one of the plutocrats, America could not be more free! If corporate America brandishes fascist qualities at the work place, it will not hesitate to impose the same qualities on society, using the federal government, bought out by soft money. The oppressive nature of modern American capitalism, is passed on to the masses through the puppet strings of government. Capitalism grande, and political favoritism is the puppet master to the plutocratic horror now unleashed in this supposed booming prosperous economy.

One thing that makes a democracy like the US, is we have more than one party. To be safe, it should have more than two fully active and functioning parties. Like I mentioned earlier, the two prominent parties today, have locked out the third parties. See how Ralph Nader wasn't allowed at the debates. Maybe he should have gotten some guest tickets, snuck in, and crashed the party. I do not think they would have arrested him in front of the whole world. If they had, maybe it could have re-awakened the sleeping giant, the people. Then the truth would be out, and our revolution would now be in full swing!

I could only guess how the two parties have joined forces, to lock out third parties. My hypothesis, based on my non-brain washed experiences and public interviews, is the third party, threatens any possibility for continuing the gradual, silent, unseen coup-de-tat by the plutocrats. It is to coincidental, that every time the third party becomes threatening to the other two, something always happens to split the party. Then the numbers plummet in the poles.

Then all you hear are the candidates throwing mud at each other, claiming the other is un-democratic, and un-constitutional. The other is oppressive, the other is treading on civil right, or some other insult. If you were an enemy power, this would be the perfect disguise, so un-believable, that nobody would give it a second thought! Maybe the plutocrats have cooked up this whole idea of Democrats, and republicans, and it is part of their larger picture. Maybe, there are no parties at all!!!! The imagination, too many times, has predicted reality!!! Sounds kind of like a great spy novel, but maybe there is a secret alliance between the Democratic Party, and the Republican Party to monopolize on the political scene. Maybe the two parties are some kind of illusion, a façade propagated to appear, as a democratic process, but in reality, they are the same political party with the same sinister plans. Possibly, CIA or some other NSA goons are infiltrating the third party, and sabotaging it. Where there is greed of historical proportions, in the richest, most powerful plutocracy in the world, anything the imagination can cook up can very likely be true. I am sorry to say so, but I am one who doesn't believe the government has come clean about John F. Kennedy. Do not rely on me, go and do your own research, and form your own theory. It will not be to far from mine! George Bernard Shad quoted: "All professions are conspiracies against the laity."

I scared up some of Ralph Nader's websites. Alan B. Morrison and Ralph put their heads together, and formed a new legal support group called the Litigation Group. Their job is to assist or represent the un-represented. Individuals like you, and I could literally take litigation on public policies to the federal courts. Under normal conditions, as individuals we would not have the fortitude, financial resources, or patience to tackle federal court litigation. The thing I like about this group, is it is in the habit of choosing causes, not clients. They take on high profile cases, with deeper meanings than the standard legal litigation at the local Bar Associations. They tackle worker's rights cases, auto industry safety cases, occupational safety cases. Mr. Morrison and Mr. Nader sound like the guys for the little guy! I could have used him in my class action pay disputes at my job. Nader quotes: "In many ways, these administrative law cases are the centerpiece of the consumer movement's litigation;

they are the chief instruments by which government, and businesses are held accountable for their actions." "Apart from these cases, the Litigation Group may be best known for it's pioneering litigation to defend the constitutional separation of powers, and reform the legal profession." Basically the federal government is bound by the constitution, to assign different responsibilities to three separate branches. The Legislative, the Judicial, and the Executive branch. Then the constitution orders the government to implement a series of checks, and balances. This prevents any one branch from becoming too powerful for it's own good. Many times under pressure of special interest groups, the President or Congress may attempt to circumnavigate the checks, and balances. This is when our Mr. Morrison's and Nader's group steps in!

This group has also fought for consumer's rights. Kenneth Lasson with the aid of the Litigation Group wrote a book, "Representing Yourself: What You Can Do Without A Lawyer". Kind of like a bully defense kit! Nader has tried to awake the American people to the various ways corporate America has been successfully deflecting consumer interests. Nader quotes; "The consumer movement has paid special attention to statutory mechanisms, that give citizens powerful new leverage to instigate reforms."

It seems the legal system has created several methods to protect Corporate America against individual lawsuits from citizens. There is a loophole that allows, the system to only look at individual cases, of a larger class action brought on by several citizens. Then the system requires there to be a humanly impossible amount of complaints by thousands, or millions of citizens, before it will even consider a case against a corporation. That way if a corporation screws a few hundred people on any one subject, there still will not be enough complaints to open a case against the corporation in question, the person who initiated the case usually throws the towel in, and drops the case. Most of the time, the corporation skates by, and gets off the hook. A built in safety net for corporations. The group has also tackled this problem.

Nader has been an adamant supporter of the Freedom Of Information Act (FOIA) This act allows citizens access to once closed information in government circles. Normal everyday citizens can use the act to force the government to cough up files, on most subjects once kept confidential. Information about a corporation doing dirty deeds can be exposed, and since the act is constitutionally bound, the government must hand it over.

Nixon, Reagan, and Clinton have been some of the presidents, who have intentionally attempted to neutralize the FOIA. Ironically, the most prolific cases of FOIA tampering, have occurred at the hands of Republicans. They are the first to harp about protecting the constitutional amendments, and they are the first to denounce communism. Do what I say, not as I do, seems to be their forte. They are flaming hypocrites! Among other agencies guilty of trying to circumnavigating the FOIA, are the Central Intelligence Agency (CIA), and the National Security Council (NSC). The FOIA has been used to open government files to public scrutiny, to allowing citizens, employees, and consumers the "right to know concept" if they are being exposed to hazardous conditions at the hands of government, and corporations.

These are just a few movements enacted by Ralph Nader, and company to ensure democracy, and prevent the formation of a kinder gentler Communist totalitarian police state.

In another Nader website, Nader uncovered "Welfare for the Rich" Kind of a rob the poor to feed the rich story. Many politicians are sucking up to corporate America, and giving massive tax breaks, cash gifts (bribes) to corporations for favors in return. We can only guess what those favors are, but I can bet money, and power is involved! Nader quotes; "This corporate socialism is for the rich only. Small and medium-size businesses don't qualify. These subsidies create competitive advantages for large corporations, which use the same city services as smaller businesses, but don't pay a proportionate share of taxes that finance them."

Sounds like another attempt by corporate America, with the help of a few good dirty politicians to circumnavigate the laws of democracy, and the free market, and to gain an unfair advantage. And businesses claim federal control is communism. It's seems more like corporations are the Communists, and do not like getting caught with their hands in the cookie jar. The typical pot calling the kettle black scenario.

There are a few other situations, that have me seriously concerned about freedoms, and rights in the Good-ole-US of A. They do not have any thing with corporate America, but are in need of mentioning anyway! Actually, it's against Slick Willie (Bill Clinton), as he is sometimes called, and Janet Reno. These next situations border on NATZI Gestapo police state tactics.; Being married to a Cuban American, I have a new hate for our cigar smoking dictator south of Miami, Castro! I was in the heat of the Elian Gonzalez scandal. I was one of the marchers valiantly rallying for the boy's freedom. I will not go into detail, as we all knew the final outcome. But my beef with the police in this particular situation, is there treatment of marchers not being rowdy. Many times, when I was at several marches, the police assaulted, and arrested peaceful picketers. They didn't give any reason, they just walked up to people, old, and young, and slung their arms around their backs, throwing on the handcuffs. One night, when I was over at my sister-in-law's home, about 20 police cruisers, 3 or 4 sheriff prisoner transport busses, and some special forces transports parked across the street. Troops of police came marching in rows of two, similar to soldier formation. There could have been at least 60 in numbers, with Gestapo style black helmets, vests, boots, and nightsticks drawn. There were no violent marches in this particular part of town. It seemed as though they were using this street as a staging area. I had enough of picketing that day, so all of my signs were put away. I attempted to walk up the street to see what all of the commotion was about. There were at least a dozen homeowners out wandering around. Soon as they got assembled, they came right at all of us, yelling, and ordering us back into our homes, and not to come back out the rest of the evening. I immediately, said from the sidewalk in front of my sister-in-law's home, this is America, and I cannot be forced in, without a formal broadcast from the city mayor, that marshal law has been instituted. At that, one club wielding storm trooper, yelled to another, "Take him down!" "Take them all down, and arrest them!" At that, I put up my hands, replying, "That will not be necessary!" My wife, and her sister herded the kids in, as we all backed up in a fashion similar to one backing away from a snarling dog. These scenes were repeated throughout Dade County, as our insider information was given to us. Our insider was one of the police officers. As we were basically prisoners in our own homes, in America, the land of liberty, and justice for all! There was a knock at the front door. Much to our surprise, it was a muscular, but rather short Italian or Spanish cop, complete with all of the Gestapo gear, resembling a Star Wars storm trooper! He kind of whispered to my sister-in-law, "May I come in for a minute?" I came rushing over to make sure all was OK! He was not in a hostile posture, but cradling his helmet in both hands. We let him in, almost immediately he blurted out, "I hope my supervisor didn't see me!" He asked us if we had something cold to drink. We offered him a soda, and a pork sandwich, as he explained, he had been on duty for more than 16 hours, and had not had a bite to eat since the following day. As we pulled a chair over for him by the table, he slowly settled in it as though he were sitting on an egg. He had a complete uniform, covered with a thick, black, padded, bullet proof vest, with all sorts of hooks, straps, and pockets filled with tear gas grenades, pistol magazines, pepper spray cans,

REVOLT AGAINST THE PLUTOCRACY

and billy sticks. Yes, he had a excellent Glock pistol, similar to the one I used to have!

As he wolfed down the Cuban style hoagie sandwich, he told us about some of the unconstitutional things going on. He exclaimed that it wasn't even like America. He even felt his own force became too oppressive. He was almost apologizing for the reactions of the law enforcement agencies. At his last hastily gulped down bite, he advised us just to put up with it, as it was happening city wide, and even though it wasn't right, it will eventually stop. He said they will not hesitate to arrest you without warning, and you could get roughed up a bit. It was pushing 9 PM, and it was starting to get dark out. At his closing words, he grabbed up his helmet, and struggled to his weary boot covered feet, as though he were a dismounting knight, laden with heavy armor. Mind you, it was very hot, and humid that time of year here, with 95 degree days, and 85 degree nights. As he walked over to the door, we gave him a Pepsi to go, as he slipped his helmet back on. With a quick look up and down the quiet police vehicle infested street, he paused long enough for some of the few remaining officers to walk past the house. Then, black uniform and all, he inconspicuously blending into the night like a black Japanese Ninja. Slipping out only with a few clicks, and clanks from all of his gear, the only remnant of his presence was the metallic odor of sweat, and heavy metal.

Never before, had I seen such open violations of ones civil rights. It gave you a tid-bit taste of what life must have been in the heart of Berlin, during World War II. Every street corner had club, and shield wielding cops. There was an un-official curfew. Every now and then armored personnel carriers, resembling some alien black moon buggies, roared by. Every time picketers gathered in mass numbers to wave signs at news cameras, reporters, and passing cars, they were told to disperse, and return to their homes, and if they didn't, they would be arrested for civil disobedience. All of this with out the issue of martial law. I kept thinking, "Is this really America?" What happened to the first amendment??? What happened to the right of public assembly?? I thought there were constitutional amendments to protect us from police state tactics. Maybe the Constitution is nothing more than an outdated list of customs!! I didn't even think we lived in a police state! But we do!

As I mentioned in previous chapters, this now has me thinking back to the late 60s, and 70s, when Florida public beaches were free for the public to use them for sporting, and recreational activities. There used to be a potpourri of Sunfish sailboats, catamarans, windsurfers, scuba divers, volley ball players, Frisbees, kite fliers, and picnickers. Today, except for a couple of surfing areas, most public beaches only allow a towel, and a bottle of suntan lotion. Private beaches are the only ones that some of these activities can be performed, but only the people who live on that stretch of beach are allowed to use them!

Then there are whole cities, and neighborhoods, that dictate what color to paint your house, how much, and what type of landscaping you can have, how many pets, if any, you could have, if you can have a satellite dish or not, if you can have a ham radio or not, if and what size of swing sets for your kids, if you can have a basketball hoop or not, if you can own an SUV, van, pickup truck, if you can have a boat or camper, and even how much Christmas decorations, if any, are allowed on your house.

As long as I do not force others to choose as I do, or I do not physically harm another in the process of my choosing, I will be able to choose as I wish! The state, corporations, or neighbors have no authority to force me to live in communism. So what, if I wish to paint my house purple, drive a pink VW beetle with yellow, and blue flowers on it, or park a work vehicle with company logos, in my driveway!

Then we are being exposed to communistic, oppressive philosophies at the work-place too. A corporate atmosphere, is far from a democracy. The CEO of the corporation is similar to a totalitarian. He has the final say so! Whether, it's to the worker's benefit, or not, is not high on his list of priorities. The bottom line is all that counts, everybody, and everything is expendable. It is an actual hive society, with the CEO the Queen, and the stock values the royal drone (King) bee. Like the Communist culture, it strips away individuality, rights, liberties, freedom of choice, and attempts to strip away individual thoughts. A prime example for social conditioning, is one of those employees, that lives, breaths, and thinks the company, and are so convinced the corporation does no evil. They are the company employee! Like the teacher's pet in school, they take whatever comes their way, no questions asked, even if it is not to their benefit. For all practical purposes, the corporate environment is a micro-Communist society.

Technically speaking, in fascist, or Communist societies, corporations are owned by the state. But do not let them fool you. There were a lot of private corporations in these Communist societies. Just the ones that were very profitable were owned by wealthy oligarchs (Communist capitalists) that were loyal to the Communist party. The corporate world in a Communist country is *very* monopolistic. Economic, political, corporate, and governmental functions are centralized, or narrowed down to the smallest denominators possible. A Bureaucracy! This led to wealth, and prosperity concentrated in the hands of the corporate, and political elite few. Even the press is centralized to promote uniformity in propaganda. Hence, the hive infrastructure, and Herculean **GREED!**

This is what American capitalism is doing to send up all of the *"red"* flags. What seems to be the ultimate goal of all mega, multi-national corporations, besides making ever-growing profits? Acquisitions!!! Yes, I mean buy outs! Mergers! Re-organizations! Basically, down-size, consolidate, and to **centralize!!!** Even the big television, and radio broadcasting companies are consolidating, and buying out each other. Therefore, narrowing down the number of sources of information, and creating the possibility of a monopolistic strangle-hold on all sources of information, and propaganda. Thus, creating a centralized hive infrastructure for the press with overwhelming **GREED!** Too coincidental. Gives me the willies!!! Maybe, I am on to something I shouldn't be here!

Illustration 20

"Little red hiding good" The enemy's motto. Know thy enemy's desires and use those desires against him! What does America hold most dearest? Free enterprise and the free market. There is a very real possibility the enemies of America are doing just that. Big plutocratic capitalism would be the ideal method to infiltrate our society with enough power, influence and capital to pull it off. Monopolize, manipulate and multiply to crush all small business and individual enterprise, then slowly manipulate the government to cater to mega-corporations at the expense of the people. Ultimately freedom, liberty and democracy is slowly inconspicuously eliminated for all citizens except the plutocrats and their families. A mirror image of all other autocratic, totalitarian and Communist cultures. Our culture will be destroyed without firing a single shot!!!

I promised to tell you of the frightening paradox, I mentioned earlier in the book. In a hypothetical situation, if you were an organized Communist political movement, or any other enemy political force, and your enemy is too strong to defeat politically, militarily, and economically, what would you do? Like I mentioned, a Japanese marshal arts Taido instructor taught me. "Do not attempt to overpower your enemy physically." "Fight intelligently!" "Use his strengths, and techniques against him!" I would attempt to find my enemy's lusts, and deepest desires. Then I would utilize them to my benefit. What does America hold most dear? What is America's pride, and joy, now that it's definitely *not* the prosperity of the working masses? Corporate profits, and ***CAPITALISM!!! LAISSEZ FAIRE***, or unregulated capitalism to be more precise!

What if it is possible that the Communists have done just that? Could they be intentionally infiltrating capitalist America? Are they attempting to sour the milk in the breast, to kill the baby? Are they meddling with capitalism as a direct attempt to overthrow us from within? Or, are they attempting to foul up capitalism, with greed to make larger income disparities, to form a severely down trodden majority, suffering from status withdrawal? Status withdrawal is what citizens, who have lost their social status, such as prosperity, the American dream, good paying jobs, and financial security. These down-trodden people are more inclined to seek reform, by revolutionary means. They are easy prey for the Communist propaganda, and movements. Could it be, the Communists, or some other enemy political force, may be forming these clicks of people, and are seeding, or provoking a revolution to make an environment more favorable for **enemy occupation????**

Is this what the plutocrats are using to hand us all directly over to the Communists, one little grain of salt at a time? Or is this new Draconian breed of capitalism just the results of self destructive, self centered greed, amongst the corporate elites, in their attempt to rule the world? The choice is yours my friend!!! One thing is for certain something "Something wicked this way comes!"

The next page has what I've coined the "Freedometer". It has the past, and present positions the US, and other friendly or hostile countries, hold in relation to America. It separates the most free, and the most oppressed. Like a thermometer, one can see where we stack up in amount of freedom, and prosperity, or oppression, and down trodden.

Jay T. Baldwin

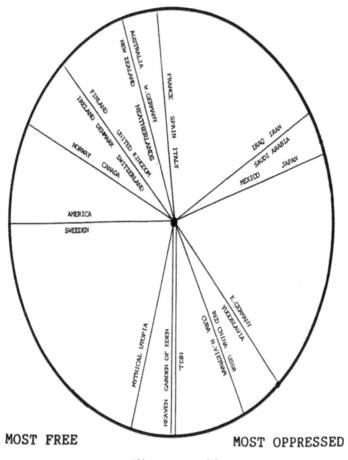

Illustration 21

REVOLT AGAINST THE PLUTOCRACY

The working Americans freedometer for the 1960s. A rough measurement of how working America's middleclass freedom and democracy is viewed and stacks up to the rest of the world in the 60s. If you were in the middleclass in the 1960s, America was the best place on earth to be. This was the closest to mass utopia we have ever been.

FREEDOMETER READING 2001

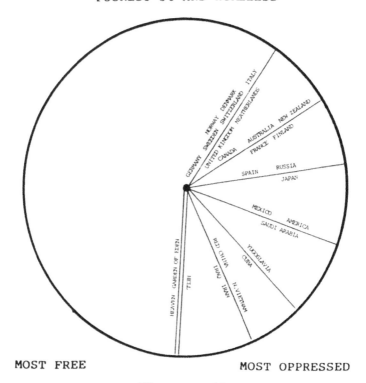

Illustration 22

Jay T. Baldwin

The freedometer for 2001 in the eyes of the poor and homeless. If the American poor and homeless could measure their pain and suffering compared to the rest of the world. This is what it might look like as they will have less freedom than if they lived in Russia. In America the poorer and less fortunate you are, the less democracy, freedom, liberty and freedoms of choice you have. A larger part of the world's democratic industrialized nations would be a better place to live for our poorest fifth than America. If you are at the lower end of the economic ladder, America is not the place to be.

REVOLT AGAINST THE PLUTOCRACY

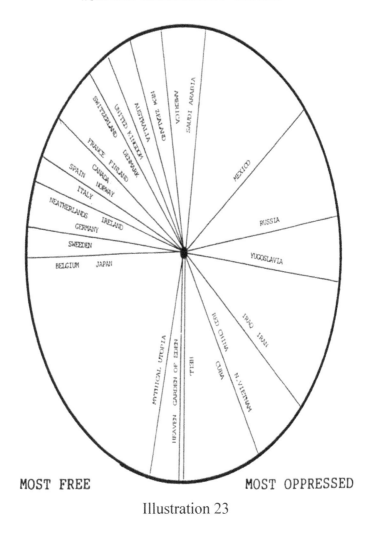

Illustration 23

Jay T. Baldwin

The freedometer for 2001 as viewed through the eyes of the working middleclass. The working middleclass is loosing a lot of ground compared to the rest of the free, democratic industrialized nations. America used to be the place to be for the middleclass, but now it is better to live in Sweden, Belgium and Japan. The middleclass citizens of other industrialized nations have much more influence in their country's plans and can reap the fruits of their ethical capitalism more readily than their American counterparts. Their minority richest elites have less manipulation of governments and legislation to become greedy capitalist consumer and labor exploiters. They are true democracies as we used to be.

REVOLT AGAINST THE PLUTOCRACY

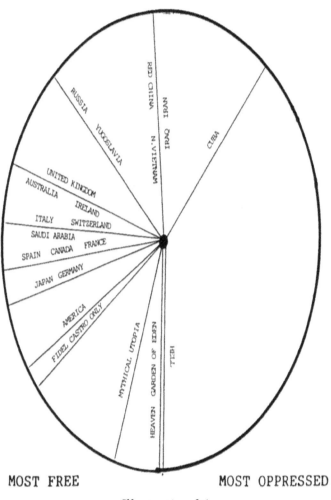

Illustration 24

Jay T. Baldwin

The freedometer for 2001 as savored by the American elite. If you are a corporate or political elite, America is definitely the place to be. Everything has a price, but money is no problem. Justice, freedom, liberty and freedoms of choice are in abundance as long as the cash flow and political contributions keep rolling in. Only Fidel Castro has more freedom at the expense of his countrymen. Just head-off the American Dream at the pass before it is accessed by the masses. If there is a social or political roadblock, just throw enough money at it until it is legislated in your favor. The epitome of an American plutocracy. The rest of the free industrialized nations impose more regulation on elites and their big corporate empires.

Imagine for a moment, the year is 2080, after over a century of bi-partisan squabbling, both parties have literally combined. There is absolutely no difference between them. This now forms what's called the Republicratic Party of the United Corporate States of America (U.C.S.A.). Third parties have been extinguished, as the U.S. Constitution has been mothballed. The colors of the flag are now red, white, and green. The star-spangled green field represents production, and profit. Public participation in the voting process has been eliminated. The actual election process has been federalized, and the Board leaders are elected from within by the power elite only. Citizen participation in the voting process was suspended in the year 2030, due to almost complete non-participation of the registered voters. The 2000 elections began what is called The Great Transition. After the many years of change known as the Great

Transition, the New World Order government is no longer responsible to the Constitution of the United States, the antiquated policies of a more free, and democratic period. Citizens have been re-named Team Members to create a sense of importance, and to assist in social conditioning preventing revolution. The Constitution of the United States was retired to the Omega section of the Smithsonian Institution next to the ancient Declaration of Independence. The Omega section is currently off limits to all Team Members, and requires a Board authorized D.O.S. clearance signed by an acting corporate CEO.

    Now the Plutocratic government, funded, and owned by several mega-national corporations, only answers to the CEOs that make up the chairmen of the board, or active members of congress. The position of politician is no longer an active position, as the privately owned government (the Board) doesn't have to answer to Team Members. All regulatory amendments have been rescinded. The descendants of the governmental Depts., when the government was still constitutional, that have survived the Great Transition, are now providing corporate housing, work credits, food allotments, health care, population surveillance, socio/psychological conditioning, and rehab-conditioning for violators, and dissenters. The Dept. of Domiciles (D.O.D.) provides Team Members corporate provided domiciles. The Dept. of Medicine (D.O.M.) provides Team Members basic medical treatments to maintain Team Members productivity levels, and emergency service for critical Team Members. D.O.M. also regulates expired Team Member cremation. The Dept of Servcon (D.O.S.)

implements Team Member surveillance through a surveillance chip installed in all Team Member's ID Cards, to guarantee complete conformity maximizing productivity. D.O.S. also provides partial productivity for Minor Team Members and socio/psychologoical conditioning seminars for minor Team Members until age 15. The D.O.S. implements rehab-conditioning for violators, and Noncon-dissenters (nonconformists), and also maintains secured Noncon dormitories until the Noncon completes his/her re-conditioning, and earns the title of Team Member again.

Noncons do not enjoy the facilities of America, and their families also known as Cohab Team Members (CTMs) or Cohabitating Team Members, must wear a yellow ID with the label Noncon CTM on their uniforms until their CTM completes re-conditioning. The Dept. of Credits (D.O.C.) heads distribution of productivity credits to all Team Members, schedules all shift assignments, deducts tax credits, issues Team Member uniforms, issues authorization of periods of non-productivity, once called vacations under the old constitutional days. They issue non-productivity time for health clearances, cremation ceremonies, and exemplary productivity performance awards. It also oversees the issuance of Team Member ID Number Cards (TMIDNC) to all Minor Team Members on their 16th birthday.

American Team Member Rights and Privileges (ATMRP) are issued by Head Team Members (HTM) in manual form (ATMRPM), in revised format by the D.O.S. annually to all team members, and new Team Members on their 16th birthdays. It is a very honorable, patriotic, and celebrated period in the life of a Team Member. This period of celebration, and the receiving of an ATMRP manual (ATMRPM), glorifies another year of Team Member productivity, and contribution to the corporate society, and the United Corporate States of America (U.C.S.A.). First year TMs are honored, not only by receiving an ATMRPM, but are issued their very own (TMIDNC) pronounced "timid NC" with an added bonus, their fist productivity schedule, and shift. A free Internet Terminal (IT), once called a personal computer (PC), is also issued, in ceremonial fashion to first year TMs, free of credit deductions. This will be the only time, in a TMs life, that an IT will be issued free.

The ATMRPMs are issued in a ceremonial fashion with a corporate dinner, not requiring use of Team Member Credits (TMC), at all local Corporate Team Member Conference Halls (CTMCH) on the eve, at 12:PM sharp, before the first day of the new year, called Team Member Recognition Eve (TMRE), once called New Years Eve in constitutional days. Noncons are forbidden at these ceremonies, and are issued an (ATMRPM) at the termination of their Recon.

TMs are responsible for reporting for productivity according to their Assignment Schedule, and Shift Orders (ASSO). TMs must wear their TMIDNCs at all times, as they cannot gain access at any entrance, and exitways, or utilize any credits in their accounts. To ensure compliance, all TMs cannot exit their domiciles each day, without first inserting their TMIDNCs into their ITs to converse with the Internet, and down load their ASSOs, and memory joggers for the day. TMs access their ASSOs, and memory joggers by touching the small clear yellow smile face on their TMIDNCs. Properly updated TMIDNCs will verbally dictate any changes, or modifications in a TMs ASSO. Any lost or misplaced TMIDNCs must be reported immediately at any street IT using the TMs numerical emergency code, or directly to an HTM, Dept. Director (DD), Corporate Chairman of the Board (CCB), or CEO. Once a tracking signal is activated, the card will be found, and discipline will be issued to the TM. Destroyed cards will result in discipline, and cost the TM one month in credits.

    TMs must present their TMIDNCs without hesitation, upon request by any Head Team Member (HTM), Dept. Director (DD), Corporate Chairman of the Board (CCB), or Chief Executive Officer (CEO).

    TMs are forbidden to own, or operate an aircar, or property of any kind. Aircars are only owned by, and for use by DDs, CCBs, CEOs, and their immediate family members, also known as the Elites, which include the wives, brothers, sisters, and children over the age of 15. Property including land, single family homes, aircars, recreational vehicles, boats, space transits, appliances or anything else desired, can only be purchased, operated, and privately owned by DDs, CCBs, CEOs, and their immediate family members. The terms, family, mother, father, grand mother, grandfather, wife, brother, sister, son, daughter, aunt, uncle, cousin, nephew, niece only apply to the Elites, and are not to be used by TMs, in the presence of Elites, or while on shift at the productivity site.

    Only authorized corporate issued items can be in a TM's domicile, or in the uniform pockets. TMs can only read authorized materials, and can only gain access to the TM levels of the Public Libraries. TMs cannot write letters, reports, musical compositions, poems, literature of any kind including books, short stories, novels, these privileges belong to the Elites, and their immediate family members. TMs cannot engage in recreational activities at corporate authorized facilities, unless under direct consent of an Elite, or they have earned authorized non-productivity time. TMs observe one authorized holiday, Team Member Recognition Eve (TMRE). This is to minimize TM non-productivity. Only the Elites can celebrate holidays such as Christmas, New Years Eve, New Years Day, Independence Day also known as the Fourth of July, Easter, Labor Day, and Thanksgiving. Labor Day is also known as laborers appreciation day, the day in which Elites celebrate their prosperity, wealth, and the productivity, and profitability of their international corporations, due to the productivity of their TMs. All of these holidays have one thing in common, they allow the Elites to indulge in materialism, bathing each other in material wealth, and their multi-national corporations to commercialize, boosting international trade.

TM mobility is monitored by the D.O.S. and is limited to TM monorails, TM shuttles, routs to, and from production sites, and recreational facilities providing the TM has authorized non-productive time status. A TM that wanders outside of authorized areas, will receive an automated verbal warning from his/her TMIDNCs, then upon arrival at his/her authorized destination, the TM will locate the nearest IT. Once an IT is located, the TM will insert the TMIDNC, and receive orders for discipline. TMs that violate this corporate policy will loose TM status.

TMs work one of two 12 hour shifts, 7 days a week. Shift A from 6:00 AM to 6:00 PM. Shift B from 6:00 PM to 6:00 AM. The 7th day, Sunday, TMs will work an alternative productivity task, different from their standard assignments, to alleviate monotony fatigue, and to maintain maximum productivity. Ex. A TM with an assignment in an office setting Monday through Saturday will be assigned to an outdoor labor position requiring physical productivity procedures on Sunday. A TM assigned to an outdoor labor assignment Monday through Saturday will be assigned to an indoor office setting on Sunday. All shift change requests will be determined on the following premises, there is currently an excess of TMs on the shift the requesting TM is wishing to vacate. There is a shortage of TMs on the shift the requesting TM is wishing to occupy. If the shift change causes a TM to be assigned to a position not in that TMs individual aptitude parameters, or training history, the request will be denied. Corporate policy dictates there will be no exceptions.

TMs wishing to procreate, must formally request authorization from an Elite. A complete inventory, both current, and forecasted, will be completed, to determine if there is an excess, or shortage of TMs in that particular corporation. If the TM's request is authorized, the D.O.S. will be notified to determine if there are any Noncon violations in the TM's history. If the D.O.S. gives a clearance, the D.O.M. will be notified for a complete health screening, and genetic code analysis to determine genetic stability, and superiority. If the TM is cleared by the D.O.M. then the TM will be pared with a TM of the opposite sex based on genetic stability, and issued a Corporate Intercourse Clearance (CIC), pronounced "chic". TMs are not authorized to participate in intercourse with out a CIC. Violation of this mandate will result in D.O.S. ordered sterilization by the D.O.M., followed by issuance of a Noncon label with the appropriate discipline measures, and mandatory Recon by the D.O.S.. This corporate policy is non-negotiable!

TMs that are suffering health complications, too complex to be treated with modern medical procedures, and prove to be non-productive in the least laborious assignments, while consuming an excess of corporate resources, will be exiled to the nearest direct descendant's domicile. The non-productive (NONPROD) TM will live out the rest of his/her life with minimal medical attention until the TM expires. Credits will be deducted from the descendant TM's account for all medical, food, and clothing supplies. TMs without immediate descendants, will be exiled to the nearest Non-Productive Omega Centers (NONPRODOC) to live out the rest of their lives with minimal depletion of corporate resources. However, TMs undergoing medical training will frequent these centers, and utilize these NONPRODs for hands on training, medical projects, and experiments. Once the NONPRODs have expired, there non-diseased undamaged organs, will be recycled to local D.O.M. medical centers. There they will be transplanted into sick un-productives (UNPROD). This greatly appreciated gesture of humanity is mandatory, to increase overall corporate productivity, and profitability. The generous NONPROD's name will appear on the Internet along with other generous NONPRODs, with an overview of their contribution to the Corporate Society (C.S.). The elites are very appreciative to these fine, former TMs for there generous stewardship.

TMs that generate ideas, to streamline productivity, to generate new productivity, or any other innovative contribution to corporate society, will report such ideas, without hesitation, to the nearest HTM, Department Director (D.D.), Chairman of the Board (C.B.), or CEO. In constitutional days, these individuals were called inventors. However, due to the in-hospitable corporate environment of the day, the inventors (NONCONs) demanded valuable corporate resources in return for their innovations. This type of inventor extortion, Communist in nature, was fought secretly, and valiantly by our Founding Liberators (F.L.), or known then as the Republican Party (R.P.). Fledgling corporations, of the day, did manage to control some of the supply of inventor's ideas, by covertly apprehending them from the inventors (NONCONs), through the cunning prowess of their primitive legal consultants (lawyers).

In the constitutional days, a very bleak, and dismal period in corporate history, the entrepreneur had little freedom due to the Communist, totalitarian directives in the ancient Constitution of the United States. These directives guaranteed employees (TMs) an unacceptable portion of corporate profits. These directives, pro-employee (TM) indeed, also forced resource depleting bribes from the corporations of the day, such as extortion payments to employees (TMs), equal employment rights, employee (TM) rights, occupational safety rights, environmental rights, minimum wage laws, family leave laws, and believe it or not, animal rights. One of the most unheard of directives of the day, enabled the constitutional government of the day, to legally extort massive ransom payments from early CEOs in the form of taxes. Failure of a corporation's CEO to relinquish these hefty ransoms resulted in incarceration of the CEO. It was as though the CEO was a NONCON, or criminal as they were called in the day, and was exiled to a primitive D.O.S. RECON facility for re-conditioning. However, primitive corporations, again with the legal prowess of their legal, and financial consultants, were able to fend off most of the ransom charges, and expenses. Also the Founding Liberators (F.L.s), the Republican Party fought valiantly, and patriotically to snuff out all of these corporate hindrances. The American patriot that started the Great Transition's momentum, under fierce resistance from the enemy party called the Democratic Party (D.P.), was named Ronaldus "Raygan". A second source of resistance, for our FLs resulted from third parties. The Reform Party headed by Ross Perot, and the Green Party headed by Ralph Nader. These criminals (NONCONs) proposed massive, terrorist style assaults against the young corporate society of the day. They basically envisioned a day, when corporations were created for the benefit of the mass majority of American citizens (TMs). This empowered these early TMs to live free, and democratic lives. Some owned property, cars (a land version of the aircar), boats, airplanes (Primitive atmospheric bound devices, to travel long distances at very slow speeds), primitive stocks (an early form of credits) and much more. Basically the citizens (TMs) were free to wander around un-supervised, work where they wished, in the tasks they wanted, get paid money (an early currency later replaced with credits), that rightfully belonged to the corporations, and CEOs, with the help of the government, and that dreaded communistic Constitution. The early TMs were almost as powerful as the early overclass, wealthy, or rich as they were called then. These "overclassmen", and socialites were the forerunners of today's Elites.

Eventually, these greedy pirate organizations, were exterminated by a process called political lock out. When it came time for elections, these terrorist organizations were not allowed to debate, advertise, or transmit their propaganda to the citizens, also known as TMs. This enabled the battered Republican Party to fend off only one opponent, The hated, and despised Democratic Party, not a whole pack of attackers.

In the end, the Democratic Party, even though it was our prime enemy, eventually halted it's offensive against the Republican Party. A new phase in politics, that was called the Quickening evolved, where the two parties cooperated in slow but decisive, strategic, covert plans, and forced legislation to give more power to the corporations, and their CEOs. The early corporations, and their powerful lobbyists, used precious corporate resources, to purchase, bribe, and manipulate the government into creating an atmosphere more favorable for corporate growth. These payments were known as soft money, and/or contributions. This so called soft money was a valuable tool in keeping the once criminal Democratic Party (DP) allied with the (RP).

The last battleground was to be fought against the citizens (TMs). They were easily defeated through combined corporate, and governmental Ideological Social Control, or social conditioning, constructive propaganda, force, intimidation, and legal prowess, to render them, and their famous ransom note, the Constitution of the United States harmless.

There were some authors (TMs) that were permitted to compose written propaganda, books, etc., against the New World Order, the World Trade Organization (W.T.O.), and the coming Great Transition (GT). They also attempted to align themselves with the leaders of the third parties to propagate, and plan future assaults against the new system. One author, that wished to remain anonymous, and low profiled, and was very instrumental in creating pockets of enemy resistance, by allying himself with other authors supporting the third parties, hell-bent on sabotaging the quickening with propaganda, was named Jay T. Baldwin.

As we have learned, the constitutional days were very uncivilized, pro-worker (TM), with citizens (TMs) running rampant like cockroaches, rats, vermin, and were very anti-corporate. They had an ancient saying that best fits this picture, "The fox was in charge of the hen house!"

Three hundred miles above the South Pacific Ocean, in a sub-orbital trajectory, a bright Titanochrome semi-delta/disk shaped craft streaks across the heavens. It's 3:00 PM South Pacific Time,

Jay T. Baldwin

New Years Eve 2085. The sounds of turbine thrusters, suddenly whining out a deep, metallic whirring cry, breaks the silence of space flight. A little boy, weightless, studying a history book, sitting strapped in the back seat of a private space transport, prepares to re-enter the atmosphere. "Well dear, we are almost there!" Mr. Garrity says softly. Mrs. Garrity responds, "We are there already?" "Yes, its only about an hour from the W.T.O. headquarters in New York, where the old United Nations building used to be, to Sydney Australia in a sub-orbital flight!". Then a deep sultry, feminine voice comes over the stereo speakers. It's the ship's computer replying, "Mr. Garrity, we are preparing to re-enter the planet's atmosphere." "The poly-alloy hull is currently re-configuring itself for atmospheric flight!" "Please fasten your seatbelts, and enjoy the view, while I interface with Sydney Navcom!" The little boy peers out of his large oval window, taller than him sitting in the seat, at the saucer shaped poly-alloy wings, glistening in the afternoon sunlight, set in a jet black background splattered with stars, morphing into a delta shape, like some computer animated program. The leading edge of the delta wing begins to glow orange, as the ship begins to shutter ever-so-slightly at first, then with a more persistent jolting. Then the sound of muffled air rushing over the hull, vibrating plastic, and leather fills the interior of the ship, as the lights, and holographic, liquid crystal avionics make a few insignificant flickers, followed by a pleasant electronic bell-tone. As the nose of the ship begins to point upward at a 45 degree angle to the blue curved horizon, the orange glow turns into bright yellow. Mrs. Garrity reply's, "Oh Dave, look at the shades of royal blue melting into lighter blue shades!" "I have always loved this part of the flights!"

The little boy says, as gravity begins to take hold with a forward, and downward pulling G-forces from deceleration, many times stronger than normal gravity, "Mommy, why was it so un-plutocratic in the past, and we weren't free at all?" Mrs. Garrity reply's, "I am not so sure, honey, but thank your lucky stars that we live in the freest, most prosperous, and most plutocratic times in human history, where you can have anything, and do anything your little heart desires!" "And nobody can say NO!" The little boy replies, "You mean I can have my very own corporation with as many TMs as I want!" "Yes dear!" reply's Mrs. Garrity As the ships nose slowly lowers, the last of the visible stars is being engulfed in royal blue skies, the buffeting, and rattling diminishes, as the ship settles into a quiet smooth flight. The ships sexy female voice interrupts, "Mr. Garrity, we are 550 miles outside of Sydney, current airspeed is 6,0205 MPH, and decelerating, the hull is configuring for atmospheric flight, altitude is 150,000 feet, I have locked into the Sydney air traffic pattern." "Mommy, I wished upon that last star before it turned light blue!", cried the little boy in an almost joyful glee. "What did you wish for dear?" The boys reply's, "I wished those mean, scary, free and democratic, Communist TMs, from the past, never come back to take daddy's corporations away, and tell us what to do!!!" "You do not have to worry baby, the TMs of today are just like this ship. If they become defective, daddy just takes them to the engineer's shop, and has them re-programmed!" calmly reply's Mrs. Garrity as the craft sharply banks, and circles Sydney, closing in on a ghostly, glistening aqua, and turquoise 4,500 foot stratoscraper condo, in the distance, with $19 billion stratosuites overlooking both the South Pacific Ocean, and the rugged Outback.

Well my reader friends, welcome back to the past. I hope you enjoyed your little hypothetical journey? Kind of left you feeling a little empty, cold, sad, hopeless and bewildered with a serious lack of self worth, if you attempted to live the story in you mind? **Didn't it????**

Welcome to the feeling my wife, my daughter, and I felt each time we lost another battle with corporate America, thanks to the growing procorporate policies being enacted with each passing year. Is this our destiny if things remain on the current path. What did Ronald Reagan really mean when he quoted; "The business of America is **business!**" Have we begun to put capitalism before the well-being of the people?

Grahm Greene quoted; "I don't think we can do entirely without capitalism, but the extremes are disagreeable and dangerous."

Janet Lowe quoted; "No matter how useful or benevolent a corporation may be, it cannot be expected or allowed to assume the functions of government. Business is not operated by a democratic process; by it's very nature, management does not represent a majority view or public sentiment. In facing the rapidly changing nature and size of corporate activity, nations must identify and affirm their basic tenets. Otherwise, they will be embarrassed, cajoled, or bullied into doing things contrary to the long-range interest of their workers, consumers, investors, and their cultural identity."

REVOLT AGAINST THE PLUTOCRACY

Education is our primary tool against the plutocrats. Education has been commonly used by the economic powers to justify corporations taking over of our society. You know, those who say; "If you get a higher education, you too can be one of those rich, and wealthy elites!" "You need an ever higher, and higher education to amount to anything today!" "College is a must today!" or something along those lines. Well you can ask any sociologist with any degree you can dream up, and he will probably tell you that it is partially true! Yes, if you do go to college, you will increase the odds of being in the top 10% of the wage earners, but it still doesn't guarantee it!" There is just not enough room at the top for every college graduate. In the corporate structure, it doesn't take a rocket scientist to figure out, that corporations aren't all chiefs, and no Indians. This is just an illusion, being passed on down the line, from those both in government, and corporate positions of authority. This is just a ruse to pacify the educated masses, but the masses really know the truth. Elites, and their kind will always remain king of the hill regardless of the education of the competition!

Maybe they have already figured out, if they do not slow the number of college bound citizens, they will be in a whole heap of trouble in the future. When all of those educated people, do not get into positions they were promised that guarantee the American Dream, what do you think will happen?? There will be a nice, little, BIG revolution, complete with educated ways, and non-educated ways to overthrow the fox from this hen house! This makes me think back to the many positions, now in the classified adds, that are requesting only college graduates apply for the job.

Jay T. Baldwin

The shocker of your life, is when you see what the jobs are, and what they are paying. I mentioned most of the real shockers in my first book, but here are just a few off the top of my head! Warehouse workers with at least 2 years of college for around $8 an hour. Security guards with at least two years of college, and minimum of five years of law enforcement experience, about roughly $7 to $8 an hour. Oh, we cannot forget about those $9 an hour avionics technicians repairing the avionics in $20 million jumbo jets! Or those $8 an hour aircraft technicians, overhauling jumbo jet engines, and airframes. And the police records keeper, that needed a bachelors degree in criminology, and paid something ridiculous like $14,000-$16,000 a year. Is this just more social conditioning to further lower the income expectations of all American employees, college educated or not? Are the American people that spineless, and gullible?? Is this another fallacy from the power elite?

In the Sunday Herald, June 27, 1999, pg. 3E by Dian Vujovich shows what we can expect.

"Facing the costs of college education can be daunting". With four-year college expenses today running into the tens of thousands of dollars, just imagine what they'll jump to in 10 and 15 years is enough to make many parents shudder. Or worse yet, not even think straight. Which, according to a recent survey, is what many are doing." "A survey conducted by the Mosaic Funds in Madison, Wisc., shows that parents have a tendency to be overly optimistic and not very realistic about where they will find the money for college expenses."

In the Communist cultures, most of the ordinary citizens do not have access to college, or the funds to even think of going. The Communist, totalitarian, and plutocratic elite mind set is not to make it possible for the masses to get higher education. It is reserved for the wealthiest few, and represents a threat to their domineering reign over the country.

By making the cost of college education gradually rise, until it is out of reach for the mass majority of Americans, the same thing is happening h ere!!! By doing it slowly over time, there will be a minimal chance of even triggering the bat of an eye! If the powers to be, were really interested in the well-being of the average American's access to college, there would have been a government imposed cap on college fees along time ago! At this rate, in a few short years, college will only be for the children of the elite. What then? Uneducated people are a whole lot easier to control, manipulate, deceive, and brain wash. In a few generations our wonderful little democracy may very well resemble the story in this book, or George Orwell's 1984. The choice is yours!

A short note for the end to this mind jarring chapter! As I might have mentioned earlier in the book, inventors in America have really gotten the royal screw, by corporate America. It seems corporate America doesn't want to pay the inventor any royalties for his idea!! I had an invention, the square pattern sprinkler head. No corporations wanted to sign my disclosure contract. But they all wanted to see the detailed plans first to determine if they wanted to pursue it further, and then they would sign the contract! My attorney said they were hoping to lure me into a false sense of security. Then they could get a peak at the plans, and run off with them like a fumbled football, grabbed up by the other team, and run for the goal themselves!!. One gave me the honor of putting my name on it as the only payment for releasing the plans. They explained how honorable it was to have a product with my very own name on it! Oh how sweet!! Kind of reminds me of what today's corporations do, to appease good performance employees, by showering them with worthless trinkets, and paper certificates, instead of giving them a raise. Something they can really use to prove their loyalty to the company! Today's employees have more worthless certificates, and trinkets hanging on the wall, than at any other time in American history!! In my first year at the pest control company, known for it's once a year pest control, I received three certificates of merit, one baseball cap, and one mug! People, that have been there over the past couple of years, have a complete wall covered from top of desk, all the way to the ceiling. As of the 2000 Christmas season, along with most of the other employees, I haven't even received the automatic 6, or 12 month raise, promised to us, over a year ago when we were hired. In the mid-to-late eighties, when I used to make almost double the money, than what I am earning today, it took me 5 years to earn 3 certificates of merit.

In this article, "They Saved Small Business, When corporate America tried to seize the patent system from independent inventors, this Boston couple came to the rescue", By Edward Robinson in FSB magazine April 2000, pgs., 75-84. Robert H. Rines a MIT-trained physicist and private inventor, that holds dozens of patents from radar to fish farming. in the Summer of 1999, a bill went before Congress that would have literally stripped all patent rights from independent inventors, and small businesses, and given them on a silver platter to corporate America. But Mr. & Mrs. Rines, with the help of U.S. Rep. Donald Manzullo of Illinois, saved the day only hours before the bill would have been signed, under great pressure from the corporate lobbyists. The bill still retains the rights to independent inventors, and small businesses.

That was a close call for all inventors, the world over. It's time for all of you mega-corporations out there to treat inventors with respect they have earned.!!

"Show us the money, you stupid morons!!!

Illustration 25

"Stop private innovation at all cost" My personal experience in dealing with corporate America as an inventor was a joke! My lawn sprinkler system ' is so efficient in saving water and uniformly watering lawns, that I figured I had a winner in the bag.

Especially in a nation wide drought. Unfortunately, that didn't make much difference, since I was asking for a modest royalty for my idea. All responses were various sneaky attempts, by corporations and their legal geniuses, to outright steal my idea. One attempted to convince me that giving them the idea for free, with the possibility of my name being printed on the side of it, and the idea of a grand contribution to society would be more than enough reward in its self. Who would reap the financial rewards for the invention if it wasn't going to be me? Who would get to keep all of the profits from the sales of the items? I wonder if they were willing to give them to the public for free as well?? Last but not least if all attempts fail, they buy the inventor out with an irresistible sum of money and shred the plans to prevent future competition. I didn't sell out to allow that!! It was royalties or nothing at all! I destroyed all plans, and will die with a revolutionary water saving devise. Bingo! Innovation in America is suppressed and stagnant! What an innovative idea!!

Jay T. Baldwin

Chapter 6 Placid Outrage, Violent Apathy. Social conditioning, the silent enemy.

Up to now, you have heard a lot about social conditioning, and have a general idea as to what it is, and how it works. But now we will get into the philosophical limits of this most effective, damaging, and destructive of all of the weapons, the plutocrats will ever throw at us. It is silent, invisible, penetrating, intimidating, and evasive. It's their secret neutron bomb, that has taken out 8 of every ten citizens that believe in reform. The side effects can be seen at the voting booths across the nation, at a less than a 35% of the registered voters. Just like it's non-hypothetical sister the neutron bomb, it obliterates all life in a shower of neutrons, and leaves the surrounding landscape un-scratched. This lethal weapon leaves no evidence except the lives it just changed forever.

If our founding fathers, in 1776, had been exposed to such a weapon from the British, they would have never risen up, and revolted. We would be called the United States of Britain today. Maybe, the British employed a primitive form of social conditioning, but the colonists were motivated enough, and saw it coming, and were able to counter its mind altering qualities.

The Herald on Sunday, October 10, 1999, an article by David S. Broder, pg 5L, "Nonvoters: America's no shows" No easy cure for apathetic electorate. "The gloomy message is that longer voting hours, easier access to absentee ballots or even Election Day registration may not do much to increase participation rates.... The nonvoters' indifference and hostility pose a clear danger to the health of the American republic." A gentleman named Henry Montoya votes every couple of years religiously. He even goes into the voting booth with his card, but never punches a selection. Then he delivers his blank card. He says this is his own way of protesting a system that presents he quotes; "no one worth my vote."

The article continues, Mr. Montoya is one of the few. Most that have been disillusioned by the process do not even show up. They are "the other America," the citizens who have lost faith in the system, and have given up the most prized rights, passed on to us from our founding fathers."

"Behind the answers that they are too busy to vote or the process is too cumbersome lies the accumulated belief of a majority of Americans that a vote has not only lost its actual value in terms of influencing the result of an election... but also its symbolic value as a democratic virtue...."

This is proof the people have quietly given in to social conditioning. They do not believe in the democratic process anymore, because regardless of their votes, the big money interests will still get their way. They represent that proverbial, "p _ _ sy" whipped individuals, I have taken great pains to snap out of their solemn daze. The whipped dog syndrome.

Maybe these individuals are the direct result of successful social conditioning, the plutocrats have implemented to slowly eliminate our most fundamental constitutional rights. If we do not use it, we will loose it! And they know this, so they do not attempt to rock the boat anymore, and just give us enough rope to hang ourselves. Then they will be free to do what ever their little rich hearts desire!

Our democracy, and freedom of choice is now under attack, from all possible angles, like a swarm of locusts gnawing at the edges, and slowly devouring everything in their path, it is slowly disappearing.

One less group of doctors to choose from, as they, and their medical center have fallen prey to big money. in the Business & Technology section, Sunday, January 16, 2000, the article by Bob La Mendola, pgs. 1G, 12G, "Medical Group lacking a cure" "Profit squeeze causes demise" Before we knew what HMOs were there was the Lauderdale Medical Group. The first multidoctor office in the Broward area. Patients had a multiple choice for any service they needed. But big money interests destroyed a good thing. "The rise and fall of Lauderdale Medical mirrors a national trend for doctors. They grew into independent titans of the community, then formed into centers of profit for corporations, and now are not sure which way to go." "Many feel they have lost control over their patients, prices and working lives in a health-care climate dominated by profit-orientated conglomerates, especially in South Florida, where half of the patients come from HMOs." "It's what's wrong with medicine today," quotes; Dr. Vincent DeGennaro acting president of the Broward County Medical Association.

We again come to the battle between our logical mind, and our emotional response regarding money. Is money the root of all that is evil? It seems to be used more for evil than good if you count up the actual uses for money. However, it could be we only see the bad effects money has on our lives. But the other question is, why do most people seem so defeated, when it comes to pay, and benefit cuts? What is held over their heads, that prevents them from asserting their rights? In other situations, if this same thing happened to them, or their family members, they would be going ballistic!!

Why do average people actually justify these aberrations of the economy. They may not agree at all, but in the other breath they will say, "Things can't stay the same!" "We are in a different economy now!" "It's been going like this for awhile now!" "You can't change corporate America!" "Greed will always be there!" "It will get better!" "No matter what, the U.S. is still the best place to be!", etc.

I have seen a dual side of some people, who for all practical purposes back the ideals in this book, but on the other hand they condemn me for my stance against corporate America. They condemn my books, and all that I am trying to do to better life in America. They even condemn, and denounce the Third Party candidates, and at the same time they support, and agree with their ideas, and regard the other party members as dysfunctional. Then they will go out, and vote for one of those dis-functionals. Are they suffering, what I've coined the "abused wife syndrome"?

They condemn the husband that brutally beats the sh _ t out of them. They may even call the police if somebody hasn't already. But when the police arrive they have a last minute change of heart, and come to the husband's rescue by dropping all charges. they will not even let the police take him away for the night. Even if the creep was killing her, she would come to his rescue, if somebody intervened and took him out.

Are we supposed to take this crap? Is this our lot in life, to be just like the TMs in the future vision? There just to be taken advantage of, like milk cows to be milked? Are we just the natural resources, that come with the territory, to be their for the greedy capitalists to utilize like crops, and just give enough in return to guarantee a new crop next year? Are we really worker bees in some grand colony hive to be there to benefit the queen? If any one bee rises up against the queen, he is stung, and thrown out of the hive to die! Is this what our founding fathers have wasted all of their time on?

Kazuo Inamori, CEO and founder of Kyocera Corporation of Kyoto Japan quoted "Capitalism and communism have similar failings." "Communism broke down because it neglected the spirituality of human beings. It's demise was accelerated by the irreversible tide of time, the rising power of the people. But these are not only the issues pertaining to Communist societies in crisis; they are the concerns of capitalist societies as well."

"A system of social checks is needed to ensure that the immense power of corporations is not taken advantage of or used for the interests of certain people, or that actions counter to the public interest and the spirit of the times are not taken in the name of corporate profits." "Corporations must be operated in a fair manner for the benefit of society as a whole."

Quote pulled from "The Secret Empire, How 25 Multinationals Rule the World." Written by Janet Lowe, business journalist, educator and public speaker. Another book I demand that you get!

Janet gave this direct quote; "Throughout the world, government leaders are exposed to public scrutiny. Writers, musicians, and artists reveal themselves through their work. We get to know, face to face, the educators, physicians, and others who influence our daily lives. But somewhere offstage in the darkened wings is a group of men who influence government officials, determine whether a local economy prospers or withers, and, too often, have a say over whether we live or die. They are the meganational corporate leaders. Even employers of these massive operations may know managers only a few rungs up the corporate ladder from where they are. The worker may never see, speak to, or even partially understand the person who can reconfigure her or his destiny with a single telephone call, the dictation of a memo, or a simple lifting of an eyebrow to the appropriate vice president."

"Who are these aloof people?" "How did they get where they are?" "Why do they do what they do?" "Can we trust them?"

If social conditioning coming from private big money interests isn't enough, the very institution installed to protect us from social conditioning, as well as assaults against our democracy, has implemented it on us. *The government!* As I had mentioned earlier, the Chairman of the Federal Reserve is instituting social conditioning, to condition Americans to accept a lower income standard, lower standard of living, and ultimately a lower quality of life. All this to minimize inflationary pressures in corporate America. What's meant by inflationary pressures, is not directly linked to products the American citizens purchase. It is referring to overhead expenses, like labor expenses, incurred by corporate America, that cuts into profits, executive pay, bonuses and perks. Then the usual comeback by the plutocrats, is "then results in higher consumer prices!" This is true, only if the elites insist on constant record increases in their own incomes. With the booming economy, if elites froze their incomes, and recycled the increasing corporate profits back into the company, in the fashion of hefty pay, and benefit raises for the employee base, there wouldn't be inflationary pressures! This way the stock market wouldn't take such a hit. In fact, it should give it a boost, by increasing the amount of discretionary income of the largest segment of the American population. The working majority!

Jay T. Baldwin

The government also uses social conditioning, to pass legislation of it's own that benefits the fat bureaucrats, also continually wanting larger incomes. It also uses it to promote larger soft money contributions from corporate America, and minimize the public backlash. Basically, government uses social conditioning to prevent reform beneficial to democracy, and the masses. It's no different than Soviet propaganda!

Most importantly, if there is some power struggle in Washington against the Constitution, and the free will of the people, then this social conditioning keeps the ignorant masses pacified. This allows the coup forces, ample time to concoct their little plan, and see it through.

The government uses polls to pass on propaganda, beneficial to their ulterior motives. Ex.; "The poles indicate that candidate _____ _____ is pulling ahead of _____ _____.", when in reality, it's the opposite. This is an attempt to stimulate "herd mentality"', to bring the poles back to acceptable parameters for the political group that best addresses the needs of those with the most amount of money. Herd mentality is the definition sociologists use, to define the sudden mass change of ideals, ethics, mood, or any other form of public opinion, upon given information that "fools" the masses into accepting an inevitable outcome. This is very powerful in campaigning months, weeks or even days before a major election. This can ultimately determine the final election results, depending on which direction the proverbial herd is running, at the final moments of voting. Like timing some giant pendulum, to be on your side at the final tally count! That is where the proverbial reference to the masses as being ignorant, gullible, easily manipulated and molded to benefit the existing power structure comes in. I mentioned several versions of this philosophy in my first book. This is where we can no longer allow those in power to manipulate us in our daily lives. This is a very powerful method used in Communist societies to propagate oppression. Facts show our supposedly free democratic society is being assaulted by our own government, and we are in a serious pickle now! This would put this form of social conditioning on the *public enemy number one list! IT IS IMPERATIVE WE DEFEAT THIS FORM OF SOCIAL CONDITIONING!!!! THIS IS THE VERY THING THAT IS UNDEMOCRATIC AND WILL CERTAINLY DESTROY OUR NATION AND CULTURE!!!*

Social conditioning also comes from the plutocrats in a variety of other ways. We have been conditioned to accept, we cannot even exercise some of our First Amendment Rights without first paying money to exercise that right. I found out in certain communities, and states most key areas, such as court houses, federal buildings, or other high profile areas, one cannot protest, unless he purchases a protest license. Who would ever have dreamed, in their wildest nightmares, that in America, a citizen would have to pay to access his founding father's given rights!

The other hidden truth, I get in my street interviews, is the fact most Americans are horribly terrified to go out, and protest openly in public! They are convinced that it is against the law to protest! They have actually asked me if it is legal to go out, and protest negative problems in society. Yet, they are more likely to think positive marching, or rallying is OK!. They have been conditioned by their parents, schools, society, and the press, their whole lives, that protesting societal insufficiencys' is not kosher, and labels one a trouble maker. Anything that appears to disagree with the status-quo, the system, the government, private corporations etc., is a sign of a trouble maker. If our founding fathers thought this way, the nation would have never been born! In Adolph Hitler's, and Karl Marxe's days, this form of social conditioning was key to keep the electorate, citizens, and any rival political forces from hindering their and/or preventing their coup-d'e-tats from taking place. This is exactly what the existing power structure in American is doing now, to guarantee continual plutocratization and not to change the status-quo!! This is where the influence of the third parties have been tripped up. A lot of people think Ross Perot, Ralph Nader, or any other political images are plane wacko, crazy, un-realistic, if they so much as preach dramatic, historic, or monumental changes for the better. So is news like this in The Politics Of Rich And Poor by Kevin Phillips on pg. 47, quoted by Harvard University's Lawrence Summers; "The U.S. is today in the midst of a quiet depression in living standards. The median income of the typical American family is right now the same as it was in 1969.", is thought as absurd, crazy, wacko, unrealistic or some other form of denial! Of course this refers to the cost to income ratio, adjusted for inflation. This is what they are expecting from us! **The elite have us right where they want us!!!**

WAKE UP AMERICA! MAN!!!

The other form of social conditioning is happen-stance, and has coincidentally fallen into the picture as another form of societal distraction, the plutocrats are using to prevent too many minds from contemplating reform revolution. Sports, Hollywood, T.V., Music, and any other form of pacifying recreation, that is all hyped up by the society, are fine, and dandy, as long as we do not allow them to pre-occupy our lives to the extent, that other more pressing things are forgotten or eclipsed. This definitely includes the economy, politics, and plutocratization!

I have seen too many people, more hyped up about the elimination of a favorite series, soap opera, movie star, famous singer, than they would be, if their jobs suffered cutbacks in pay, or benefits. Or, if a particular right, privilege, or tradition is permanently outlawed, rescinded, or revoked. Even the fleecing of consumers by companies is less advertised than the World Series, the Super Bowl, the Stanley Cup Playoffs, or some other form of sports. These forms of pacification have also been used by the worst of commies (Communists slang), and other oppressive leaders, and regimes. Hitler, advocated and promoted sports, acting, music, and other forms of the arts in Germany when he was in control. The Soviet Union took great pride in it's athletes, and broadcasted any sporting events openly. I know Fidel Castro allows the broadcasting of all sporting events in Cuba, to pacify the people! While on the other hand, oppressing other more pressing matters more likely to effect the masses. Harriet Beecher Stowe quoted; "Looking over the world on a broad scale, do we not find that public entertainments have very generally been the sops thrown out by the engrossing upper classes to keep the lower classes from inquiring too particularly into their rights, and to make them satisfied with a stone, when it was inconvenient to give them bread; wherever there is a class that is to be made content to be plundered of it's rights, there is an abundance of fiddling and dancing; and amusements, public and private, are in great requisition."

The message is, as I quote, to; "watch your back more persistently, when there is an abundance of sport, song and dance in front of you!"

"School and professional sports work to reinforce conforming attitudes and behaviors in the populace in several ways." (Eitzen and Sage, 1993). D. Stanley Eitzen and Maxine Baca Zinn authors of the seventh edition of "In Conflict and Order", a college psychology book issued to my wife at Barry University. This book basically sees society as I do, even though I had read it, after formulating my ideas for the first book. This book is backed by the Barry University staff. "This identification with athletes and their cause of winning for the nation's glory tends to unite a nation's citizens regardless of social class, race, and regional differences. Thus, sport can be used by political leaders whose nations have problems with divisiveness." "Virtually all homes have television sets, making it possible for almost everyone to participate vicariously in and identify with local and national sports teams. Because of this, the minds and energies of the viewers are deflected away form hunger and misery that are disproportionally the lot of the lower classes in U.S. society. The status quo is thereby preserved."

"The sports smoke screen serves two functions. Besides serving as a pacifier and uniter of citizens, it perpetuates the notion especially to the youths of lower classes, that sports is the elevator out of poverty and is a symbol of society as a whole. *"The poor youth who might otherwise invest energies in changing the system work instead on a jump shot. The potential for revolution is thus impeded by sport."*

Now I am on to something really big! Just maybe, by making advanced education less accessible, to more and more of the average masses, the plutocrats are deliberately attempting to prevent books like the "In Conflict and Order, and the accompanying classes, from ending up in the hands of the majority! I think, if more of the population had access to books like In Order and Conflict, they would be less socially conditioned! This would make more of the people harder to manipulate, accepting the status quo. Because of this I am, hereby, declaring this book one of the most important books for you as my reader to check out or purchase. **Sit back and weep all of you plutocrats!!**

"In Conflict and Order" by D. Stanly Eitzen & Maxine Baca Zinn, seventh edition copyright 1995. Allyn and Bacon publishers A Simon & Schuster book. **GET IT! READ IT!**

The media is another tool of social conditioning, the power structure uses, to pass on propaganda in it's attempt to preserve status quo! Parenti quoted; "Along with products, the corporations sell themselves. By the 1970s, for the first time since the Great Depression, the legitimacy of big business was being called into question by large sectors of the public. Enduring inflation, unemployment, and a decline in real wages, the American people became increasingly skeptical about the blessings of the corporate economy. In response, corporations intensified their efforts at the kind of "advocacy advertising," designed to sell the entire capitalist system rather than just one of it's products.... Today, one-third of all corporate advertising is directed at influencing the public on political and ideological issues as apposed to pushing consumer goods. (That portion is tax deductible as a "business expense", like all other advertising costs.) Led by the oil, chemical, and steel companies, big business fills the airways and printed media with celebrations of the "free market," and warnings of the baneful effects of government regulation." (Parenti, 1986:67)

Direct social control, is a direct, and deliberate intimidation, to render powerless, neutralize, and silence any person, persons, and organizations, who dare to challenge the current status quo regardless of it's benefits to the democracy, masses, the Constitution. It is usually directed toward nonconformists (NONCONS), political dissidents, and organizations, the poor, minorities, criminals, and the psychologically challenged. I fit the bill of a NONCON, and a political dissident, wishing for reform! **OH NO!! WHAT DOES THAT MEAN FOR ME??** The publishing industry, authors, and radio talk shows that supports reform, Ralph Nader, Ross Perot, John MCCAIN, Martin Luther King, Art Bell, Green Peace, labor unions, environmentalists, me, and all of my written sources, as well as my first book, and any others that dare to butt heads with the current plutocracy, status quo, then fit the bill of political dissidents or dissenters!

Let's do a little test, in an attempt to determine how successfully you have been socially conditioned!

The following questions have a scale of 1-10 at the end of them. 1 being farthest from a trouble maker/bad social influence and the most democratic. 10 being the most of a trouble maker/bad social influence and the least democratic.

Jay T. Baldwin

		trouble maker	bad social	democratic
1)	Government regulation?			
2)	labor unions?	____	____	____
3)	environmentalists?	____	____	____
4)	picketing?	____	____	____
5)	protesting?	____	____	____
6)	Martin Luther King?	____	____	____
7)	Ralph Nader?	____	____	____
8)	union strikes?	____	____	____
9)	political dissident?	____	____	____
10)	political dissenter?	____	____	____
11)	Karl Marx?	____	____	____
12)	Nelson Mandella?	____	____	____
13)	George Washington?	____	____	____
14)	The Constitution of the United States?	____	____	____
15)	social conditioning?	____	____	____
16)	John Hancock?	____	____	____
17)	Ronald Reagan?	____	____	____
18)	Democrat?	____	____	____
19)	Republican?	____	____	____
20)	capitalist?	____	____	____
21)	George Bush?	____	____	____
22)	Jay Baldwin?	____	____	____
23)	Al Gore?	____	____	____
24)	Adolph Hitler?	____	____	____
25)	Communist?	____	____	____
26)	work slow down?	____	____	____

REVOLT AGAINST THE PLUTOCRACY

27) corporate downsizing? ____ ____ ____
28) W.T.O. World Trade Organization? ____ ____ ____
29) N.A.T.O. North Atlantic Treaty Organization? ____ ____ ____
30) Union busting? ____ ____ ____
31) Stock Market? ____ ____ ____
32) money? ____ ____ ____
33) Ku Klux Klan? ____ ____ ____
35) skin heads? ____ ____ ____
36) N.A.A.C.P.? ____ ____ ____
37) Robin Hood? ____ ____ ____
38) Fidel Castro? ____ ____ ____

For fun, compare your results with your other family members! It probably varies considerably, with a few exceptions like Hitler, communism, George Washington, Constitution, etc., unless you are a pro-totalitarian dictator supporter. The variables are so diverse, depending on your race, color, political orientation, economic class, and last but not least, exposure to social conditioning. Mine differs in some aspects, compared to a multinational corporate CEO. Yet, the CEO, and I most likely feel the same toward Castro. A black man would vary compared to a K.K.K.

This proves some social conditioning is good. Like do not take drugs!, Do not drink and drive!, Eat a balanced diet!, Pray if religious!, Keep your children from physical harm!, Killing humans, not in self defense, is a crime!, Lock up all child molesters!, The stove is hot!.

Social Conditioning becomes harmful when it's used to deceive, and oppress a segment of the population for the benefit of a few. Slavery! Racial discrimination!, The Jews in Nazi Germany!, Plutocratization of the U.S.! To manipulate people, in order to keep them naïve! Lies!, Etc.

What comes to mind when political dissident is mentioned? I know from my street interviews, that most people tend to think of a dissident as a criminal element? Political dissident is probably, an enemy form of a politically inclined person. Communist, Marxist, anarchists, uni-bomber Theodore Kazinsky, etc. Who would ever think that George Washington was a political dissident? He was, if you were the British! To the colonists, he was a hero! Robin Hood was a political dissident! Robin Hood was a hero to the poor!

The term dissident is usually seen in a negative light. We have been socially conditioned, by our power structure, to view dissidents as no-good-for-nothings, crooks, etc. This is then spilled over into education, the media, Hollywood, and even our parents.

dis.si.dent 1. disagreeing or dissenting, as in opinion or attitude. **2.** a person who dissents. (also dissenter)

The actual definition is very benign. Social conditioning makes us view political dissenters, in what I've coined, the "Robin Hood factor". Depending on who in power makes the label, also makes the choice of who gets the unlucky privilege of wearing the negative connotation. We have been conditioned by our existing power structure to view people like, third party people, political reformers, authors against the status quo, environmentalists, anti-capitalists, and libertarians, etc., as bad.

In reality myself, all of those other people, and organizations mentioned a few pages ago, are really not bad people. We are just individuals, and organizations wishing political, and socio-economic reform for the benefit of the masses, democracy, and America. It just doesn't sit too well with the power elites, political elites, greed, and Ideas. **Status Quo 1.** the existing state or condition.

Working hand in hand with social conditioning, the United States is under going another undemocratic, un-American transformation beneficial to an elite few only. Bureaucratization! Bureaucratization is defined in sociological term as changes in an organization to create greater rationality, and improved operating efficiency, with more efficient attainment of organizational goals. 1) Work is parceled out into routine tasks performed by specialists. 2) There is a hierarchy in the chain of command, with each link having it's clearly defined duties, and responsibilities. 3) Then behaviors, and tasks are governed by an inflexible, standardized, written, and precise set of rules, regardless of the circumstances dictating likewise. 4) All decisions are made on technological, corporate, or scientific needs, and knowledge, with no consideration for personal considerations such as personal limitations, human limitations, legal limitations, and physical limitations. 5) Members are judged solely on efficiency, accuracy, and un-questionable loyalty to authority, with no regards for experience. Discipline is uniformly distributed, and unbiased.

It operates as if it was a machine. All aspects in American life from churches, schools, to corporations are rapidly converting over to bureaucratization.

"The majority of social scientists have viewed with alarm what they see as the trend toward greater and greater bureaucratization. Individuals will, it is typically predicted, increasingly become cogs in a very big machine. Narrowly defined tasks, a rigid chain of command, and total impersonality in dealing with other people will be our lot in the future. Human beings will be rigid conformists-the prototype of the organization man or women." "Several aspects of bureaucracies as they operate in reality work to promote the status quo. First, the blind obedience to rules and the unquestioned following of orders means that new and unusual situations cannot be handled efficiently because the rules do not apply. Rigid adherence to rules creates automatons."

These bureaucracies tend to stagnate. They choose only those people down the ladder, who have blindly followed orders, been the most efficient and fastest, and who have not proverbially rocked the boat. The Peter Principle (Peter and Hull, 1969) states the advancement of individuals that have been very successful at lower levels, until they reach the limits of their abilities, and competence. The bureaucracy is the most impersonal, and un-adaptable. "In sum, the bureaucratic form of organizations inhibits social change because it tends to encourage sameness."

REVOLT AGAINST THE PLUTOCRACY

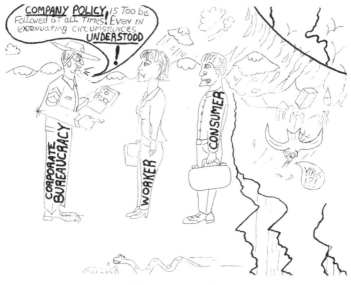

Illustration 25

"Company policy must be followed no-matter-what!!" Today's corporate policies are so unflexible that they are literally useless. The company policy must be followed even if worlds collide! If a particular variable scenario doesn't show up in the company handbook, it isn't addressed! Forget about any form of customer service, or employee relations. Basically it is up to God, fate, the law of physics, coincidences, consumers and the workers to adapt to the goals and operatives of the corporation.

They also tend to concentrate vast wealth, and power in the hands of a few or one. This allows that few, not only to create social resources for desirable ends, but also, and more likely, to other more undesirable ends. If left unchecked, they can result in total un-adherence to regulations, laws, safety, employee rights, consumer rights, innovation, technological progress, quality of goods, and services, and even human ethics, and rights. Even the Constitution is fair game!

I basically see these corporate bureaucracies as the ultimate stagnation of society, culture, identity, and humanity. When a society reaches the bureaucracy status, it signals the final end, and total corruption of society! Even social, technological advances, and innovations are fiercely suppressed, and condemned. Personal identity, and freedom of choice assassination is their primary function for their employees, and consumers. As a consumer, you no longer have any rights, or choices. "The customer is king!" no longer applies. As an employee, the individual relinquishes all civil, human, and personal rights, and takes an oath of complete unquestionable obedience to authority, even if it is in violation of societal ethics, safety, benefit or well-being.

Kind of reminds me of most of the places I've worked! Especially the relinquishing of all rights part, including, personal ones, like the right to use the bathroom, eat lunch, or my wife's situation, where family plans, and obligations are not to interfere whatsoever, with the corporate operatives. Hey, it is beginning to resemble our so called "hive mentality", or the Borg collective! Is it my imagination, or does everything we have discussed so far, seem to be coming together like some vast frightening, Orwellian puzzle? I think this is the largest and most influential revelation of biblical proportions, our future will hold! For the sake of democracy, it's time for the American people to sabotage, and bring these horrible monsters to a grinding halt NOW!!!

The life blood of these bureaucracies is social conditioning. The life blood of social conditioning is greed for money, control, manipulation, and power. What did I say, earlier in the book that comes inherently, or hermetically attached with power? Money and sex! Money, power and sex are the life blood of ***PURE UNADULTERATED GREED!!!***

More proof, that our country is taking abominable means to some haunting ends. "The government has been active in all major changes in U.S. history. Government has not been a disinterested bystander but rather an impetus for change in a particular direction. Most important, the government has tended to promote changes that benefit those already affluent segments of society. Actions providing equity for the lower strata of society generally have occurred when there was a threat of social unrest (Laur, 1973:156-157; Piven and Cloward, 1971)."

The proof is in the pudding! Our nation is no longer the democratic reality brought forth by our revolutionist forefathers. All that they stood for, and all that they died for is almost gone! Contrary to the order theory, a theory that claims the state exists to maintain order and stability, laws are enacted by representatives of the people for the benefit of the people. According to order theorists, the state, and law exist to promote equal distribution of prosperity, and justice without favoritism, and bias. Therefore, the interests of all people are guarded. But the sickening reality is we've strayed way off course set by the Constitution. The conflict theory model supported by most sociologists, dis-enchantingly proves the unthinkable. "The assumptions of this model are that (1) the state exists to serve the ruling class (the owners of large corporations, and financial institutions), (2) the law, and the legal system reflects, and serve the needs of the ruling class, and (3) the interests of the ruling class are served by the law when domestic order prevails, and challenges to changing the economic, and political system are successfully thwarted. In other words, the law does not serve society as a whole, but the interests of the ruling class prevail."

Basically, our nation today is a shell of it's self. Freedom of the ability, and will to change injustices, *A CONSTITUTIONAL RIGHT!!!,* in the political, and economic system, are now considered crimes against the state, and are punishable, by what ever means the communistic state deems necessary. Then it permanently silences, and eliminates the individuals exercising their given rights. Here is the actual section of the Constitution of the United States that is being unconstitutionally neutralized by our very own, new kinder gentler totalitarianism!

THE FORGOTTEN CONSTITUTION, A FAILURE OF THE HUMAN SPIRIT!

"Governments are instituted among men, deriving their just powers from the consent of the governed. That whenever any form of government becomes destructive of these ends, the rights of life, liberty, and the pursuits of happiness, it is the right of the people to alter or abolish it, and to institute a new government, laying its foundation on such principles and organizing its powers in such a form as to them seem most likely to effect their safety and happiness."

I can already hear the socially conditioned masses! "What can we do?" "There is nothing we can do, it's a shame!" "You can't change it!"
"The U.S. government, then, is faced with a dilemma. American tradition and values affirm that dissent is appropriate." "the well-off in society benefit from the existing power arrangements so they use their influence (which is considerable,), to encourage the repression of challenges to the government. The evidence is strong that the U.S. government has opted for repression of dissent." And has violated it's own oath to the responsibility of office and Lady Liberty!

WAKE UP!!!!!!!!!!!!!!!!

Because of these ungodly violations by government, corporations, and the ruling class (the power elite), against the people, and the democracy, government agencies have started a campaign of surveillance of the American people. Maybe, they feel paranoid about citizens exercising their constitutional rights, as they present a serious threat to planned social conditioning, and the status-quo. Then this makes the Constitution a serious road block, a ball, and chain hindering the maintenance, or advancement of pro-power elite operatives. Therefore, the power elite expects the government to do its part of the bargain, and squash the perceived threat, before it becomes a problem.

Jay T. Baldwin

"The scope of these abuses by the FBI and other government agencies such as the CIA, the National Security Agency, and the Internal Revenue Service is enormous." The Federal Bureau of Investigation (F.B.I.), the National Security Agency (N.S.A.), the Central Intelligence Agency (C.I.A.), now monitor the American people in a frantic search to snuff out all forms of dissent and reform. Positive democratic dissent and reform to return America to a democracy, not catering to the power elite plutocrats, are very high on the list of surveillance.

The following well known American authors have been vigorously monitored and intimidated by the supposedly "government of the people, for the people, by the people." Nelson Algren, Pearl Buck, Truman Capote, William Faulkner, Ernest Hemingway, Sinclair Lewis, Archibald MacLeish, Carl Sandberg, John Steinbeck, Thornton Wilder, Tennessee Williams, James Baldwin, and Thomas Wolfe. Is there any particular reason the government is especially concerned about authors? Possibly, it's because authors were the minds behind the American Revolution, and the writers of the Declaration of Independence in 1776. An author was responsible for the formation of the Third Reich, Adolph Hitler's "Mein Kampf". An author was responsible for the formation of modern day communism, Karl Marx's Communist Manifesto. An author was responsible for ultimate revolution against status-quo, Moses with the Ten Commandments. It's also because authors represent the foundation of the First Amendment, the peoples guardian of the most powerful transfer of information, anti-social conditioning tools, and propaganda in our Constitution. "The pen is mightier than the sword."

"The private industry also uses surveillance to keep tabs on their employees. "The privacy of workers is also in question. Some employers require prospective employees to take extensive psychological tests that ask about, among other things, sexual behavior, religious beliefs, and political attitudes (Lacayo, 1991)"

"Workers using telephones and computers may find their work watched, measured, and analyzed in detail by supervisors (Kilborn, 1990).

"Employers can (and do) peruse employees' E-mail, tap their phones, and even secretly film them in the restroom (Smith, 1993).

Social conditioning has been so successful in American society, that the vast majority of the people, I've interviewed, feel our plutocracy is wrong. They show complete condemnation of the biased economic system, and the overbearing government, but when serious attempts to change status-quo are mentioned, they seem to recoil. It's as though the mentioning of non-conformity, and challenging the system, is a sign of deviance. They even recant their adamant stand a few minutes earlier, as just a wild flight of fancy, if they didn't already give in to the "abused wife" syndrome. They even condemn themselves for deviating in thought, thinking that something can be done to change the system, then the "whipped dog" syndrome (the "there's nothing anybody can do!"), kicks in.

"Most people define deviance as behavior that deviates from the norms and standards of society." But what then, if the norms of society are now abnormal? According to sociologists; "Because people do not ordinarily question the norms and standards of society, they tend to question the exceptions.", no matter how positive the deviance would improve society. It's still deviance and must be eliminated! "The key to this approach, then, is that flaw is within the deviant and not a function of societal arrangements." Even if society is clearly the functional flaw. The absolute power, and perfection of ideological social control!

We are now socially conditioned to accept, beyond reasonable proof, the downward mobility, and slow methodical demise of the middleclass as the norms of an irrational, abnormal American society. That is exactly what the power elite have been striving for!

American history has taught us, that each preceding generation is going to do better than the previous. But the plutocrats had other plans for us, and their social conditioning was their bomb! "Sometime around 1973, the American dream stopped working. That's the year that real (inflation-adjusted) hourly wage for nonsupervised workers-almost three-quarters of the workforce-peaked. Since then, it's fallen (with little interruption) almost 13 percent." (Henwood, 1992:195)

"The gap between the rich and the nonrich is wider now than at any time since the end of World War II. The top fifth of the people in the United States now earn more than the other four-fifths combined. During the 1980s, the wages and salaries of those earning more than $1 million a year increased by 2,184%. The increase for people earning between

$200,000 and $1 million per year was 697 percent. But for people making $20,000 to $50,000, wages and salaries increased only 44 percent during the 1980s (and, if inflation were considered, their wages and salaries would have actually declined) (Timmer and Eitzen, 1993:4)"

Now our lovely power elites have socially conditioned (brain washed) Americans to settle for unfair tax distribution, skewed toward the wealthiest fifth! Every little domestic affairs policy is designed to appease them at the expense of the majority!! What form of revolution should we reserve for them? ***One is definitely on the way!!!!***

"Tax policies have also exacerbated growing inequality in the United States. Between 1980 and 1990 there was a 16.1 percent increase in the tax burden for the poorest fifth; for the next fifth of households the tax increase was 6.0 percent. In sharp contrast, the richest fifth experienced a 5.5 percent decrease in their federal tax burden. Federal taxes declined 9.5 percent for the richest 5 percent and 14.4 percent for the richest 1 percent of U.S. households. And while the poorest fifth of the households had a 5.2 percent decline in after-tax income between 1980 and 1990, the richest fifth, 5 percent, and 1 percent of U.S. households all claimed huge increases in after-tax income-32.5 percent, and 87.1 percent, respectively (Timmer and Eitzen, 1993:4-5)."

"Thus, an increasing number of people in the United States have experienced declines in their purchasing power. Affording adequate health care, child care, mortgage payments, and the like has become increasingly problematic for people who once considered themselves middle class. For example, homeownership, the cornerstone of the American dream, has declined dramatically since 1973. As wages declined since 1973 the price of homes has increased. "Between 1973 and 1989 the average price paid by first-time buyers increased 19 percent. Meanwhile, the average incomes of the nation's young renters decreased from $27,860 to $26,000" (Newman, 1993:34)."

The sociologists insist the reason for the decline in American incomes is due to a changing economic environment, but they didn't factor in the rapid increase in the richest fifth income. If the richest fifth, only gave themselves a 44% increase in their income in a ten year period of time, and took all of the extra 2,140 percent corporate profits and "trickled" them down to the American workers, as Ronald Reagan had predicted, the average wage would be more like 4 times what we are making today! So if you were a story clerk working for the big chain retail dept. stores at $6.25 an hour, today, you would be earning $25 an hour, or $52,000 per year. An auto mechanic, working at the local gas station, at $13 an hour, would be earning an outstanding $2080 per week, or $108,160.00 per year! Social Conditioning, with greed as the pupetmaster, strikes again! **SAT IT AIN'T SO!!! NOW PONDER THAT ONE, MY SOCIOLOGICAL GEEKS!!!**

"Because the cost of basic necessities at the minimum standard rose more rapidly than the general price index...the official poverty line fell ever further behind economic reality over the years. By 1991, the poverty line for a family of four was $13,920. Yet if the government officials had simply reapplied the same formula for measuring the cost of necessities that was used to calculate the original poverty line, they would have discovered that a family of four needed at least 50 percent more than that. Our own independent measures of the smallest amount needed by a family of four to purchase the basic necessities in 1991 totaled $21,600 or 155 percent of the official poverty line. This is the poverty line that government intended to measure along-what we call the real poverty line. (Schwarz and Volgy, 1993:191-192)"

As my reader, you can't be that brain washed! Do you think the government really made a mistake like forgetting to update it's formula? GIVE ME A BREAK! This was not just a simple error on their part, the a _ _ holes had it planned all along. What do you think they would get, in the way of political contributions, if corporate America was forced to pay $12.50 an hour minimum wage! They would have spaz attacks, at mentioning a $1 an hour increase in the minimum wage. If it's just an innocent little mistake, **FIX THE F _ _ _ ING THING,** and raise the minimum wage to a living wage of $12.50 an hour!!!

This Orwellian social conditioning is also effecting the average American's view of politics. As we already know, political status quo was destructively altered by soft money back in the 1980s, and the power elite put their social conditioning to work immediately, to brain wash the American masses into accepting it as, the new norm. But the other area, the social conditioning, has dramatically effected America, is the two party system. As I mentioned earlier, the Democrats and the Republicans are basically two wolfs, with one wearing sheep's clothing. For all practical purposes, both are plutocrats, one from the left, and one from the right, and they really look out for the best interests of the power elite. Daniel B. Jeffs Founder of The Direct Democracy Center in Apple Valley California quoted; "Those who continually beat the drum for the two-party system are, in fact, handing down an indictment of a failed political system that panders to the center with lies, deceit, and political terrorism, then returns to its base and does what it wants after winning elections ["A Fight 'for People, not the Powerful,'" August 21]. During election campaigns, independent centrists are the first order of business for politicians. After the elections, we're absorbed and ignored by the warriors of the left and the right. No wonder we feel the pain from an exercise in futility each time we vote. Independent voters decide every national election and prevent party stalwarts from ruling from either side. So why not just do away with the two-party system and make all elections and government nonpartisan? Maybe then we can add most of those 62 million abstainers to the rolls of independent thinkers and make representative democracy work, directly."

The key here is ***independent thinking.*** We can overcome social conditioning by formulating our own ideals, something those powerful plutocrats do not like! Mortimer Zuckerman's Editorial ["Voting for Grown-ups," August 21] was clear about both majority party candidates' tickets filling the requirement to "not simply maintain our prosperity but also address issues of "moral drift"-is the bureaucratic rule from Washington apparently trying to regulate morality by destroying the "no laws" freedom of religion, taking away the freedom to bear arms and to assemble freely, and other Bill of Rights issues and peer pressures to behave as the government dictates. It is clear to me that the N R A gun lobby, anti-world traders, anti-A C L U activism, and anti-immigrationists all have one fear in common: that their native country, the United States of America, is being taken away from them one rule after another by Washington, D.C."

And social conditioning has brain-washed the American public to accept gradual elimination of American rights, and freedom of choice. The American public is standing there with their mouths open, catching flies, and doing absolutely nothing! What a shame!!

Here, feed on this my revolutionary friends! If you still do not agree that big business is behaving as unconstitutional as pure communism, then why is big business on the death prowl, of the very carriers of the First Amendment? Radio has been the most popular expression of the First Amendments, decades before T.V.. One would not expect in a democracy, that any organization, including corporate America would attempt mass, across the board, silencing of this American right, much less, attempt to recruit government to do the dirty work. These type of things occur in Fidel's Cuba, Red China, and through out history in the Third Reich, the Soviet Union. But social conditioning is attempting to convince the American people, it's OK, because, it is in the name of money, capitalism, and profits!

In the Herald Sunday, October 29, 2000, the Focus section pgs. 1L, 5L, "A high-powered effort to kill low-powered radio", by William E. Kennard. "With the same energy it takes to light your table lamp, new 10-to 100-watt-power FM service will create radio for the people. Low-power FM will allow schools, churches and other local organizations to use public airwaves to make their voices heard. In short, low-power FM enhances democracy on the dial: It fosters new opportunities for true community radio to flourish in an age marked by the increasing consolidation and homogenization of the industry and the market place of ideas."

"This attempt to kill low-power FM is not about ideology; it's about money. Low-power FM has been embraced by the National Association of Evangelicals, the Leadership Conference on Civil Rights, the National Education Association and the National Council of Churches."

"The only group siding against the establishment of low-power FM is big radio, which in a textbook case of protectionism is trying to use government to smother potential competition."

"As a smoke screen for their financial interests, incumbent broadcasters consistently cite the remote possibility of signal interference as the reason to stop low-power FM." "This attempt to kill low-power FM behind closed doors smacks of everything Americans have come to distrust about our democratic process."

Remember what I said about communism? It has a habit of sneaking up on you, behind closed doors. The economic reasons, and the lame duck excuses of dial interference, is just an attempt to unleash social conditioning on to the masses. If it is said enough times, the masses will begin to accept these ant-

REVOLT AGAINST THE PLUTOCRACY

democratic encroachments against the freedom of speech. They may also be inclined to believe no corporation is capable of harming the democracy, due to successful infiltration of social conditioning! It can't happen in America!! Naïve we are!!!

Thank God there are good men to help fend off big radio. Of these patriots is Sens. John McCain, R-Ariz., and Bob Kerrey, D-Neb. "How any self-respecting representative of the people could think of colluding with big radio to stifle the voices of our schools, churches and local organizations is beyond me."

I wouldn't be surprised that big corporations have a lot to fear of churches, education, and individualists. They are the first to be stamped out in any Communist coup d'e tat! My first book had suffered mighty attempts, by large publishing companies to prevent publication. As a professional member of the National Writers Association (N.W.A.), I was exposed to thousands of publishing companies. After two years of membership, I received a call from the N.W.A. president. She told me they have attempted to find a publisher, but to no avail. Once the publisher read my galley draft, they kicked it back like some hot potato. They said, regardless of the First Amendment, those words cannot be circulated, as they have gone over the line! She even told me about some other author, who attempted to uncover political corruption in Capitol Hill. His life was made so impossible, by threats to him, and his family by governmental officials, he ended up moving out of the country! She said I was playing with the tail of the dragon, and would suffer the same fate, if I get that book out! I can just hear all of the Order Theorists out there saying' "You have to have control of the freedom of speech, or it will lead to anarchy!" "Status quo must be preserved for the benefit of social calm!" "We must give up some of our rights to preserve peace in society!" These are examples of a lazy society, unwilling to face up to a social problem, so monumental, that it warrants a social revolution by the masses. I feel our democracy is on it's last legs! We have really gone fascist if these accusations are true!!!!

Damn it America, cross check my sources, and **SNAP OUT OF IT!!!**

Social conditioning has really been successful in the wonderful world of the Stock Market. The Stock Exchange Commission has no legal authority, to protect investor's money from greedy corporations, that want to use the peoples money for their own demonic purposes, such as expanding, consolidating, or paying the CEO a larger paycheck! That then makes the Stock Market a legal ticket for corporations to further fleece the American people for capital, and financial resources. This further agitates the disparity of incomes in America!

Talk about leaving the fox in charge of the hen house! In The Herald Sunday, November 5, 2000, an article in the Making Money section, pg. 3E, by Meg Green. Mark in Coconut Creek Florida wrote a question to Meg. "I don't understand the rules that cover dividends. Auto Nation has never paid dividends. Isn't there an SEC rule that requires companies to pay dividends?" Answer: "Decisions on dividends are made by the board of directors of a corporation. They vote to determine whether a dividend should be paid to shareholders of not. If you've invested in a company that is looking to grow, then it's very likely the board of directors will vote to spend money to expand rather than pay the shareholders a dividend."

WHAT THE SAME HELL??? You mean to tell, me it's legal for a corporation to use the American people's money, and not pay them in return for that privilege!!! **What is this corporate charity??? Charity for the elites??** I can't understand, why there aren't mass marches, and protests on government buildings, by the very investors attempting to make a little profit for loaning corporate American their hard earned life's savings. Are we that socially conditioned, to accept our role as an exploitable commodity for the fancy of the power elite? **A REVOLUTION OF BIBLICAL PROPORTIONS IS LONG OVER DUE!!**

Elite charity seems to be the word for the day! If anybody with, half a brain, was told their charitable contributions were going to an elite family, in the form of elite charity, they would go ballistic! However, the system has kept these horrible abominations under wraps. If they splattered these crimes all over the morning paper's front page, you wouldn't hear so much as a peep! We have resigned ourselves to the supposed inevitability, that there is nothing we can do about it! Yet, if the permanent canceling of the Super Bowl, was splattered all over the front pages, there would be a damn civil war! It seems most government welfare assistance goes to those least in need! It's called **"wealthfare",** "the receipt by the nonpoor of financial aid and/or services from the government."

"We should recognize, first, that most poor do not receive welfare. Only one-third of poor families receive public assistance payments, and only about 40 percent of the poor receive public noncash benefits such as food stamps, free or reduced school lunches, public housing, or Medicaid. Second, the average welfare recipient stays on welfare less than two years (Sklar, 1992:10)." Third welfare was short financial handouts, in order to meet the poor's needs."

"The upside-down welfare system, with aid mainly helping the already affluent, is accomplished by two **hidden** welfare systems. The first is through tax loop-holes (called tax expenditures). Through these legal mechanisms the government officially permits certain individuals and corporations to pay lower taxes or no taxes at all. In 1975, tax expenditures amounted to about a $93 billion savings for the already fortunate. By 1990, the amount was about $294.3 billion (US Census Bureau, 1991a:320) In an interesting and telling irony, the government tax breaks to homeowners who were able to deduct interest and taxes amounted to a housing subsidy of $47 billion in 1991, which was five times the Housing and Urban Development's budget for low-income housing (Dreir and Atlas, 1992)" "In a perversion of progressive tax policy, the homeowner deduction gives the largest subsidy to those with the highest incomes and the most expensive homes. About one-third of this year's $47 billion homeowner subsidy goes to the 3.8 percent of taxpayers with incomes over $100,000. About 12 percent of this subsidy goes to the wealthiest 1 percent of taxpayers with incomes over $200,000. (Dreir and Atlas, 1992:93)"

"The second hidden welfare system to the non-poor is in the form of direct subsidies and credit to assist corporations, banks, agribusinesses, defense industries, and the like. Some examples (from Goodgame, 1993)" "Business meals and entertainment are 80 percent deductible to businesses. "Tax deductible meals are virtually a federal food-stamp program for the benefit of the corporate class, since the average taxpayer enjoys no such ability to write off the cost of winning and dining" (Goodgame, 1993:36)"

"Owners of business in oil, gas, and mining receive special tax breaks for depletion of mineral reserves and for the purchase of drilling and mining equipment. This saves them $1.7 billion annually." This further accelerates the upward flow of the nation's capital from the middle classes and the poor, to the power elites. "Rob Peter to pay Paul!"

"socialism for the rich"-that is, they supply money and support to the corporate businesses, not according to the much-applauded principles of the free market, but according to need as determined by the government.... We should recognize that government welfare to corporation or an industry may be necessary to avert an economic disaster. This is also the principle that underlies government spending for individuals who have floundered in the "free" market. There, the government seeks to maintain the individual as a productive member of society. Applauding the government's commitment to corporate welfare while condemning its support for individuals facing economic difficulties seems less than consistent." (Currie and Skolnick, 1984:139-140)

More proof the power elite, is doing it's best to socially condition the American people, by showering them with untrue facts, until they are widely believed to be true. I have been hearing the number of homeless has continually dropped over the past several years. The homeless amount to about 350,000 to over 3 million (information from Timmer and Eitzen, 1992: and Timmer and Eitzen, and Talley, 1994). "Whatever the actual number, two points must be underscored. First, the proportion of people who are homeless is the highest since the Great Depression, with a rapid rise in the past fifteen years or so. Second, the numbers actually minimize the seriousness of the problem because many poor people are on the brink of homelessness and many who lack housing are hidden by doubling or tripling up with relatives of friends. Jonathan Kozal estimates that there are more than 3 million families are living doubled up. When these households are added to the poor people paying more than half of their income for rent, more than 10 million families are living near the edge of homelessness in the United States (Kozal, 1988:1, 14) November 2000, the Census claimed that food assistance has skyrocketed 17%, and temporary housing for the poor has risen 15% for the year.

Mind you, all of this during, the supposed most prosperous economic times for all classes of Americans, in US history, as depicted by the press, and economic reports! Love that propaganda! Hip! Hip! Hooray!! Social conditioning to the rescue once again!!

"Even though the number of homeless in the United States is disputed by politicians, activists, case workers, and social scientists, there is widespread agreement that the number has increased dramatically in the past decade or so. The question is why? What factors explain this spreading social problem now? The current and expanding crisis of homelessness results from the convergence of two incompatible forces: (1) the rapidly dwindling supply of low-income housing, and (2) the increased economic vulnerability among the poor. Let us examine these forces in turn. The homeless problem is fundamentally a housing problem, that is, there is not enough low-cost housing available for people in U.S. society who are economically marginal. The availability of low-income housing has shrunk dramatically in recent years. Inflation is one source of this shrinkage. The cost of housing at all levels has risen rapidly. The median price of a single-family dwelling has quadrupled since 1970. Prices vary by locality, of course; the median cost of a house in some areas such as Honolulu, San Francisco, and Anaheim, California, is well over double the national median, and Los Angeles, San Diego, Newark, Boston, and New York City is just below the national median (USA Today, 1993a:10B)."

"The cost of renting followed this inflationary trend of the 1970s and 1980s, in fact, rising faster than renters' incomes. This inflation in the housing market at all levels has placed increased pressures on the poor, who simply cannot afford the increased rents or must sacrifice such essentials as food to pay the higher rents. The federal standard for "affordable housing" is paying less than 30 percent of household income for rent. A survey of 44 cities by the Center on Budget and Policy Priorities found that 75 Percent of low-income households (those earning less than $10,000 annually) pay more than 30 percent of their incomes in rent (reported in Gugliotta, 1992:A6). Data from 1989 indicated that nearly one-half (47 percent) of those households below the poverty line spent more than 70 percent of their incomes for housings (De Parle, 1991:1)"

Oh, they forgot to mention social conditioning to make us accept lower income standards than in the past! This is more likely to be a factor than all of the things mentioned here.

Oh, they haven't included the power elites attempt to gradually buy up all housing in the US, to profit from the renting of those properties. Hey all the pieces of the puzzle are coming together now! Get the American people to work for less, raise the cost of owning the American Dream, change the government to a plutocracy, socially condition the people to accept diminishing constitutional, and American rights, work them harder, to exhaust them, so they do not fight for their rights, shower them with lies to the point of acceptance, and socially condition them to accept all of this as inevitably the way things are! You commie jack_ _ _ _s think you can fool some of us out in the American masses, think again!

"There are several important reasons for the loss of low-income housing units. Most conspicuous has been the loss of single-room occupancy (SRO) boarding houses, often the housing of last resort for the economically marginal population. About a million SRO units have been torn down nationwide since the 1970s. The number of SROs and other low-cost rental units has decreased because of two related trends. One trend is gentrification-the process of converting low-income housing to condominiums or upscale apartments for the middle-and upper-middle classes. Another trend has been the demolition of low-income housing and their replacement with office buildings, apartments, and stores to revitalize downtown centers. Both developers and real estate interests to increase their profits result in removing affordable rental housing from the market, driving up rents in the remaining apartments, and displacing tenants from their homes and communities."

"These actions by the *private sector*, which have decimated the supply of low-cost housing, have not been overcome by governmental policies. Federal housing programs, which provide government subsidies for the construction of low-cost housing declined dramatically during the Reagan presidency. Federal support for another way, the Department of Housing and Urban Development (HUD) authorized the construction of 183,000 subsidizes dwellings in 1980 but only 20,000 in 1989. Moreover, the relatively meager federal budget for housing was mismanaged by HUD due to outright fraud; moneys that were targeted for the poor actually often were allocated for housing for the non-poor. Ameliorating the problems of the poor was clearly not a priority of the Reagan administration (Appelbaum, 1989:9)." Basically, the *private sector* = corporate fascism!!!

Now they are using their heads! If the corporate power elite did not hog all of the government's welfare subsidies, there would be enough to increase substantially the number of low-income units. But through force of fraud the power elite overclass gets it's way, unless we throw every last one of them out of positions of authority!!

The government's infallible rule of thumb, backed wholeheartedly by the Republicans, "the costs and burdens of all domestic affairs policies, must be born by those least able to bear them", have converged, "Finally, at a time in U.S. history when powerful forces were converging to lead more and more people to the brink of real poverty, government policies shifted dramatically toward more austere social programs. In essence, the government pulled away the safety net, leaving more and more poor vulnerable to the ravages of poverty. Each of the Reagan budgets lowered programs that helped the needy in society by tightening eligibility requirements and reducing moneys for the poor that were reduced by $51 billion. The situation did not improve during the Bush administration and has not improved during the Clinton administration."

I bet the moneys allotted for the low-income housing, have been diverted to the welfare for the rich! **How much do you want to bet??**

As we have learned, social conditioning is the largest and most effective weapon the corporate elites, and the plutocrats are using against the people. When I went to the library in Coral Gables to ask about donating my first book, I got an ear full from the librarian, proving my point. When he looked at a summary of my book, the first thing out of his mouth was, "It's a thought provoking book, but, You can't change the system!". I could not believe somebody of such intelligence has given in to social conditioning, and unchallenged authority. It is reminiscent of George

Orwell's 1984, even the great minds in the story are totally whipped by social brain washing. This form of ideological social control, is the same abhorrent tool, used by the worst of dictators, the most oppressive of Communist societies. We must, under no circumstances, fall into the false belief, that the implimentors of ideological social conditioning expect us to, that declining wages, lowering standards of living, less benefits, fewer American rights, and privileges, and fewer freedoms of choice (basically total concession to corporate, and political plutocratic fascism), is inevitable like some abhorrent natural phenomenon like hurricanes, tornadoes, or earthquakes, etc. These societal problems are man-made, and therefore, can be un-made! Remember that, the next time you find yourself coming up with another "there is nothing anybody can do!", "you can't change the system!", or some other total concession to the fascism of the power elite. ***This is exactly what they expect from the masses!*** I refuse to accept this, and I am attempting to wake you (the American masses) up, and allow you to think for yourselves, so you will also refuse to accept this as the inevitable. You must be a patriotic American exercising your founding father's Constitution, and Bill of Rights.

    Do you really believe the predictions in my future story, will eventually come true, if we stay on our current path? It will, if you do not do something **RIGHT NOW!**

Jay T. Baldwin

Chapter 7 Wake up America! Hello! Protest now or revolt later.

"The history of human progress can be written in terms of revolts against the status quo prevailing at any given time."

"An attempt to record all these struggles would be tantamount to writing a history of the human race since its emergency from primitive tribal life."

"It is besides the point whether progress is conceived as a real advancement for the bulk of the human race or as a change from one form of minority rule to another, whether it results in the improvement of the status of merely some of those who had risen against the powers that be, or, to be still more modest, whether the memory of the crushed revolts served to nourish the rebellious spirit of the underprivileged of later generations."

"The growth of the cities, the development of modern industrialism, and the concomitant decline of feudalism and agrarianism in general brought to the fore and increased the ranks of three social strata which were henceforth to dominate the historical stage of modern society: the capitalist employer, the hired manual worker, and, between the two, the noncapitalist man of education, the privileged and not-so-privileged managerial and technical employee-in short, the intellectual worker. Of these three forces, the uppermost stratum, the capitalist bourgeoisie, has in the course of the last centuries secured its ascendancy as a result of a number of violent and peaceful revolutions."

"From its inception the very basis of the profit system was to meet a theoretical and practical challenge issued by many representatives of the propertyless men of education, intellectuals, professional, technicians, and other mental workers. They questioned the wisdom or the justice of the wealth of the world being concentrated in the hands of a small minority of property owners and suggested various forms of collective ownership under which, as they claimed and believed, the despoiled majority would come into its own." "Is the challenge against social injustice slated to convert the dream of individual liberty and universal welfare into the infernal reality of universal collective submission to the all-powerful bureaucracy of the Moloch state?"

"Are we to accept the aristocratic, or rather plutocratic, gospel of those critics of the coming slavery of totalitarianism who would make us believe that every intervention of the state beyond its role as mere thief-and-murder-catching policeman is a sinister transgression of the sacred principle of individual liberty, a sinister concession to the infernal idea of socialism, which to those critics is one step removed from what the disciples of Lenin call communism? Or are we to reject their "libertarian" arguments as the special pleadings of hired apologists of the sordid interests of the supermillionaires whose "rejection" of the state is the "ideological" fig leaf of their hostility to the income tax, and of their readiness to deliver to private charity-to starvation-all the present beneficiaries of social security?"

"Are we to accept the defeatist idea that dictatorial collectivism, now in the ascendancy, is the only historical possible "inheritor" or "grave digger" of the continually changing modern industrial system?" (Quoted from Political Heretics by Max Nomad, the University of Michigan Press, 1963.)

It was another late Summer Saturday that was scheduled for me. We work on alternate Saturdays taking a Wednesday off on those weeks. I had about 4 stops scheduled, with one new account and three call-back services. The new customer was first thing in the morning. His work order called for a regular pest control for $395, with an additional flea treatment for an extra $175.

I introduced my self as usual, and proceeded to explain all of my treatments. I asked him where the pets were, and explained they had to stay off the carpet for about two hours until the flea treatment dried. He then got a puzzled look, and said he didn't have any animals. I then said, "The salesman sold you a flea treatment, didn't he?" I said to myself, we just do not have customers ordering flea treatments, if they didn't have pets, or haven't recently moved into a house that the previous owners had pets. The customer responded with a yes, and volunteered to show me his fleas. I then figured he just moved into a new house previously occupied by pets, and the fleas have gotten desperately hungry chewing him up as an alternative meal. He walked me to his kitchen and pointed to a swarm of small flies hovering over the garbage can. I immediately realized they were fruit flies. I diplomatically told him there was a mistake as they were not fleas, but fruit flies. He angrily said the salesman told him they were dog fleas, and the entire carpet would have to be sprayed. I again reassured him they were just fruit flies, and the way to get rid of them is by throwing the garbage out, also making sure not to leave any dirty dishes around. He then said he still wanted the regular pest control to get rid of his ant problem, but to remove the flea charges. I proceeded to call my supervisor to get permission to alter the contract. There was no answer at the office. The supervisor is always in on Saturdays. I proceeded to service his home for regular pests and would try again later. After three hours to complete a thorough new production, I attempted again to call several more times to no avail. I then took it upon myself to change the contract only charging him for the regular service, but explaining, in writing on the comment section of the contract, the reason for dropping the extra charges. He was very satisfied, and honored me for being truthful. He didn't know a bee from a butterfly.

Jay T. Baldwin

The next morning I turned in my paperwork as usual. My field supervisor immediately asked me why I dropped the flea service. I said, "It's all there in writing, but I will explain again." After a brief explanation, she went to the branch manager and filled him in. He immediately asked me to come to see him in the sales managers office. Upon entering, he closed the door behind me with a concerned look on his face. The sales manager also had an angry look on his face. I was asked to again explain the whole story to both of them. Once again another brief explanation, but before I could finish, he said in a stern voice, "You can not cancel services sold by a salesman!" I said it was a pest mis-identification, and I wasn't going to charge a customer for something he doesn't have. He stalled for a moment, and impatiently replied, "I do not care, you are not to question a salesman's judgment, it makes us look like idiots, and you cost us $175 in lost revenues!" I couldn't believe what I was hearing from him. I then said, "It's not right or professional to fraudulently charge a customer for something he doesn't need. He again said, "It is not your call, and our salesmen are trained to identify all pests, besides you are there to do everything the salesman writes on the order without any question what-so-ever!!!" "If it happens again, you will be terminated immediately." He then asks the service manager to get a disciplinary form.

I was written up for insubordination and costing the company a lost revenue. This was to be put into my file permanently. I couldn't believe this pest control company, known for it's once a year pest control, could be part of an international department store, with a household name made famous with it's appliances and tools would stoop that low.

I thought to myself, "What would happen if I write a letter directly to corporate headquarters addressed to the president of the company?" That night I wrote an intense letter explaining my love for my career with over fourteen years, and how I was honored to be a member of the team. I told him about my attention to details, and my desire to be honorable and truthful at all times never to cheat a customer. I then explained the company's name is honorable, and I will make sure that as long as I am there it will remain that way. Ironically the vice president of the company has the same name first name as I do. He also got a copy of the same letter.

Almost a month went by, and it was just another day at the job. This day would turn out to be yet another day to never be forgotten. One of the regional managers was down from Orlando, the company's headquarters. A young lady was also with him. I completed my paperwork and turned it in. The field supervisor told me to wait awhile as I will receive my work later. As the last technician left for the day, I was invited to the field supervisors office along with the branch manager, the sales Dept. manager, both field supervisors, the regional manager, and this young lady that came with him. I was introduced to all by my service supervisor. It turned out this young lady was the corporate attorney. Every person in that room had a yellow legal pad in their lap and a pen in their hands. I was then told my letter was received by the president, and the vice president. I was then asked to explain the flea incident once again. As I proceeded to explain, I noticed everyone was intently writing on those legal pads. Each question was asked very precisely in chronological order by the regional manager as though I was a murder suspect undergoing a police interrogation.

After a ½ hour of explaining every tiny detail, I was told to never question any sales representative. I was lectured by every person in that room, as they said, in various versions, of I dragged the company's name through the dirt, and made fools out of the company management, and the salesman. They told me to ignore future pest mis-identifications, and in a nut shell, if the work order called for treatment for pink elephants, you are to treat for pink elephants! The s.o.b.s basically said to look the other way while committing consumer fraud!!!

They dismissed me, but they all stayed in the room behind closed doors and had a phone conference with the president and vice-president. The walls are very thin in this building, as I could hear the conversation. The vice-president on phone conference said something along this line, "I want you to do a very through investigation on Mr. Baldwin's background!" "I want to know where he was born, where he went to school, where he lived, I want to know what he has for breakfast!!!"

About a week later, I came in as usual one rainy day. My field supervisor told me the operations manager from Orlando was in the office. He was possibly a year or two younger than me, and could vouch about ten years in the industry. I had never met him before, but he sure knew who I was. He introduced himself, and said that he was going out with me to evaluate my performance the best he could with the weather. Well, I was literally criticized at almost every move I made, and was humiliated as though I was on my first day. I guess God was looking out for me, as it was raining buckets all morning, which caused one of the three stops planned for me to be canceled, and the other had to be given to another tech as we got tied up in traffic for a very long time. We only did one stop, a new customer.

The following morning the branch manager explained I was to take all of the training modules over as though I was a first week trainee, and be completely re-tested. Ha!! A fourteen year veteran being humiliated so persistently and for such a long time like this! No wonder most people do not even attempt to challenge corporate America. They used me as an example to all of the other employees to socially condition them that "RESISTANCE IS FUTILE!" "YOU WILL BE ASSIMILATED!"

Little as they know it, each time they run me through the corporate meat grinder, I come out much stronger, more cunning, more obstinate, more rebellious, and ever more determined to institute change for the better. IT reaffirms my resolve, and solidifies the real truth about corporate America for all to see.

It was early December 2000, the height of the holiday season. This is the busiest time here in South Florida. All of the snow birds are down escaping the snow and ice of their home towns.

It was just another busy day at my pest control company. I had at least 5 services, some would take at least 2½ to 3 hours, and others 45 minutes. I had customers scattered throughout Broward County, with some at opposite ends of town. My last two were at least 30 miles apart. I finished my second to the last customer out in west Pembroke Pines by Interstate 75. The next customer was over in East Ft. Lauderdale by the beach. The time was about 4 PM, the beginning of traffic grid-lock. What would normally be a twenty five minute drive can turn into an hour and a half or more nightmare. I finally arrived at my last stop at about 5:30 PM. It was a service call that only took 45 minutes to complete.

  I arrived at the office the next morning to turn in the following day's paperwork, as we take our trucks home at night, and do not report back at the office until the next day. I completed the completion log, and my time sheet for my hours. As we were waiting for that day's work orders, the supervisor called me to his office, along with two of the field supervisor lead-techs. Upon entering, the door was closed behind me, and all three of the supervisors were quiet as mice. I was calmly asked to have a seat, and upon sitting was asked what my two last stops were. I answered, one was a renewal, and the last one was a service call. I was then asked why it took an hour and a half drive to get to the last stop. I immediately said, the stops were at opposite ends of the county, and the traffic was unbearable. Again, I was asked the same question, as though I hadn't answered it the first time. I again repeated the same phrase. Then one of the lead-techs said to me "It doesn't take that long to drive that distance. I turned to her and said, "Only if there is no traffic, then it might take only 25 minutes!" She paused for a second, then commented, "If there is that

REVOLT AGAINST THE PLUTOCRACY

much traffic you can find a different rout around the traffic!" I immediately replied "If I take the back streets, which are also grid-locked, it would take even longer!" She calmly said "You can find a rout quicker than that!"

Here I am, a 14 year veteran being lectured, like some sort of imbecile, by a field supervisor with only 4 years experience in the pest control industry. I replied quickly "If I knew of a quicker rout, I would have taken it, as I have been driving these streets for at least 20 years." The branch manager then interrupted, as he was handing me my time sheet and a pen, and said you will have to take a longer lunch break out of your time. I made the correction, unwillingly, and initialed the corrected area under duress. I was then instructed if it happened again, I would be terminated. Well this meant another trip over to the Dept. of Labor office with all of my copies!

Good God man! Was I supposed to sprout wings and fly over the traffic!!!

It was another November day 2000, I had about 6 stops, all service call-backs. I had one stop in Hollywood for carpenter ants. Upon knocking on the customer's door, I introduced myself as usual. "Hello Mrs. Smith, I am Jay, and I came to get rid of your carpenter ants." The customer says to come in. She points at her rattan living room set says, I have drywood termites eating it up. I get closer, "sure enough drywoods." She then says the _____ (oops! I almost said the company's name) salesman told her they were carpenter ants, but her neighbor came over and told her they were termites. She then angrily says she was deceived by the salesman, and he told her I was coming out as a courtesy call to spray the furniture to get rid of them. This is because she had purchased the subterranean termite protection program. These are two different species of termites, requiring totally different treatments. Our company no longer treats for dry-woods.

I then realized she had been had, (this salesman is no rookie!) and explained embarrassingly, that the salesman made a mistake, and spraying the furniture would not get rid of termites, only carpenter ants. It should be thrown out before they get into the house, or they could be gassed with Vicane. I explained it would be more cost effective to buy new furniture. She then commends me on my honesty, and expertise.

I went about my day not worried, as I didn't cause the loss of a sale, as she planned on keeping the subterranean treatment. I explained to her that it is advisable in South Florida.

I came to work the next morning to turn in the following day's work, only to be told by my lead field supervisor, the sales manager along with the other supervisors wanted to have a word with me in his office.

Once again, the gang had their little yellow note pads ready to write! I then realized, once again another day to never be forgotten. The sales manager cuts right in and says, "Why did you make one of my sales reps look like a total idiot?" I then said, "When did I do this?" He said yesterday at the carpenter ant courtesy service. I immediately respond, "that lady didn't have carpenter ants, she had drywood termites!" "Besides, I took great pains not to degrade your salesman!" He then said, "Haven't we told you about questioning the judgment of our sales staff." "You are supposed to do what's on the service order!" I then said, once again, "I didn't disrespect him, in fact I gave him a good word just maybe he made a mistake as we are all human." "Besides spraying the furniture would not kill them, you should know that, you have many years in this industry!" Then they all took a whack at me, writing on their little note pads, basically saying something along the lines of "you screwed up again, and could have possibly cost the company another sale." Again the sales manager had another discipline form filled out and ready for me to sign under duress. I was accused of insubordination, not following company policy, and a whole host of other violations! IRONICALLY, THERE IS NO COMPANY POLICY ON HOW TO DEAL WITH COVERING UP FRAUD!, other than playing along with the game. And I said just basically that, "What company policy?" I was then told, "The part on disrespecting fellow team-members!" "How would you like it if one of my salesmen went out and told a customer that you didn't know what you were doing when you treated their house????" I then said there is a big difference, as I didn't say he didn't know what he was doing, but he made a mistake!" I was then reassured that there was intentional disrespect, and to sign the disciplinary form, and if I have one more write up, I will definitely be terminated.

Well my fellow readers, welcome to the life of an honest blue-collar worker with good morals. This is exactly what corporate America is all about, right from the horse's mouth!! No wonder the average American worker is so frazzled and ready to go postal with a typical day at the office! And society wants us to be more family orientated!!!!

In Time magazine, May 6, 1996, pg. 63, by Jill Smolowe. "The Stalled Revolution" "Since the '70s, women have poured into the workplace, compelled by economic necessity and personal ambition, to the point where duel-wage-earner families are now the norm. Yet somehow neither work nor family has changed enough to make this a tenable situation. Day care is still catch as catch can. Employers still demand 110%, while spouses and children still need clean socks and a ride to the dentist. Add stagnating wages and layoff anxiety, and for millions of Americans, each week becomes a stressful triage between work and home that leaves them feeling guilty, exhausted and angry."

The Public Policy Institute at Radcliff College did a study called the New Economic Equation. According to the discussions among at least 36 different business and labor leaders, economists as well as family experts agree on one thing. "People have accommodated all they can accommodate. They have made the trade-offs to get a better quality of life, and it is still insufficient,"

They forgot to mention that people have sacrificed all of this for what? So the boss can have more profits, and give himself a big fat raise??? Is this what capitalism is all about??? Is this civilized, and American??? If I have my way, capitalism is finished if it doesn't take a more ethical responsibility geared for a respectful, civilized America! And that is a promise, so-help-me God!!!!

REVOLT AGAINST THE PLUTOCRACY

"Multigenerational housing is closing some gaps", the New Homes section, Sunday, January 30, 2000, pg. H13, in The Herald, by Patricia Dane Rogers. "The traditional nuclear household-Father, Mother, Dick, Jane, Puff and spot-is now the fastest-declining family type in America," quoted David Pearce Snyder, an investigative reporter for Futurist magazine.

And that's just the beginning. "In 10 years, that number could easily be 15 percent." "People are banding together for societal and economic reasons. Everybody's looking for an anchor of stability," remarked Garald Celente, the New York State Research Institute's director. "This is the future, and it's multigenerational."

Think about this my readers!! Now think about some of the poor third world nations. What comes to mind when you picture the family setting other than those living in grass huts or cardboard boxes? You picture two, three, four or more families living in the same run-down house. There is usually a car, if they are lucky. Guess what? All of the adults and teen-agers work long hours, with no benefits, seven days a week, for some multi-national corporation, if they do not have a town farm with agriculture positions. For what? Just to make a few fat cats filthy rich! Is there a similar future for America, as fewer average working Americans' wages will keep pace with the cost of home ownership inflation? Then add the true fact that all other expenses of life are also increasing, and most working wages are not just stagnant, but steadily declining!!! ***Wake up America! This is the stuff third world families must endure.***

Work-place injuries are one of the most taboo subjects for the corporate elites. "Treating On-the-Job Injuries as True Crimes" by Ann Davis, Wednesday, February 26, 1977, pgs. B1, B5, The Wall Street Journal. Jorge Torres suffocated to death when a 60-ton mountain of salt, in a storage bin, swallowed him like quicksand. The company failed to provide platforms for the workers to stand on. Two supervisors from Chicago's Morton International will stand trial for his death.

The owner of a scrap-metals plant was charged with manslaughter when one worker was sucked into a giant metal shredder called the "cyclone", and another was crushed to death by a loading truck. The owner was warned multiple times to erect proper guards around the shredder, and to repair the brakes on the truck, but in his attempt to save money refused to.

Owners of two affiliated metal companies were also charged for exposing workers to lead vapors, and in another separate case, exposing workers to solvent fumes. The companies refused to repair the giant exhaust vacuum, that was broken, that sucked the fumes away from the workers stirring molten metal in huge kettles.

"The case is among a growing number involving businesses and bosses charged with what most people think of as street crimes. Calling their conduct everything from assault and battery to reckless homicide, prosecutors in at least 14 states in recent years have sought hard time for employers who ignore warnings to improve safety on the job or, in the case of corporations, steep fines. States have jailed close to a dozen employers in the 1990s-handing one plant owner a sentence of nearly 20 years."

State prosecutors claim to be stepping in on behalf of the Occupational Safety and Health Administration, because it no longer enforces workplace safety. OSHA was downsized by a third during the Republican administrations of Ronald Reagan, and George Bush senior in the pro-corporate policies designed to reduce corporate expenses at the cost of the safety of working America. It has literally been rendered dysfunctional, and is little more than a paper tiger, a wall-flower there as a symbolic deception to convince the masses that the government really cares about the safety of our workplaces. Then add the pressure of lobbyists to be pro-corporate, so as not to interfere with corporate donations, you are actually left to fend for yourselves at the mercy of the wolves. All to enable an elite few ever increasing pay raises!!!

"Protect yourself from consumer fraud" The Herald, Sunday, May 16, 1999, pg. 2BR, by Amy Merrick. "Given the pervasiveness of financial fraud, consumers may think they're being assaulted from all directions. They are."

Being attacked from household international mega-corporations to the swindling self employed scam artist, consumers may think there is nothing they can do. However there is a lot they can do to protect themselves. Before making all financial obligations, thoroughly investigate companies and get all agreement in writing.

Check it out: Before signing away money, call the State comptrollers office to research a company's fraud history. Phone number available through information.

Never give personal information over the phone to a solicitor.

Don't be swayed by a polished sales pitch. Experienced swindlers look respectable and are skilled in deception.

Deposit outgoing mail in a post office box so petty thieves can not access financial information, and shred junk mail that might have personal information.

Refuse to deal with investment brokers that are not licensed and registered with the state.

Do not deal with those firms that charge fees in advance for loans, guarantee high returns or no-risk investments, and pressure you to invest your whole life's savings. ***Turn and walk away!!!***

The organized labor union is one of working America's strongest pillars of labor justice and preservers of the American Dream. They literally turn the corporate greed machine against the very corporations that unleash their monster on society. Labor unions are democratic, and condoned by our constitution.

Article I-Legislative Department, Section 8-Powers of Congress,
Cl. 3-Regulate Commerce.

National Labor Relations Act.-The case in which the court reduced the distinction between "direct" and "indirect" effects to the vanishing point and thereby placed Congress in the position to regulate productive industry and labor relations in these industries was NLRB vs. Jones & Laughlin Steel Corp. Here the statute involved was the National labor Relations Act of 1935, which declared the right of workers to organize, forbade unlawful employer interference with this right, established procedures by which workers could choose exclusive bargaining representatives with which employers were required to bargain, and create a board to oversee all these processes.

However, our constitutional right has been under attack for at least 20 years by Republicans, and corporate America. Most unions are a shell of what they used to be. Many states in the union, such as Florida are called "right to work states", which offer a very hostile pro-corporate anti-worker environment. These states must be returned to pro-labor status at all costs. One direct way to get attention on this subject is to send a letter to your state senator and your governor. A copy already to send, is at the back of this book. All you have to do is make a copy of it, enlarged on a copier, put your name, address, sign it, and mail it to your state senator at;

Name of your senator
The United States Senate
Washington D.C 20510-0904

The next is to join the union wherever you can, and disregard the corporate propaganda that unions are not democratic, and offer workers no freedoms what-so-ever. They will try their best to make you think unions are not in the best interests of the working American. They will even attempt to create corporate sponsored employee organizations as a substitute for labor unions. They also use corporate psychology to socially condition America's workers that the corporation is one big happy family, and the bosses are your big brothers looking out for you needs. They give employees the feeling of empowerment with names like public relations expert for a receptionist, logistics engineer for a truck driver, rout manager for a pest control technician, or a whole host of other flatterable headings. They also glorify employees that suggest ways to be more efficient, ironically the employees just may be signing their own death warrant, as the efficiency efforts may result in further staff lay-offs. At the same time they brain-wash the employees that the efficiency tips will result in higher wages, and better benefits. The only ones here getting the higher wages are the management, and the CEO!!!

Do not give into social conditioning!!!!!

"Big Labor Flexes Its Muscles", Fortune, June 10, 1996, pgs. 24, 26, by Justin Fox. One would think that in a booming economy, with record corporate profits and record CEO income increases, workers incomes would be exploding, and worker job security would be guaranteed. But something is interfering with the natural laws of the market economy. One would then think union come-back is guaranteed, due to pure rage on behalf of workers that have been jilted, with unfulfilled promises on the bosses part of healthy wage, and benefit increases. Especially when they were promised these things when profits soar, as Reagan and republicans promised of "trickle down" benefits, that never materialized. But the American economy is further becoming less hospitable legally, and politically for labor. "We've been virtually stripped of our right to organize and represent the people," cries George Becker, chief of the United Steelworkers of America. Join! Join! Join the union! The last vestiges of American prosperity, and democracy.

With this realization it is now up to us, as citizens to form unions of our own as Americans to Preserve the American Dream and Democracy. This would be literally impossible for corporate America or the political plutocrats to stifle out our cries even under direct threat from the power elites.

Here is an example of American citizens, that are immune to ideological social conditioning, because they came from previously oppressed fascist societies. They have can do winning attitudes with out the aid of an organized labor union. "Truckers strike takes heavy toll", the Herald Sunday, February 20, 2000, pg. 2E. Truckers from all walks of life, Cuba, the Caribbean, South America, post Soviet block nations, and patriotic Americans, "although not represented by a union, the solidarity effectively shut down the seaport." They united in one mass front against rising fuel prices, skyrocketing insurance premiums, and sub-standard pay.

Within a couple of weeks the trucking firms were raising the pay to all of the drivers. This proved the proverbial "gun to the head diplomacy" is the most effective way of dealing with corporate America. This also proves that some people from once oppressed societies are not so defeatist like most Americans. They are not so p _ _ _ y whipped!

Jay T. Baldwin

Good paying American jobs, that once guaranteed the American Dream, being shipped overseas is another front to battle corporate America on. I take my car now to mom & pop garages as a revolt against the large conglomerates. I buy off-name brands as often as possible. I purchase generic prescriptions. I drive long distances to get the cheapest gasoline. I go out of my way to make life hard on greedy corporations, with an eye for an eye, tooth for a tooth attitude. Yet, I reward those who pay me more with superior loyalty, and production. I religiously deal with corporations, as a consumer, that treat me with respect. I shop at mom & pop stores, even if it's not always cheaper. These family owned small shops are just one step up the ladder from company employees. They are at the mercy of the mega-corporations almost as much as we are. They must deal with cheaper merchandise, sold at the mega-firms, because they can't purchase in such large quantities. If any firm treats me with indifference, I just walk out. You already know what I do to employers that attempt to give me a screw deal. The revolt has to become a way of life not just a once in awhile crusade. This is not always the cheaper, or easier rout. Each American must take responsibility to change, and force the laws of the free-market down the throats of the plutocrats, altering it to once again work for our benefit. We must shift the tides once and for all in the working man's favor. We have seen record growing anti-capitalist sentiments world wide in 2001. In Canada, the Philippines, Australia, England, Russia, and even our arrogant, cigar smoking, Communist pig's Havana, Cuba. What were the warnings I gave in my first book?

All of the Castro's of the world are laughing and rubbing their hands together! We are sinking our own ship. Capitalism has shot it's self in the foot. It's now imperative we take action now before it's too late. This is an emergency tantamount to an asteroid on a collision with earth. ***Wake up people!!!*** We must not allow the failure of true ethical capitalism in America. It worked once, but it will work again. Now on with the revolution!!

"Keeping commercialism out of maternity wards, Nader urges hospitals" http://www.nadir.org/releasees/82799.html Nader's example was George Washington University Hospital where a new mother received two bags chuck full of corporate baby products, coupons for clothing, toys, movies, chocolate bars to three credit card offers, life insurance, and seven requests for more personal information. in response to Nader's letter, the hospital's CEO Phillip S. Schaengold agreed to stop passing out the commercialized products. "After our review of the bag's contents we found our complaints to be valid," "Over the next month, we will be working to create a GW Hospital diaper bag of our own which will include items such as: baby bibs and generic safety instruction cards. The purpose of this new bag is twofold. It removes the need for bags you found offensive and provides gifts for new moms who deliver their babies at our hospital."

We are even fighting them at the beaches of Normandy. "State prepared to pull Lauderdale condo's beach barrier", by Brittany Wallman, Sun-Sentinel, Wednesday, December 1, 1999, pg. 3B. The large twin towers of L'Hermitage attempted to rope off the entire beach front to reserve it for their wealthy residents.

Mickey Havens a Ft. Lauderdale entertainer sat next to the signs and ropes running all the way down into the surf. ""Everybody's been walking over and saying, 'I can't believe this,'" Havens remarked. "You can't do it. There really is no such thing as a totally private beach."

Barry Manson-Hing, engineer for the Florida Department of Environmental Protection quoted; "they have no right to do that. they can't do that." "Anything to hinder public access is not allowed, even on the private part." They were forced to remove the barriers. This is just another victory against a rich, greedy socialite class, attempting to corner their unfair share of America.

"Justice uses spy tactics to unlock global price fixing" "Whistleblowers, bugged lamps, FBI raids reveal plots that cost consumers" USA Today, Monday, July 10, 2000, sect. B, pg. 1, by Jayne O'Donnell. Like something from America's Most Wanted, 20 FBI agents storm a building. But it isn't a crack house. "But they were raiding U.S. offices of Japanese industrial giant Toray Industries near Seattle, part of an orchestrated group of raids at manufacturers around the country." Once a tedious time consuming process of subpoenaed documents, now is performed in lightning fast stings.

"And many of those tactics have been used in an investigation of the carbon fiber industry, including the March 1999 raid on Toray."

Now with another Republican administration, I wonder if these tactics are still in use today? Corporate

America, and the conservatives insist on allowing corporations to police themselves. But every time they are given this privilege, they abuse it. Labor, consumers, safety, and the environment end up paying the price. The Nader Page "In the Public Interest", February 22, 2000. A book "The Poor Pay More", by David Caplovitz revealed some startling evidence of relentless consumer abuses against citizens least able to protect themselves legally. The National Consumer Law Center (NCLC) in 2000, published a report revealing corporate fraud, crime, and abuses are thriving at the expense of the poor.

1) Auto fraud—"an astonishing percentage of car sales involve fraud, deception, or unfair conduct. Consumers are sold both new and used cars that are "lemons" or are defrauded by car dealers who do not give a full disclosure of the car's wreck or salvage history, its prior use as a rental vehicle, history of mechanical problems, or other defects."

2) Auto title pawn—"These transactions are a recent phenomena in which the car-owner pawns title to the car in exchange for a sum of cash. The effective interest rate of an auto title pawn can be astronomical (sometimes over 900% APR)."

3) Home equity fraud—"Home improvements scams and deceptive lending practices are among the most frequent problems experienced by low-income homeowners." "Often in desperate need of home repairs (e.g. roof replacements, structural reinforcements), unsophisticated homeowners fall prey to unscrupulous home improvement contractors who promise easy access to credit. Many of these loans

have inflated interest rates, outrageous closing costs and unaffordable repayment terms."

4) Payday lending—"This exploitive form of short-term lending can devastate the finances of cash-strapped consumers." "Payday lenders charge exorbitant fees for the loans, and the effective interest rates can top 1,000%."

5) Rent-To-Own (RTO)—"RTO businesses are essentially appliance and furniture retailers which arrange exorbitant lease agreements for those customers who cannot buy goods with cash. Consumers who buy from rent-to-own businesses often pay two to three times the cash price for their purchases."

6) Arbitration of Consumer claims—"Creditors and merchants are increasingly inserting clauses into fine print of their contracts that prohibit consumers from filing lawsuits and forces all disputes to mandatory arbitration hearings. Arbitration clauses are carefully drafted to stack the deck against the consumer: they allow companies to select the arbitrators, arrange for the arbitration in places convenient for the companies but not the consumers, forbid class actions, limit discovery, and prohibit recoveries such as punitive damages and attorneys fees."

This center has also elected to assist elderly Americans who loose billions of dollars per year to home improvement fraud, telemarketing scams, fraudulent medical aids, and insurance scams.

These and many other abominations of capitalism came about due to the repealing of all state usery laws. What was illegal, warranting severe punishments, is now perfectly legal. Corporate America calls this reform!!! More like reform to a fascist, corporate dictatorship.

"Toughen Up the Rules of the Sky", by Ralph Nader. "The federal government is expert at recovering wreckage, but not so good at preventing wrecks." The F.A.A has consistently stalled on taking action to prevent accidents. In 1997, after the T.W.A. Flight 500 off Long Island, the F.A.A discovered that 30% of the airliners center fuel tanks got dangerously hot from external sources such as outflows from A.C.s. Instead of taking drastic action, it only recommended better tank maintenance inspections and to look at possible new tank designs. After the Value jet accident in Florida, and an airliner off Newfoundland in 1998, the F.A. A neglected to force US airlines to install fire suppressant systems in inaccessible areas of the plane. It has also neglected to force the airline companies to install updated black boxes with their own internal batteries, and can record cockpit voices much longer, as required in European aircraft.

Airplanes at Chicago's O'Hare International Airport had increasing incidents of more than one plane using the same runway, inadvertently causing near misses. In some instances American airports are now allowing airplanes to start their take-off roles before the others taxing have cleared the runway.

Cargo and package shipments are still being allowed on passenger jets without being screened for explosives, hazardous materials, and radioactive elements. Two presidential administrations have insisted the F.A. A put a stop the this practice.

Jay T. Baldwin

The F.A.A. is not living up to it's own regulations when it comes to airplane evaluations. Instead of evaluations based on actual inspections and tests on real airplanes, it is settling for analysis based on past test results, mathematical hypothesis, and computer simulations. Emergency evacuation tests on the Boeing 777-300, a 550 passenger airplane, were foregone, and the test results of the smaller Boeing 777-200, a 419 passenger plane were used in it's place.

Over 300 waivers and exemptions from federal safety mandates are graciously extended to mega-airline industries. The F.A.A safety regulations require a 20 inch spacing between seats at emergency exits. The agency has allowed airlines to shorten it to 14 inches, and is even considering a 10 inch spacing. Guess why? Money! Airlines can pack more passengers in airliners that allow smaller spacing at emergency exits. This then boosts profitability, at the expense of our lives. Like I mentioned in my first book, the Federal government gets massive corporate contributions from the powerful airline lobbyists. Ironically, some of the best contributions are always timed with government safety reviews. This to prevent too many regulations from actually being enforced. The hell with human lives, just so they can allow airlines to maximize profits, so they can maximize their contributions. Nader quotes, "Neglecting air safety is like stretching a rubber band. At a certain point, the rubber band snaps." **HIP! HIP! HOORAY!! Another two point for corporate greed!!!**

"In a democracy, the highest office is the office of citizen." Quoted Supreme Court Justice Felix Frankfurter. It seems when crusaders of democracy like Nader gum-up the greed works of corporate America, they get real nervous. Over a twenty year period, Nader's consumer and employee rights advocacy groups have been attempting to keep the law caught up with the relentless assault launched by corporate America.

At a senate hearing on General Motors' harassment of Nader, Nader quoted to the Senate, "The requirement of a just social order is that responsibility shall lie where the power of decision rests. But the law has never caught up with the development of the large corporate unit. Deliberate acts emanate from the sprawling and indeterminable shelter of the corporate organization. Too often responsibility for an act is not imputable to those whose decision enables it to be set in motion." Nader's groups stumbled across problems in the trucking industry, resulting in unsafe American roads. "Drivers were being forced to drive long hours without sleep or bathroom breaks, and to drive equipment they believed to be unsafe. Some 40 percent of truckers said in response to questionnaires printed in trucking magazines that their trucks were unsafe." Hey!, sounds like several companies I have worked for!

Ralph Nader's "Nurturing the "Consumer-Side" Economy" reinforces my conviction of turning the laws of the market economy against the plutocrats. Adam Smith in 1776, quoted in his Wealth of Nations address, "Consumption is the sole end and purpose of all production; and the interest of the producer ought to be attended to, only so far as it may be necessary for promoting that of the consumer.." Obviously something today's corporate leaders have forgotten, and have reversed to read something like this; "Profiteering is the sole end and purpose of all production; and the interest of the entrepreneur ought to be attended to, only so far as it may be necessary for promoting that of the entrepreneur."

President John F. Kennedy said in his famous "Consumer Bill of Rights," message to Congress urging it to strengthen consumer protection programs. "Consumers, by definition, include us all," said Kennedy, "They are the largest economic group in the economy, affecting and affected by almost every public and private economic decision. Two-thirds of all spending in the economy is by consumers. But they are the only important group in the economy who are not effectively organized, whose views are often not heard…"

Nader's organizations from the 70's to today have found indisputable proof from a myriad of independent sources of the abomination of the supply side of America's economy (the corporate owned side). This includes price-fixing, price-fixed products, deceptive packaging, corporate oppression of private, and small business innovation (inventor suppression) leading to stagnation of research and development, false advertisement, product built in obsolescence, and planned cooperation between corporate America and federal regulators as they work hand in hand to manipulate the free-market economy resulting in the fleecing of American society for profit and gain.

In Nader's book "The Great American Gyp," he remarks, "What most troubles the corporations is the consumer movement's relentless documentation that consumers are being manipulated, defrauded, and injured not just by marginal businesses or fly-by-night hucksters, but by the U.S. blue-chip business firms whose practices are unchecked by the older regulatory agencies." Nader adds these are not isolated, rare occurrences, "Nader asserted, by systemic: "It is becoming apparent that reform of consumer abuses and reform of corporate power itself are different sides of the same coin and that new approaches to the enforcement of the rights of consumers are necessary."

The Equal Employment Opportunity Commission (E.E.O.C.) charged a large American railroad corporation for genetically testing it's workers for carple-tunnel syndrome, to avoid workers compensation cases, and medical treatments. The genetic tests were kept secret so employees didn't know they were being genetically examined. This is an outright violation of workers' rights and privacy, and the American Disabilities Act of the Constitution! If employees refused the company's doctor exams, they would be fired immediately. The tests were done when a routine blood test was administered. These tests can, and often are used to black-ball workers, genetically prone to sickness or injuries, for the rest of their lives. Basically, they would find it difficult, if not impossible to ever find work again. These violations have become so wide-spread, the E.E.O.C. is working for a court order to forbid corporations from performing genetic tests, and from disciplining workers who refuse to take these tests. (Source: 60 Minutes, April 10, 2001.)

However, to spite these outrageous, un-democratic, and un-American violations, it seems that few politicians and public figures, who have the power for reform, seem brave enough to take corporate

America head-on! This would entail challenging the entire capitalist system, in it's trenched in greediest form, so all segments of society can benefit.

However, there is still more we could do hand in hand with the consumer movement, or on our very own as I mentioned earlier in this chapter. The problem with America is those with most of the money, depending on the size of their corporate status, can do what they want with society, consumers, employees, and politics. Smaller mom and pop firms find it hard, or impossible to reap any corporate welfare funds, or manipulate politics to benefit them.

By holding the entire free-enterprise capitalist system, to it's own overly flaunted claims, and laws of the free-market, the consumer movement has concentrated on three key economic goals.

1) "To foster genuine competition by making structural reforms of the marketplace and generating more consumer information." You and I can do our part by shopping at smaller less known family owned firms, and buying off name brands.

2) "To eliminate corporate welfare, both by cutting wasteful government subsidies to business and by reclaiming taxpayer-owned assets from private control." You and I can write protest letters to our governors on corporate welfare, and refuse to use goods and services from firms that have been built on corporate welfare. Nader quotes; "Ours is a system of corporate socialism, where companies capitalize their profits and socialize their losses....In effect, they tax you for their accidents, bunglings, boondoggles and mismanagements just like a government. We should be able to dis-elect them."

3) "To build alternative buying institutions that give consumers greater control over what they buy. You and I can help foster positive civil disobedience, such as I mentioned earlier in the book, to embarrass firms that try to give us a screw-deal.

Society seems to be wising up to the elites, who seem satisfied to make as much money as they can at our expense. One CEO named Kevin Clark believed in actually sharing the fruits of the company's tithings with the employees who were instrumental in creating these profits. He added; "When profits runneth over, employees drink deep." "what Are You Worth?", by Peter Carbonara and Abby Shultz, April 2000, Fortune magazine, pgs. 45-54. Ambrose Bierce Quoted, "self-esteem" should be defined as "an erroneous appraisement." Alan Johnson, a compensation expert said a lot of business owners who set their own salaries, "can't separate themselves from their own general wonderfulness."

Business owners are quickly finding out that employees, clients, customers, creditors, and backers do not think highly of those who seem to exhibit greedy tendencies. "Don't plan on keeping any secrets. As highly paid CEOs like Disney's Michael Eisner have discovered, even citizens bent on making their own millions don't take kindly to guys who seem too eager to rake it in. Even if you don't report your salary to the press, the shareholders, or the Securities and Exchange Commission, don't think affairs of the wallet will stay under wraps. If you take a huge salary, pad the payroll with relatives, or pamper yourself with bogus expenses, you can be sure that before long your staff will learn of it and hate you accordingly."

There are a few corporate owners still willing to share the profits to build a stronger America. "In steps with families" "Companies are offering on-site schools to attract new employees, build loyalty and increase productivity.", by Lona O"Connor, the Sun Sentinel, September 5, 2000, pgs. 1B, 5B. "Imagine your employer offered full-time day-care for your child as young as 6 weeks old. Now imagine that the company adds an on-site elementary school with after-school care and summer camp." One employee had this to say, "I feel blessed," said Heather Lyn, a financial analyst at Ryder Systems in Miami. "My daughter is in a special place."

JFK Medical Center plans to open a charter school in 2001. The executives at both companies say the multimillion-dollar start up cost will more than pay for itself.

A stainless steel products co., Yard Metals is also practicing this employee friendly altruism. In house child care, above average progressive profit sharing programs, and even an afternoon nap period. This has resulted in below average employee turnover, above average worker loyalty, and record breaking employee productivity resulting in 5 times the profit levels from previous years.

To spit the few exceptions, who do not just look out for themselves, and their own interests, the general flow in free-market America is still the me, myself, and I attitude. This has caused record numbers of Americans to seek the American Dream in other lands. These average Americans are forming cozy communities outside the US.

"Disillusioned chase 'America dream' abroad", by Paisly Doods, the Herald, September 10, 2000, pg. 21H. John Ham sits on his horse looking out over his tropical wonderland of bean fields, sweet smelling fruit trees, and fantastic Inca ruins in Chirusco, Ecuador. This is reversing the flow of immigrants rushing to the Untied States in search of a better living. Laird Schaub at Fellowship for Intentional Community in Rutledge, Mo. said, "today, these communities are what people want out of life, and there's a growing number of people who are finding that easier and more affordable to get it overseas."

"Like others, Ham and Michilena aimed for the American dream, the notion that equality gives everyone the same opportunity to succeed. It was the centerpiece of historian James Truslow Adams' 1931 book, The Epic of America."

"Ham and others say their reasons for quitting the United States are simple: expensive housing, scarcity of prime farm land and, especially, the emphasis on material things." In the United States it now takes a lot of money to realize equality, justice, and the American Dream. If one doesn't have money, it is very unlikely, to spite hard work and loyalty at the workplace, that he will ever have money, or ever realize the American dream the way it used to be.

Ham and his family says the American dream needs to be revamped. "America is a lot different now." You give up a lot to live in the United States, he says, and, "I knew I couldn't do that."

Like mentioned earlier, we have been seeing a surge of anti-capitalist movements, and protests at major cities throughout the world. These protesters consist of a variety of people protesting a variety of ills they associate with globalization. Some are just ignorant anarchists looking for a reason to dispense chaos, pillage, and loot. Some are there for environmental reasons from furs to nuclear power. But the bulk of the protests have been about unfair disdtribution of world wealth into the pockets of a few wealthy mega-national corporate elites. This results, not only in exporting good paying jobs from America overseas, but, to the relentless exploitation of smaller third world nations whose governments cannot compete with the financial brawn of a mega-national corporation. Then the corporations can openly fleece the entire nation for cheap labor, and natural resources giving little in return. "The long-term danger is that if the world's poor see no benefits from free trade and IMF austerity programs, political support for reform could erode. The current system is "unsustainable," says United Nations Assistant Secretary General John G. Ruggie, who, as a political economist at Columbia University, examined how previous golden ages of global capitalism, such as the one at the turn of the 19th century, unraveled." "From 1990 to 1996, only 33 countries managed to sustain 3% annual growth, and 59 countries saw their economies contract." The United States now generates ¼ of the worlds wealth. But the big question is where is this ¼ of the worlds wealth going, if it isn't belonging to the nations of the world?? If corporations are supposedly so profitable in these cheap labor, cheap resource, and cheap overhead expense countries, then where is all of that money going, if it is not going to assist the third world country gracious enough to allow these mega-nationals to settle in their backyards????

Then ironically, the cheaply made products produced there are sent back to the US along with all of the profits, to be sold to Americans who lost their good paying jobs creating those very items. Except the profits part. These exorbitant profits now go into some corporate bank account, on US soil, and do not always raise the living standards of the host third world nation!! All so a handful of wealthy fat-cats could explode their profits to historic levels along with their pay, perks and prestige. (Source of some information Business Week Special Report, November 6, 2000, pgs. 73, 74, 75, 76, 77.)

Illustration 26

"Sharpening claws for a larger prey" Multinational mega corporations, once small cubs in the land of the American Dream, moved abroad to exploit cheap labor and natural resources in smaller defenseless third world nations. Once paying working Americans an excellent salary, now they can pay ignorant third world workers substandard pay, even by their poor standards. This after an inferred promise, that upon being allowed to set up shop in their countries, the quality of life would improve considerably for their workers. however, these hollow-promises turned out to be lies in most cases. After 20 years of working for these multi-nationals the citizens of these nations are still waiting for the Americans to make true on their promises, while the American executives reap unheard of profits. In fact in some situations the citizens of these nations are worse of than they were under their old agrarian system before the invasion of the mega-nationals. Now they have stripped all of the bark off, the chickens are coming home to roost and take the citizens of America on. Now their mission is clear, to come back home to challenge organized labor, workers and consumers rights and lower all American's wage expectations. Bring the third world back to our own backyard. Like a leach, when it's host runs out of blood, it seeks out newer jucier hosts. Under the cloak of globalization the world will be ripe for economic conquest!

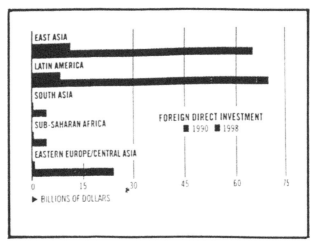

Illustration 27

Jay T. Baldwin

"Foreign investment skyrockets" The wealthy American firms invest billions in third world nations. Did they do it for a charitable cause to increase the living standards in these nations, or did they lead us and the world to think so? If they didn't have the heart to pay their own fellow American citizens a decent wage when they were here, what makes you think they are going to go to poor third world countries to boost their economy out of the goodness of their hearts? They wouldn't be there if there wasn't some good chance they could exploit these ignorant people for profits of biblical proportions. PURE HUMAN EXPLOITATION!!!

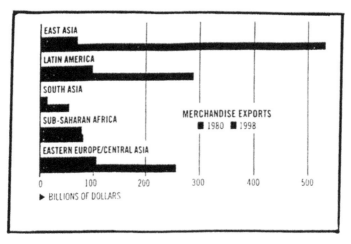

Illustration 28

"Third world exports surge, breaking records" The hard work of the poor, ignorant peoples of the third world pays off in the form of record export of merchandise they toiled with substandard pay to produce. Then one would be falsely led to believe the pay of those people, and the economies of their nations should be breaking records as well. After all, they promised higher wages and boosted economies to these poor people if they were profitable. If a country is exporting at record levels, according to logic, it's economy should be booming, and it's people should be earning more as well. The same promises were made to home grown Americans here in the USA, but never materialized. Boy were they profitable!!! But think again! Who was profitable as it is clearly not the third world countries, or its hard working people? If the trickle-down theory of the conservatives didn't work here in the good ole USA, why would it ever work in some banana republic. It seems only the elite fat cats at the top, back here in America, are benefiting and living the life of Riley at the expense of masses at home and abroad!

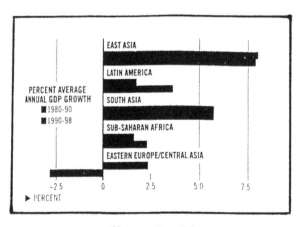

Illustration 29

Jay T. Baldwin

"Where is the money that was promised???! Gross Domestic Product (GDP) of the globalized third world has literally stagnated, but in the case of Eastern Europe and Central Asia it has regressed. Who is sucking all of value out of these nations like a blood thirsty vampire? Yet we hear of how beneficial globalization has been to them according to corporate strategists. Mark Weisbrot co-director of the Center for Economic and Policy Research in Washington, DC. says "But what if it weren't true? Is it possible that globalization has been a loosing proposition for most of the countries and people of the world?" "The real world results look very bad. For the vast majority of countries, the last two decades have shown considerably-and often drastically-slower growth than was seen in the previous 20 years (1960-1980). The average country in Latin America increased its income per person by about 7 percent since 1980, as compared to 75 percent in the previous two decades" "The last 20 years of globalization have also shown substantially diminished progress in health outcomes such as infant and child mortality, and life expectancy." Yet those who oppose globalization will be accused of turning their backs on the poor nations. "American labor and citizens' groups should ignore these self-righteous, self-serving accusations and carry on against the FTAA-as well as the IMF, World Bank and World Trade Organization-with a clear conscience. They are not only protecting American jobs, wages and forests-they are also saving the rest of the world."

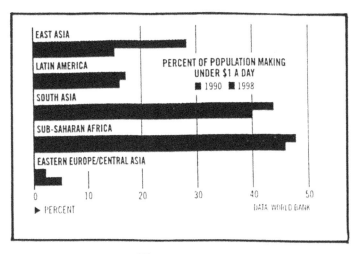

Illustration 30

"Where is all of the money going?" For people making less than a dollar a day, incomes have improved in-significantly. In Eastern Europe and Central Asia, incomes have actually declined with the help of the mega-nationals.

On the final few days of my writing, I was out and about servicing my pest control customers. I came to a large intersection and had to stop for a light. I noticed some of those newspaper vendors handing out what looked like small papers. Then I noticed they were wearing bright pink shirts that said "The Homeless Voice". I pulled out a dollar of the five left in my wallet for the week, and got the "Homeless Voice" The front page had an article about a homeless teacher in New York City. A documentary was done on Russian TV in it's attempt to embarrass the United States in a propaganda style to the Russian people. This stirred up a media frenzy. Almost immediately the homeless teacher was invited to Network Television. There he commented that before he was interviewed by the Russians, nobody would give him the light of day. Most Americans assume that all homeless people are drug users, drunks, criminals, and lazy bums. They deserve to be out in the street. However, when a full-time working American can not earn enough even in a profession such as teaching, this points to a larger social problem in American society. Most Americans would be homeless if they abruptly lost their jobs, if it wasn't for friends and family. "I discovered that you do not have to drink, use drugs, or be mentally ill to be homeless." Quotes Demitry Marin, Esq. a graduate from the New York Law School who found himself homeless in Ft. Lauderdale. "Homelessness exists in the US for the simple reason that it serves an important social function for the powers that be." This is why in America, no matter how well the economy does, there will always be those who lack the necessities of life. The masses will be reminded as to what will happen to those who do not conform to the exploitive capitalist structure now flourishing. "Fitting in may often involve slaving away, taking abuse, disrespect, bending over, and, increasingly in today's corporate culture, kissing the bosses butt." Mr. Marin also adds how the employer must wave the stick of homelessness and poverty, as a course of social conditioning, to maintain defeatist, submissive, docile employees. Why is this true? "The answer is that what is called "US market economy" is a system of dominance and exploitation which makes sure that the cards are always stacked in the bosses' favor." In America there is a combination of laws, legal and illegal, that favor corporate America leaving some long term unemployable. With no more welfare safety nets and the rising cost of home ownership homelessness is a growing, and lasting problem here to stay. On May 23, 2001, I was notified by another mortgage lender, this being at least ten different firms, that even with two full-time salaries, we will not quality for enough to even consider a home purchase. We would have to have an un-godly amount for a down payment in access of $50,000. According to our current income, according to national statistics, since my wife started teaching in late 2000, we should have no problem owning a property. In the past couples with our careers could qualify for a very nice home, hands down. I sarcastically asked the broker if there will be a deluge of houseless, one step above homeless, Americans, not ever able to purchase a single family home. His very words were, "Yes, unless the President steps in and changes our current economic system!"

The revolution in Seattle by activists against the global plutocrats, was like none seen since the seventies. "Not until they pay attention to suffering of their fellow citizens and fight for their fellow poor Americans with equal vigor things would change" Source The "Homeless Voice" written by: Dmitry Marin Esq.

I see a lot of parallels in the life of the homeless as that of the average working Americans. I and millions of Americans are living proof!

Here are still more direct ways, you and I can literally make it less lucrative for corporate America to exploit American labor, in their attempt to bring third world pay standards to the American masses, in our own front yards.

1) Truck drivers who have been forced to operate broken and unsafe equipment, or expected to complete impossible delivery quotas keep the phone number of the local Department Of Transportation officer with you at all times. They drive cruisers like the highway patrol, and the cars are usually light blue with the D.O.T. logos on the side. They can be found at weigh stations on state highways, or at truck stops. Do not hesitate to give him a call if your boss makes you operate in an unsafe manner putting the safety of the public, as well as your own in jeopardy. If you explain the situation to him, he will work with you, keeping the fact you sought him first, so as to protect your job, and he is not going to give you the ticket, as he would if he finds you first. You just might have saved lives, and prevented a lawsuit against the company, if you gave a rat's a _ _ . After all your boss sure didn't seem to care about your well-being. Also do not race around like a three alarm fire truck, and wind yourself up emotionally all to keep up with your boss's expectations. You will increase chances for accidents, and you will not benefit financially. Pace yourself. Remember the American worker has accommodated all he/she can accommodate. America's RPMs are all wound-out and red-lined. The boss is the only one benefiting here!!!

REVOLT AGAINST THE PLUTOCRACY

Illustration 31

"Red-lined with nitro" US labor is maxed out, and the stress is intolerable. When is enough!?, enough!? Corporate America is expecting more production and performance each year. Like Olympic athletes, each year must be a record breaker. Like a hamster on a wheel, the US workers are just spinning their wheels faster and faster. Reward for loyalty and performance is now reserved for the upper management and not the working masses, who are ultimately responsible for moving the gears of corporate America. This seems to be contradictory to the true goals of capitalism in raising the living standard of all people. It seems modern capitalism will eventually gobble itself up due to it's own greed. Is this the ultimate paradoxical failure of free-market capitalism??

2) Service rout people forced to cheat, and defraud consumers, use un-approved chemicals, drive neglected service vehicles, and complete impossible quotas. Do the above for trucks, as well as do not rush through your services. Pace yourself to your own comfort. Some services, such as pest control, are regulated by government standards by the Dept. of Agriculture and Consumer Services.

3) Airline pilots forced to fly neglected aircraft, short cut on pre-flight safety procedures, carry un-approved hazardous materials, and race around the skies in an attempt to stick to rigid schedules. Call the Federal Aviation Administration at once. If they seem not concerned, go to the local TV news agency and blab it on the public scene. Whatever, ***DO NOT FLY THAT PLANE!!!*** You will be risking the lives of hundreds of people, both on that plane, and the ones who just might be on the ground in the event of a crash. Your career is second to the safety of your passengers, and your own life. This is if you are a pilot with good ethics! A supervisor that fires you for this is deserves the worst public image you can draw to him.

4) If you are working with a corporation that requires using computers, computer software programming, or are directly involved with producing

software and the like, and you know that your company is illegally copying software, you can call your local Business Software Alliance office. They will be more than happy to make their day. Any corporations that have disgruntled employees aware of their dirty deeds, done dirt cheap, beware, they will have the last laugh!

5) Construction personnel, that have been wronged by their bosses, can retaliate to the Building Code Authority. Especially if they also know of shortcuts in construction to save money at the home buyer's expense and safety. Unite with fellow construction workers, and go to the local TV news press specializing in uncovering raw-deals. Do what ever you can to louse up their day!

6) Office personnel, that have had a screw deal, can really throw a monkey wrench into the works. He or she can secretly open up a web-site on the internet blabbing the wrong doing to the whole world. If the company is corrupted, they can release facts, and figures meant to be kept under wraps for the eyes of the world to see. Use your imagination, as you best know of the angle to become their worst nightmare.

7) As civic oriented citizens, we absolutely must not tolerate the free-press being manipulated by government, and corporate interests, filling our society with propaganda. On National Public Radio, May 17, 2001, 11 AM Eastern time, a talk show had some shocking revelations about our country's free-press. It seems large mega-corporate conglomerates are purchasing the nation's newspapers at a record pace. Quality of reporting, and content is openly being sacrificed for profit margins, and stock market status.

Jay T. Baldwin

The public trust based on the first amendment and democracy as a whole is in serious danger. Big money interests are determining what, how, and if stories are printed or broadcasted, depending on how it will effect their financial and political standing. Or if it may work the masses into an unfavorable mood. Jay Harrison CEO of the San Jose Times Mercury News, owned by a conglomerate, resigned, and basically stated there is no more virtue in news reporting and couldn't continue his career with good conscience in its current state of press reporting. He stated this is a serious crisis of democracy. Remember what I said about finding any European and asking him about our current state of democracy, and you will be in for a surprise!

8) Most importantly, do not be a pu _ _ y whipped, pessimist, defeatist saying and believing that there is nothing we can do, you can't change the world, that's life, or some other fooling yourself attitude. Remember if our founding fathers thought this way, American would have never been born. Do not look down on your fellow citizens in labor unions, as trouble makers. They are the fore-runners of our rebellious founding fathers, as modern day sentinels of democracy and freedom. Be like me when people hit me with these looser statements, I become stronger and more determined to prove them wrong, and aid in making society better for the masses. Every single living and breathing American should have an ax to grind with today's capitalist abomination. **We must be that fly in their ointment!!**

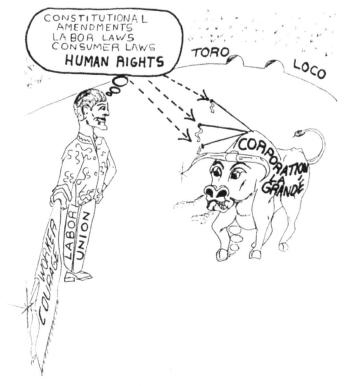

Illustration 31

"Ole' Ole' Only through pure courage can plain powerless workers take the bull by the horns and defend their liberties. Unity amongst individual workers (collective bargaining) is preferable in all corporate challenges, but we must be realistic and accept the fact most Americans will not join with their fellow workers. Courage must then be used by individual workers, like a Matador's red cape to entice the corporation to challenge them on a one on one basis. When a worker doesn't back down to the shear might of a corporation, the corporation will come on like a charging bull in it's attempt to subdue him. This is just one of the many ways a corporation attempts to make an example for the rest of the employees to keep future challenges to a minimum. However, it can backfire on the corporation if the employee is informed of his rights and liberties and knows he is right beyond a reasonable doubt. The old saying "Give them enough rope to hang themselves is a reality". As the charging bull charges the cape of courage, a sharp barbed banderilla of workers' liberties is hidden and waiting to be thrust into their side. Let them think you are ignorant, then let them take the bait. Wham! Bam! Jab! Let them have it! I have been very successful with this approach at my last job with the pest control firm named after the department store known for it's tools and appliances.

The theory of trickle-down supply and demand economics, as the Republicans and conservative economists portray it is no longer a valid statement. For one of the longest periods in US history, the unemployment rate has been the lowest. It is a labor sided economy, supposedly. Wages and benefits are suppose to boom, as they have in past economic haydays. If this is the case, why do wages stay stagnant, or continue to drop for the working majority? ANSWER THAT ONE ALL OF YOU ECONOMISTS, AND CONSERVATIVES OUT THERE!!! I am sick of all of those machiavellian right-wing wackos claiming that the corporate elites have earned their wealth fairly and squarely, because of their unique God given ability, and resourcefulness to manipulate situations, society and people for profit!! For some wealthy far-right-wing nuts, that claim that god has chosen them as the chosen ones, then in their own arrogant minds the rest of us are the condemned ones. So If I choose not to be an entrepreneur, but instead, a proud tradesman, who used to live comfortable performing his trade, that makes me a damned by God, lazy, unmotivated citizen. Then because I can no longer achieve the American Dream because some brainaics somewhere decided to hog more of the American pie, **THEY SAY ITS ALL MY FAULT**, or its inevitable!!! Isn't that the same as the crook saying he has a special blessing, then blames the victims of his crimes for being his victims?? If there are people out there that think this is the American way, then they are part of the problem. Well my friends, millions of us supposedly damned, lazy, but hard working, professional, honest, no-good-for-nothings are not going to go down without a fight!!!! That's a promise, not a threat!!

There could possibly be some other force at work here besides the usual rules of the free market economy. Or is it pure greed? Who is behind these forces, and what are their goals? It could be some darker sinister plan. What ever it is, it is our civic duty to stop this negative market force as our government leaders are not doing much to intervene themselves. The message to the President, Congress, and Allan Greenspan is as follows. If these leaders are purposely allowing this capitalist abomination to exploit the masses, then according to the Constitution and mandates from our founding fathers, they are committing treason. They should be impeached and prosecuted to the fullest extent of the law. The message to the Republicans; "Do not mix family values, democracy, and religion with corporate freedom to exploit the people and society for profit!" The message to the Democrats is; "Do not mix compassion, charity, and democracy with scandals, deceit, and lies." This slaps at the intelligence of the American people!!!

The need for cultural change from the ground up is imperative. Capitalism used to be a blessing, but with a new group of elites inhabiting earth, catering to the stock market without morals, ruled by pure greed, is now a curse. In pursuit of this relentless, insatiable greed of the worst human character, society will burn-out causing a complete collapse of society. This fast paced life, pressed on us by our job supervisors in there race for greater profits, and performance or our own greed factor, is destroying our culture and society. We have become too commercialized, and materialistic, trading off tradition, sanity, and humanity in our pursuit of the dollar. This baby boomer and gen-xer crowd addicted to materialism is setting us up for civil unrest, and civil disobedience ending in an apocalyptic collapse of society. Thus changing our whole human character for the worst. With daily pressure for better performance, we are sacrificing contentment, and virtues, resulting in shocking cases of anger control problems, and totally inhumane behavior. We should seriously consider abandoning the money system, as it caters to pure primal greed.

As a class of working Americans we will proudly request that corporate America return our American Dream, ***WITH RETROACTIVE INTEREST!*** As warriors of democracy, we hear the battle-cry to defend the spirit of freedom and democracy. This is not a Mafia nation where money buys freedom, human rights, and civility. God help the ones that do not yield to the power of the masses, as we will hold their precious economy hostage, and force compliance down their throats!! The choice is theirs, the easy civilized way, or they will have to accept a class war where they will definitely loose. After declaring war on us for twenty years, the message is now clear, no more Mr. Nice Guy!

Illustration 33

"Fair deal or fish meal" As American employees and consumers we literally have the power to make or break the country's economy. Our political and corporate friends (plutocrats) will tell us likewise, something more like "with out us, there is no economy!". That's because they are scared stiff! If the masses united and held the entire economy hostage, the all powerful corporations or greedy politicians will be reduced to humbled, inert bags of hot air. They would no longer be able to manipulate laws, words, and our sacred Constitution to allow them to continually plunder and pillage American society. We will not allow them to "Enronize". Example: The Enron fiasco of free market capitalism. We would be a very powerful force to be reckoned with. By using our mass numbers, our employee bargaining power (several employees not belonging to a union, but mad enough to join forces to manipulate corporate policy to their benefit) and our wallets (the choices we make as consumers) to literally hold the economy hostage until we get our share too. Make the forces of the free market work for us!

In The Politics of Rich and Poor, a New York Random House book, I strongly suggest you also read, by Kevin Phillips, pg. 47, 72, 74. David Gordon from the New School for Social Research quoted; "The most important story about the U.S. economy in the eighties is the economic warfare that the wealthy and powerful have been waging against the vast majority of Americans."

Conservative commentator George F. Will quoted; "Politics is about who gets what, especially as a result of government action. In the Reagan years, a particular social stratum has gotten a lot….If Marx had been scribbling away in the Library of Congress (our equivalent of the British Museum, where Marx scribbled), in January 1981, as Reaganites marched into Washington, he would have said: The class struggle is about to intensify. During the Reagan terror, labor will lose ground to capitol."

Ross Perot quoted; "To say these guys are entrepreneurs is like saying Jesse James was an entrepreneur." "In my day, you could make lots of money creating a new product or backing a new company. But now, if you're an investment banker, you can make many times that among of money in three or four weeks-and through the miracle of junk bonds and leave all of the risk with pension funds, S & Ls and banks, all of which are insured by the government...Now its' the taxpayer, the average citizen, who's become the entrepreneur in fact, with all of the risk and very little of the reward."

It has been proven time, and time again throughout history, when the elite have a booming economy, the rest of us must be sacrificed for their benefit. The "rob from the poor to feed the rich." The only way we will return to a strong middleclass majority nation, with the natural process of capitalism is to limit the amount of capital going to the top 5%. We must seize the controls of the economy by any means possible, and return the quality of life to the majority. A study of the economy during the 20s and 30s showed that when the elite's economy declines, the rest of the classes flourish. "Most of the decline took place by World War II. Between 1929 and 1948 the share of the total U.S. personal income received by the 5 percent of the Americans with the highest incomes fell from nearly a third to less than a fifth of the total. Dividends, interest and rent-the characteristic income of the wealthy dropped from 22 percent to just over 12 percent of the total family personal income. Income from wages, salaries and pensions climbed from 61 percent to 71 percent." (Source Selma Goldsmith,

Geroge Jaszi, Hyman Kaitz and Maurice Leibenberg, "Size and Distribution of Income Since the Mid-thirties," The Review of Economics and Statistics, February 1954, pgs. 16, 18.) Quoted from "The Politics of Rich and Poor", Kevin Philips, 1990, pg. 107.

Henry Kissinger quoted; "The management of a balance of power is a permanent undertaking, not an exertion that has a foreseeable end."

Former Republican White House Aid and Columnist Benjamin J. Stein added; "This is a television nation. Maybe its' time for a mini-series about the second American Civil War. This time it would be the haves versus the have-nots: Harlem against the Yupper East Side, Beverly Hills against Compton, the suburbs against the inner cities, the displaced against the entrenched. This time it would be guerrilla war, in neighborhoods, in cities, with block against block until people walked across the gulf and discovered the unique idea of sharing."

Here is a hard pill for our current President, with Texas roots, to swallow. Texas Agriculture commissioner Jim Hightower quoted; "The economic agenda of the past seven years produced one of the quickest and most regressive redistribution of wealth in U.S. history. For all of its' impassionate rhetoric about removing government as a force in our financial affairs, the Reagan government injected itself more enthusiastically into the economy than any administration since Lyndon Johnson's Great Society. Indeed Reagan's administration took so much money from the pockets of the middle and lower-income Americans and shove it up to the wealthiest 10 percent in our society that a top heavy structure now threatens to come crashing down on us." (Source: "Politics of Rich and Poor" by Kevin Philips.)

When we ask "Who stole the American Dream?", we can say with confidence, the bourgeoisie, the corporate elites, and the dysfunctional, corrupted, biased federal government. When we ask how this could have ever been allowed to happen, we can only blame ourselves for being naïve, passivist, defeatists successfully brain-washed. This publication, my first book, and the many other books by patriotic American authors are shots across the bow of corporate America, if you do not become more egalitarian as our founding fathers planned, further action on behalf of the people will be necessary. Our founding fathers chose to flee from this type of plutocratic totalitarianism from the British Crown in 1776. They sought a land where all are treated equally and no-one-class had the authority to rule over another.

The best mind of all time saw the evil potential in capitalism. Albert Einstein quoted; "We can have great concentrations of wealth or we can have great concentrations of democracy, but we can not have both."

For the first time in our history, we have come to cross-roads in our society where we will have to make hard decisions between civility, freedom, and democracy. Or we will choose wealth, power, freedom, and democracy for a scant few, while the majority will toil as a proletariat working class living in social, financial, and civil oppression. The future of democracy is up to us! I have always said, "Those who complacently accept oppression, complacently exalt oppression."

Protest now or revolt later! We must give corporate America a badly needed attitude adjustment. We are the majority in a democracy, where the majority should have been flourishing greatly since the past 15 years. We should have had a booming economy for all Americans.

Ralph Nader quoted; "We do not grow up learning how to be a citizen. If you want to learn how to dance, you go to an Arthur Murray clinic. There should be citizen training clinics." "There can be no daily democracy without daily citizenship. If we do not exercise our civic rights, who will? If we do not perform our civic duties, who can? The fiber of a just society in pursuit of happiness is a thinking, active citizenry. ***THAT MEANS YOU.***"

The road isn't going to be smooth my friends, but the alternatives are much worse. Ann Landers, Syndicated Columnist. "Our First Patriots Knew Freedom Is Never Free", Tuesday, July 4, 2000.

"Have you ever wondered what happened to the 56 men who signed the Declaration of Independence?"

Five of the signers were captured, and tortured to death by the British as traitors.

Twelve of them had their homes searched, and burned to the ground.

Two lost their sons who had served in the Revolutionary Army. One more had two sons captured.

Nine perished from wounds from the war.

Twenty four were lawyers and court jurists.

Eleven were merchants by trade.

Nine owned plantations, and were farmers.

These were well educated men. They knew that signing the Declaration of Independence would mean certain death.

Carter Braxton of Virginia owned a plantation, and had a fleet of trade ships. He saw all of his ships obliterated by the British Navy. He sold his house and all of his properties to settle his debts. He died homeless and in rags.

Thomas McKean was constantly intimidated by the British secret agents, and was constantly forced to keep his family in hiding. All of his possessions were confiscated. He served as a Congressman without pay, and ultimately ended up in poverty.

In the Battle of Yorktown, Thomas Nelson's house was captured by British General Cornwallis and used for a British outpost. General George Washington was hesitant to open fire on it, even though he knew Cornwallis was there. But Nelson constantly urged Washington to proceed with the attack regardless. Washington ultimately took his advise and opened fire. His home was destroyed, and he died bankrupt, and in rags.

Francis Lewis had his home destroyed, and his wife was imprisoned and died.

John Hart was attacked and forced to leave his dying wife behind. His thirteen children fled into the countryside for their lives. His properties and businesses were destroyed, and he was forced to live in caves out in the forests. He returned home more than a year later to find his wife dead, and his children missing without a trace. He died in poverty, heartbroken and in rags.

"Such were the stories and sacrifices of the American Revolution. These were not wild-eyed, rabble-rousing ruffians. They were men of means and education. They had security, but they valued liberty more."

This is what happened to brave, patriotic men who dared to cross wits with a wealthy, biased British plutocratic status-quo.

I have chosen to risk my own life, security, and family, and all that is sacred to me to tackle a new threat to American life, liberty, and happiness.

If you are not willing to do the same, this new American plutocracy with ideological social conditioning has become your new master. Do not say I didn't warn you, make yourself comfortable, if you can, and take your defeat in humiliation.

Take this book and America over to the garbage, and drop it in!!!

www.APADD.com

Jay T. Baldwin

A. P. A. D. D.

Americans to Preserve the American Dream and Democracy

America, the land of the free, and the home of the American dream. A democratic wonderland, where the masses enjoy freedom of choice, and are catered to by a civil service government loyal only to the people. A socio-economic paradise, based on a capitalist free market economy, which in the past, gave rise to the largest and strongest middleclass, living comfortably the American dream, in human history. Well my fellow Americans better, think again! This is the way it used to be! However, today amidst a roaring economy for the corporate elite, booming Wallstreet figures, record corporate profits, and greed of historical proportions, the American middleclass family, barely able to make ends meet, with two full time incomes, under the spell of ideological social control (social conditioning), is slowly being dismantled, into a proletarian worker servant class. To rub salt into the wound, a record number of freedoms, and privileges are being altered, neutralized or purged from our constitution, and law books, while American freedoms of choice are slowly being revoked, with authoritarian oppression, by the vary elected individuals installed to protect them. Our country is beginning to resemble the worlds largest autocratic plutocracy, or a kinder gentler, totalitarian police state.

Yes! A plutocracy, where a band of wealthy powerful corporate and political elite, in high places, create legislation, rules and regulations, that benefit mainly this power elite, all the while, they dominate, manipulate, economically and socially the American masses, greedily exploiting them for their labor, resources and political votes.

Yes! A police state, which continually, but slowly attempts to erase the first amendment, right to free public assembly, freedom of choice, American liberties, American rights, and a strong independent middleclass using social conditioning over

REVOLT AGAINST THE PLUTOCRACY

a long period of time. Americans are finding it harder to protest in public, without police harassment, outlandish city, county, state protest permits, and fees. Americans are now having to pay to exercise their given rights. The right to free public assembly, is being challenged by government, and law enforcement authorities. Today, a man's home or castle is no longer his to do with, as he likes. Some counties, cities and communities dictate, what color to paint your home, what kind, and how many cars you can drive, what kind and how much landscaping you can plant, what kind, how much, and where to enjoy recreation, how many children, if any, you can have. Homeowners can not keep boats, campers, and recreational vehicles on their property, in a growing number of cities. If, you do not believe me, a typical day at any south Florida beach, speaks a thousand words. In the 60's, 70's and early 80's, a typical Sunday afternoon, at any south Florida beach, showed a myriad of recreation activities, from wind surfers, small sail boats, catamarans, jet skis, scuba divers, skin divers, paddle balls, frisbees, kites, model boats, and a whole host of free, and happy people frolicking in the waves. Today, like some transformation into a George Orwell science fiction novel, after decades of authoritarian oppression, new regulations, and state, county and city ordinances, a day at the beach consists of masses of poker faced bathers, umbrellas, towels and sun tan lotion bottles glistening in the sun, while dozens of multi-million dollar yachts sail slowly by. Most beach front counties, and cities, now limit the number and class of people privileged, to have access to any beach property, by limiting parking, with less spaces, or charging outlandish fees. Some, no longer allow access, unless you belong to a certain economic class, who can afford waterfront property. Unless, you live on the beach, and have a Miami Beach resident sticker on your car, it will be towed to city impound. Citizens cannot visit residents overnight, as cars without stickers are not even allowed to park. Ft. Lauderdale has 9:00pm to 6:00am beach curfew, anybody parked, or walking the beach is ordered off! Only elite beach front residents have access to, most of the counties, ocean front property, during curfew times. Now, you have millions of landlocked people. It seems only a wealthy, privileged few can reap freedom of choice anymore. Ask anybody what happened to the middleclass recreational American dream pie and you will get the same answers. Too many rules, regulations, and laws, so all we do now, is take a towel, and sun screen, and watch the yachts go by. Just take a look at the signs on most American beaches; No boat launching!, No scuba diving or snorkeling!, No surfing!, No picnics!, No food or drinks!, No balls!, No frisbees!, No kites!, No inner tubes!, No playing!, No fun!!, No smiling!!!, No anything!!! I thought this was America? Seems more like the late Soviet Union.

Are you tired of politics as usual? Are you tired of the current system locking out third parties from debate, and advertisement rights. Are you sick of an irresponsible dis-functional government? Do you feel the government has forgotten who it works for? Do you feel we are now the servants of corporate America, and government? Do you feel the government is laced with greedy, and corrupted political leaders? Do you feel our government has become too intrusive into the lives of the average citizen, but does not exercise enough control over it's self, or wealthy powerful corporations, and the power elite leaders? Do you feel the constitution, laid out by our founding fathers, is slowly, and inconspicuously being dismantled? Do you feel our society is full of greed, bias, and double standards? Do you feel freedom of choice is being slowly narrowed with each passing day? Do you feel the government is too apathetic in dealing with the needs, and desires of the middleclass average citizen? Do you feel that wages have not kept up with inflation? Do you feel the middleclass, as we once knew it, will be gone in the, not too distant, future? Do you feel the middleclass is no longer living the standard of living or quality of life it used to? Do you feel the wealthy power elite, and corporate leaders, a scant 5% of the population, will continue to reap record profits, and incomes while most families, now even with two incomes, can no longer make ends meet? Do you feel our society will soon become a two class society, with a dominating power elite overclass, while everyone else struggles by as the proletariat working class? Do you feel most labor law violations, against working Americans, by wealthy powerful corporations go unpunished? Do you feel, most consumer law violations by wealthy, influential corporations against the American consumer, go unpunished? Do you feel American justice has become twisted, distorted, and is no longer effective? Do you feel criminals have more rights than the victims? Do you feel most laws apply

REVOLT AGAINST THE PLUTOCRACY

only to the masses, and not to wealthy, famous, or influential individuals, the government, and mega corporations? Has our country become the laughing stock of the world, in the face of rampant scandal, and political corruption across the board, including capital hill? Are you ashamed to be an American? Is this the America our founding fathers, and our brave service men have fought and died for? Is this the America you want your children growing up in? Must rights, liberties, privileges and freedom of choice be reserved for the wealthiest, highest bidders? Is America for sale only to those who can afford it?

If you said no to the last four, and yes to the rest, join a shocking 80% of the middleclass, and poor who share the same view point. Now, it's time to become a self declared member of A.P.A.D.D. We can no longer afford to have an apathetic, that's life, there is nothing we can do, or some other tuck your tail between your legs and give up attitude. If, we refuse to do something now, we may witness the delight of the overclass, and the demise of the middleclass, ending in an apocalyptic class war, where nobody will win. Are you willing to take that chance with our future? (See graph courtesy of the Internal Revenue service on last page of introduction.)

There are no out of pocket expenses, dues or fees, to join A.P.A.D.D. or any other requirements, other than being a citizen of the United States, registered to vote, and have an overwhelming desire fore a fairer, more free, prosperous, and democratic America. A.P.A.D.D. is not a conventional organization, but faith in the Constitution, and a frame of mind! You must also be willing to bravely stand up for American rights, liberties, and what you believe in! It is also a non-conformist attitude, to counter ideological social conditioning, proving our thoughts, beliefs, and freedoms of choice, are ours, and ours alone!

The A.P.A.D.D. United Declaration of Virtues, on the preceding pages, does not have a copy right, and is there fore you to make copies of. Please be free to make as many copies, by copy machine enlargement, as you can! Hand them out to your friends, and family members, who may not have printers or computers. Next sign, and date, inserting your address, place in an envelope addressed to the President of the United States, and mail at once.

Jay T. Baldwin

President _____ of the United States of America
1600 Pennsylvania Avenue
Washington D.C. 20599-001

Next mail a copy to your senator, congressman, all the way down to your local elected officials.
Consider this a formal warning from the American people united!
"United we stand, divided we fall!"
"Pad the American Dream and Democracy!" with A.P.A.D.D.

Concerned citizen
President and founder of A.P.A.D.D.
Jay T. Baldwin

REVOLT AGAINST THE PLUTOCRACY

A.P.A.D.D.
Americans to Preserve the American Dream and Democracy

United Declaration of Virtues

We, the people of the United States of America, in order to restore a more perfect union, have united as Americans to Preserve the American Dream and Democracy, and as a people united of all races, religions, and national origins, in an American democracy, as a majority, will no longer tolerate the following unethical, undemocratic, and unconstitutional, plutocratic, autocratic activities in democratic free America.

1) As a people united, we will no longer tolerate corruption and fraud in the office of the President of the United States.

2) As a people united, we will no longer tolerate corruption and fraud in the federal, state and local political offices.

3) As a people united, we will no longer tolerate corruption and fraud in law enforcement offices.

4) As a people united, we will no longer tolerate suppression of freedom of speech by corporate America and government.

5) As a people united, we will no longer tolerate suppression of the right to assemble, by corporate America and governments.

6) As a people united, we will no longer tolerate presidential, federal, political, corporate and law enforcement abuse of power, or elitism in any form.

7) As a people united, we will no longer tolerate authoritarian or totalitarian tactics enacted by corporate America, government and law enforcement agencies.

Jay T. Baldwin

8) As a people united, we will no longer tolerate police state tactics enacted by corporate America, government and law enforcement agencies.

9) As a people united, we will no longer tolerate martial law enacted permanently by government, and law enforcement agencies.

10) As a people united, we will no longer tolerate curfews permanently imposed by government and law enforcement agencies.

11) As a people united, we will no longer tolerate taxation without first democratic representation presented to the people, in a clear and non-deceptive manner.

12) As a people united, we will no longer tolerate careless spending of taxpayers dollars by government.

13) As a people united, we will no longer tolerate unfair tax loopholes utilized by corporate America that shift greater tax burdens on the middleclass and poor.

14) As a people united, we will no longer tolerate experimentation on the people, society, and the environment by corporate America, military, or government without first democratic representation to the people, in a clear and non-deceptive manner.

15) As a people united, we will no longer tolerate development and use of any product or service by corporate America or government that knowingly compromises the safety of the people, society or the environment.

16) As a people united, we will not tolerate corporate and government non-adherence to federal, state, and local laws.

17) As a people united, we will no longer tolerate unethical, destructive exploitation of society, commerce, American workers, American consumers and the environment by corporate America, and government for greed, profit, and personal gain.

18) As a people united, we will no longer tolerate the government's procrastination toward raising the minimum wage to a living wage.

19) As a people united, we will no longer tolerate apathy and incompetence on behalf of the government toward corporate and political crimes.

20) As a people united, we will no longer tolerate violation of labor laws, consumer

REVOLT AGAINST THE PLUTOCRACY

laws, safety laws, and environmental protection laws by government and corporate America.

21) As a people united, we will no longer tolerate corruption, fraud, apathy, and incompetence on behalf of government agencies created to protect labor laws, consumer laws, safety laws, and environmental protection laws.

22) As a people united, we will no longer tolerate substandard wages, declining wages, benefits and declining quality of life imposed on American workers as a direct result of corporate greed, exploitation and profiteering.

23) As a people united, we will no longer tolerate unsafe, unethical employment conditions forced unwillingly upon American workers.

24) As a people united, we will no longer tolerate the exporting of sound, stable American jobs to foreign countries leaving American workers in low paying jobs, or unemployed.

25) As a people united, we will no longer tolerate early release program for violent criminals.

26) As a people united, we will no longer tolerate crime severity reduction, crime record deletion practices, or other forms of apathy by cities and law enforcement agencies to intentionally reduce crime percentages.

27) As a people united, we will no longer tolerate racial, religious, sexual, age, or handicapped discrimination by corporate America and government.

28) As a people united, we will no longer tolerate, refusal to treat any life threatening or serious injury/illness, by medical care facilities because of medical insurance carrier, cost reduction pressures, on medical physicians and staff, patient's inability to pay, or patient's lack of insurance.

29) As a people united, we will no longer tolerate social disrespect, medical negligence, and apathy toward any veteran of war, veteran of law enforcement, or any causes, injuries, or illnesses relating, by corporate America and government.

30) As a people united, we will no longer tolerate additions, alterations, deletions, or any attempts to repress or neutralize articles of the Constitution of the United

Jay T. Baldwin

States, and The Bill of Rights, without first democratic representation, presented to the people, in a manner easily understandable to the average citizen, and free of deception and fraud.

31) As a people united, we will no longer tolerate deception and fraud by corporate America, political leaders, law enforcement, or governments to gain public support, votes or legislation.

32) As a people united, we will no longer tolerate the government's infallible rule. "The costs and burdens of all domestic affair policies, must be born by those least able to bear them."

33) To ensure adherence to the plans, visions, and dreams set forth and bestowed upon the American people by the founding fathers, and to prevent further decay of democratic principles, processes, freedoms of choice, American prosperity, and the American middleclass, we the people united will no longer tolerate, ideological social control, manipulation, and oppression of democratic free America by the power elite, corporate America and governments.

The government, it's elected officials, and corporate America, are hereby presented with this formal ultimatum, and are to answer only to the American people united, exercising their Constitutional rights bestowed upon them, by the founding fathers of America, or said government and economic institutions will be dissolved, by democratic process, as directed by the founding fathers and replaced with new government, and economic institutions created by the people, for the benefit of the people, honoring the Declaration of Independence, Bill of Rights and the Constitution of the United States on this _____ day of _____ the year _____.

Sincerely _____

name _____
street _____
city, state, zip _____

American citizens, the following letters are protest letters for a variety of subjects effecting the citizens, and are to be copied by copy machine enlargement. Make as many copies as you can, give them to your family members and friends, sign, date, and mail them to the prospective political head. I hereby give you written permission to copy the following letters. Mail them a copy once a year, once a month, or as many times as you want, at least until the situation is remedied. If there is no reply, do not let that rattle you. They get millions of letters, it is the fact they are being mailed. By the millions we can preserver!!

Jay T. Baldwin

Date _____

Name

_____

Street

_____

City / State / Zip

_____

President

_____
1600 Pennsylvania Avenue
Washington D.C. 20599-001

Dear President

_____

As American citizens united, in an American democracy, we will no longer tolerate destructive corporate, political, and plutocratic exploitation of American society. This causing stagnating, or declining incomes, less safe working environments for America's employees, and also causing unsafe, inferior products for consumers. All for the profit and personal gain by an elite few.

We will not tolerate political manipulation, and spin of American Constitutional rights, and liberties handed down from the founding fathers, with intent of public deception to justify the plutocratic exploitation of American society for profit by a wealthy elite minority.

As a public servant elected to an office of civil service, by the people for the people exercising democratic principles, we expect you will address this growing problem, and honor these demands of a united people in a democracy. We demand that you uphold your sworn oath to the service of America, the Constitution, and worker's liberties not to big money, and corporate interests. Thank you.

Sincerely signed,

_____

Jay T. Baldwin

Date _____

Name
_____

Street
_____

City / State / Zip
_____

President
_____

1600 Pennsylvania Avenue
Washington D.C. 20599-001

Dear President
_____

The federal standard for America's minimum wage has not kept pace with cost of living increases for the past twenty years. This has also kept other working wages from increasing resulting in the decline of the working middleclass, and a lower standard of living for most Americans.

As American citizens united, in an American democracy, we will no longer tolerate failure of government, elected to serve the people, to address implementation of the living-wage for both state, government workers, and employees of private corporations. The facts show that a majority of Americans support this living-wage legislation.

As a public servant elected to an office of civil service, by the people for the people exercising democratic principles, we expect you will address this growing problem, and honor these demands of a united people in a democracy. We demand that you uphold your sworn oath to the service of America, and the constitution, not big money, and corporate interests. We will not allow America to become a thriving plutocracy, allowing a select wealthy few access to liberty, happiness, and the American dream at the expense of the liberties of working American people. Thank you.

Sincerely signed,

Jay T. Baldwin

Date _____

Name
_____

Street
_____

City / State / Zip
_____

Governor
_____

Street_____

City / State / Zip
_____

Dear Governor
_____

As united citizens of the state of _____, we will no longer tolerate pro-corporate "right-to-work" policies that permit state agencies, and private corporations to inhumanely exploit employees, and consumers to create an environment of profiteering for an elite few.

We will not tolerate policies, and legislation that strip American workers of their rights, liberties and abilities to seek a functional salary, fair humane treatment, compensation, retribution, and powers in the preservation of their American liberties by corporate and state bureaucratic interests.

We will not tolerate policies, and legislation that strip consumers of their rights, liberties and abilities to seek quality, safe, products and services, free of deception, fraud, and price gouging.

As Governor and public servant, elected to an office of civil service, by the people for the people exercising their democratic principles, we expect you will uphold your sworn oath to the service of the people, and address these concerns of a united people in a democracy.

We will not allow this state, and America to become a thriving plutocracy, allowing a select wealthy few access to liberty, happiness, and the American dream at the expense of the liberties of working American people. Thank you.

Sincerely signed,

_____

Jay T. Baldwin

Date _____

Name

Street

City / State / Zip

President

1600 Pennsylvania Avenue
Washington D.C. 20599-001

Dear President

    As American citizens united, in an American democracy, we will no longer tolerate federal moneys from taxpayers, budgeted for welfare purposes to assist the less fortunate, and poor, being diverted to corporations and wealthy individuals. This is done in the form of corporate grants, promotionals, low interest loans, and gifts or loans for wealthy individuals to purchase high-end homes, home improvements, and properties.

    We see this corporate welfare as an abomination of society, liberties, and human ethics to assist those least in need, and most capable of being financially self-sufficient at the expense of those incapable of supplying the basic necessities of life.

As a public servant elected to an office of civil service, by the people for the people exercising democratic principles, we expect you will address this concern, and honor these demands of a united people in a democracy. We will not allow America to become a thriving plutocracy, allowing a select wealthy few access to liberty, happiness, and the American dream at the expense of the less fortunate, and the taxpayers. Thank you.

Sincerely signed,

_____

Jay T. Baldwin

Date _____

Name

_____

Street

_____

City / State / Zip

_____

President

_____

1600 Pennsylvania Avenue
Washington D.C. 20599-001

Dear President

_____

As American citizens united, in an American democracy, we will no longer tolerate dysfunctional or corrupted state, and federal regulatory agencies designed to protect the Constitutional, human rights, safety and liberties of American consumers and employees from corporate, bureaucratic crimes.

We will no longer tolerate understaffed regulatory agencies resulting in unacceptable waiting period, and dismissal of valid cases for action on citizen complaints.

We will no longer tolerate internal limitations secretly practiced by these regulatory agencies on legal action against violators resulting in dismissal of valid cases for action on citizen complaints.

We will no longer tolerate internal limitations secretly practiced by these regulatory agencies on legal action against violators resulting in dismissal of valid cases, to minimize political repercussions from the corporate sector.

As a public servant elected to an office of civil service, by the people for the people exercising democratic principles, we expect you will address this concern, and honor these demands of a united people in a democracy. We will not allow America to become a thriving plutocracy, allowing a select wealthy few access to liberty, happiness, and the American dream at the expense of the American people. Thank you.

Sincerely signed,

_____

Jay T. Baldwin

Date _____

Name

_____

Street

_____

City / State / Zip

_____

President

_____
1600 Pennsylvania Avenue
Washington D.C. 20599-001

Dear President

_____

    Congress constantly slows, freezes, or reduces the budget for the U.S. Fish and Wildlife Administration for environmental causes, and endangered species under relentless pressures from corporate, and big-money interests.

    As American citizens united, in an American democracy, we will no longer tolerate the complacent, reckless neglect of these important environmental concerns to allow corporate profiteering. Thousands of endangered plant and animal species are in financial backlog due to this form of exploitation. This prevents them from being entered on the endangered species list, and having the appropriate preservation legislation. The time is running out for some of these life-forms. Once gone, they will never be replaced.

As a public servant elected to an office of civil service, by the people for the people exercising democratic principles, we expect you will address this concern, and honor these demands of a united people in a democracy. We demand that you uphold your sworn oath to the service of America, and the constitution, not big money, and corporate interests. We will not allow America to become a thriving plutocracy. Thank you.

Sincerely signed,

_____

Jay T. Baldwin

Date _____

Name

_____

Street

_____

City / State / Zip

_____

_____

President

_____

1600 Pennsylvania Avenue
Washington D.C. 20599-001

Dear President

_____

As American citizens united, in an American democracy, we believe in a free, un-biased press. Free to report the truth, cover stories, and depict the facts without pressure from big money interests, corporate pressures, and political influences. We believe the press should hold itself to a higher standard, totally free from plutocratic, and stockmarket influences.

The American people united will no longer tolerate conglomerate buy-out of free-press agencies. This suppresses democracy, and leads to diminishing sources of information. The passing of propaganda then becomes much more viable, and efficient for plutocratic interests.

As a public servant elected to an office of civil service, by the people for the people exercising democratic principles, we expect you will address this growing problem, and honor these demands of a united people in a democracy. We demand that you uphold your sworn oath to the service of America, and the Constitution, not big money, and corporate interests. We will not allow America to become a thriving plutocracy, allowing a select wealthy few access to liberty, freedom, happiness, and the American dream at the expense of the American people. Thank you.

Sincerely signed,

_____

Jay T. Baldwin

PUBLIC ALERT!

As of March 7, 2001
Dear American citizen,

On March 7, 2001, broadcasted on World News, only on International syndicated Radio, broadcasted on 91.3 WLRN FM. House Republicans had proposed a bill to speed through the Senate, on what is known as fast-track, which basically prevented any form of debating in the Senate, a principle of democracy, from taking place.

This bill has removed certain labor/worker safety mandates that require corporate America, America's employers, to create safe, worker friendly environments, reducing the likelihood of on the job injuries, especially from repetitive tasks. This to reduce corporate expenses, and to even further boost corporate profits, all at the expense of the well-being of all American workers. This bill on fast track passed the Senate in less than 48 hours from its debut on the radio press, and was signed into law by March 9, 2001.

This was only heard on the world radio news. To minimize any chance of public outcry, and organized labor backlash. This was not heard on the mainstream American television news broadcasts as of March 7, 2001. Only after the fact was it made public on the mainstream press. This form of fascist press censorship is not going to be tolerated. As well as the fact of not bringing this matter to the public to be voted on.

This Republican autocratic tactic, smacks of everything fascist, or Communist. It is our responsibility as American citizens to take immediate action, in the name of American democracy, the American dream, and the American workers.

Please make as many copies as you can, hand them to all friends and relatives, then ask them to make copies and do the same. Fill out the last page with your name, address, and sign it at the bottom. Mail the last page immediately to the President of the United States, George W. Bush.

We must not allow further incursions on the rights of Americans. This will not be tolerated!!!!

Jay T. Baldwin

Citizen _____
Address
_____
City/State
_____

Zip _____
Date _____
President
_____

1600 Pennsylvania Avenue
Washington D.C. 20599-001
re: Repeal of Federal employee ergonomic safety work place laws.

Dear President
_____,

As American citizens united, we will not tolerate the repeal of employee ergonomic requirements, or any other labor/worker protection mandates from the labor laws, or constitutional laws exposing workers to unnecessary physical injury, without first due democratic processes offered to the people, in the form of a public voting process. It must be presented to the people in a manner easily understood, and free of fraud, and deception.

As an official elected by the people, for the people, in a position of public service, we expect you will make decisions based on the needs, and desires of the mass-majority, not the wealthiest few, for the sake of American freedom, and democracy.

We will not allow America to become an unchallenged autocratic plutocracy, catering to corporate America, in the name of profiteering at the expense of the American workers, and American democracy!

Thank you,

Sincerely a concerned, united American citizen.

Jay T. Baldwin

PUBLIC ALERT!

Dear American citizen,

On or about March 20, 2001, again for the second time, in less than two weeks, another bill was proposed by House Republicans, placed on fast track, and was not debated in the Senate. It was placed in front of President Bush, signed and made into law by March 22, less than 72 hours, again another end-run around American democracy! Once again the mainstream American press was kept in the dark, or was ordered to downplay this incursion on more American liberties to keep citizen backlash, and organized labor outcry to a minimum. Again the American people were not allowed to vote on a matter that effects every single working American for generations to come.

Another pro-corporate mandate that removes Constitutional, and civil rights of American to legally sue their employers for injuries due to negligence, discrimination of any kind, breach of employee contract, or for any reason. Instead Americans workers will be forced to negotiate with corporate America, in what is known as binding arbitration, without the presence of their attorneys, or a twelve member jury panel. This will greatly decrease the chances of a fair settlement for the employee, giving more power to the employer. Again, all in the name of increasing corporate profiteering at the expense of the American worker.

How many more American liberties, human rights, or Constitutional Amendments are we going to allow to be purged, altered, or neutralized before we unite and end this plutocratic fascism once and for all?? We must not allow democracy to fail us! For the first time, America has endured more incursions against the sanctity, human rights, and American virtues than at any other time, and in less time than in any other administration in our history.

According to our rights handed down to us in the Constitution of the United States, by our founding fathers, we the people united will not tolerate any more violations of American liberties as a sacrifice for the benefit of the wealthiest few, and corporate America.

Jay T. Baldwin

Citizen _____
Address
_____
City/State

_____

Zip _____
Date _____
President

_____

1600 Pennsylvania Avenue
Washington D.C. 20599-001
Re: Repeal of employees right to sue their employer.

Dear President

_____,

As American citizens united, we will not tolerate the repeal of employee legal rights, and options to legal action against a negligent employer that results in injury, discrimination, breach of employment contract, or any other reason, by President, government, Senate, State, or any other source. We will definitely not tolerate further incursions against employee rights, liberties, and American democracy.

As a civil service official elected by a people using democratic rights, and principles, under the Constitution of the United States, we demand that you halt further autocratic, plutocratic incursions against the people, without first presenting proposals that effect this majority in a democracy, in the form of a public vote, free of deception, and in a manner easily understood. If these mandates by a democratic people are not met, said government will be altered, or abolished, and new government will be instituted laying its foundations on such principles that most likely effect their safety and Happiness, as our Founding Fathers dictate.

We will not stand by idle and allow America to become an unchallenged plutocracy, for the benefit of a corporate, wealthy few. Thank you!!

Sincerely a concerned, united American citizen,

Jay T. Baldwin

Internal Revenue Service April 15, 2001
Atlanta, Ga. 39901
Re: The mistake on our tax return that we didin't make.

Dear IRS,

I have received your letter on the amount of money you think we owe you. Unfortunately, we do not owe you this money as I have reported all income that I have earned! I have been a law biding citizen, and have always paid my taxes.

I am just your average blue-collar worker who can barely make ends meet as I am earning less today than I earned 15 years ago. Yet the cost of living is much more now than then. I have realized the loss of the American Dream, only to live a life of pure survival.

In the meantime, wealthy millionaire corporate leaders have so many loop-holes and tax shelter privileges, that by the time they add them up, they end up paying next to nothing. Yet, when I filled out my tax return from last y ear, I couldn't even declare our medical expenses because they didn't add up to 7,000 or more per year. I can not even declare my auto expenses on the one car we have been able to keep as we've sold our second car due to continual pay cuts at work. The corporate millionaire can deduct all auto expenses, living expenses, mortgage expenses, travel expenses, recreation expenses, clothing expenses, dining out on the town expenses, and for god's sake even gets to deduct taxes from his taxes! ***WHAT THE***

SAM HELL IS THIS CORPORATE WELFARE AT MY EXPENSE????

So I think you have a many more bigger fish to fry unless you want another homeless family living on the streets of America!!!

So I think you better get your priorities straight, and stop bothering the poor little people!! Has this country become a thriving plutocracy?? One that rewards, glorifies the rich man, wealthy corporations, and spits on the carcasses of the of the once prosperous middleclass, and brutalizes the poor man?

I will never pay this extortion payment!! Up till now, I have always paid my taxes, but after this, I will not be so obliging, and will look for ways to reduce my taxes any way I can, whether you approve of it or not. ***Have a very GOOD DAY!!!***

A struggling American.

Jay T. Baldwin

REVOLT AGAINST THE PLUTOCRACY!

The following are addresses of governors for all fifty states. The address stays the same regardless of whom is elected to office. This is for your convenience in writing letters to your governor. Just write the name of your governor into any correspondence.

ALABAMA: Office of the Governor 600 Dexter Ave., Montogomery.

ALASKA: Office of the Governor P.O. Box 110001, Juneau.

ARIZONA: Office of the Governor 1700 West Washington St., Phoenix.

ARKANSAS: Office of the Governor State Capital Room 250, Little Rock.

CALIFORNIA: Office of the Governor State Capitol 1st Floor, Sacramento.

COLORADO: Office of the Governor State Capitol Bldg. Room 136, Denver.

CONNECTICUT: Office of the Governor Executive Chambers 210 Capitol Ave., Hartford.

DELAWARE: Office of the Governor Tatnall Bldg., William Penn St., Dover.

FLORIDA: Office of the Governor The Capitol, Tallahassee.

GEORGIA: Office of the Governor 203 State Capitol, Atlanta.

HAWAII: Office of the Governor State Capitol 415 S. Beratania Ave., Honolulu.

IDAHO: Office of the Governor P.O. Box 83720, Boise.

ILLINOIS: Office of the Governor Capitol Bldg. Room 207, Springfield.

INDIANA: Office of the Governor State Capitol Room 206, Indianapolis.

IOWA: Office of the Governor State Capitol Bldg., Des Moines.

KANSAS: Office of the Governor State Capitol 2nd Floor, Topeka.

KENTUCKY: Office of the Governor 700 Capitol Ave., Frankfort.

LOUISIANA: Office of the Governor P.O. Box 94004, Baton Rouge.

MAINE: Office of the Governor 1 State House Station, Augusta.

MARYLAND: Office of the Governor State House, Annapolis.

MASSACHUSETTS: Office of the Governor Executive Office 360, Boston.

MICHIGAN: Office of the Governor P.O. Box 30013, Lansing.

MINNESOTA: Office of the Governor State Capitol Room 130, St. Paul.

MISSISSIPPI: Office of the Governor P.O. Box 139, Jackson.

MISSOURI: Office of the Governor P.O. Box 720, Jefferson City.

MONTANA: Office of the Governor Capitol Bldg., Helena.

NEBRASKA: Office of the Governor P.O. Box 94848, Lincoln.

NEVADA: Office of the Governor Capitol Complex, Carson City.

NEW HAMPSHIRE: Office of the Governor State House 107 N. Main Room 208, Concord.

NEW JERSEY: Office of the Governor State House CN 001, Trenton.

NEW MEXICO: Office of the Governor State Capitol Room 400, Santa Fe.

NEW YORK: Office of the Governor Executive Chambers State Capitol, Albany.

NORTH CAROLINA: Office of the Governor 116 W. Jones St., Raleigh.

NORTH DAKOTA: Office of the Governor 600 E. Boulevard Ave., Bismarck.

OHIO: Office of the Governor 77 S. High St. 30th Floor, Columbus.

OKLAHOMA: Office of the Governor State Capitol Room 212, Oklahoma City.

OREGON: Office of the Governor State Capitol Bldg. Room 254, Salem.

PENNSYLVANIA: Office of the Governor Main Capitol Bldg. Room 225, Harrisburg.

RHODE ISLAND: Office of the Governor 143 State House, Providence.

SOUTH CAROLINA: Office of the Governor P.O. Box 11369, Columbia.

SOUTH DAKOTA: Office of the Governor 500 E. Capitol Ave., Pierre.

TENNESSEE: Office of the Governor State Capitol Bldg., Nashville.

TEXAS: Office of the Governor P.O. Box 12428, Austin.

UTAH: Office of the Governor 210 State Capitol, Salt Lake City.

VERMONT: Office of the Governor Pavilion Office Bldg. 109 State. St., Montpelier.

VIRGINIA: Office of the Governor State Capitol Bldg. 3rd Floor, Richmond.

WASHINGTON: Office of the Governor Legislative Bldg., Olympia.

WEST VIRGINIA: Office of the Governor 1900 Kanawha Blvd. E. Capitol Bldg., Charleston.

WISCONSIN: Office of the Governor P.O. Box 7863, Madison.

WYOMING: Office of the Governor State Capitol Bldg. 124 200 W. 24th St., Cheyenne.

BIBLIOGRAPHY

Alexander, Keith. "Machinists' strike stalls jetmaker", *USA Today*, June 6, 1996, pg. 3b.

Bousquet, Steve, Charles, Jacqueline. "The High Cost of Being Broke", *The Herald*, August 8, 1999, pgs. 1L-3L.

Bouza, Tony, *The Decline and Fall of the American Empire*. New York: Plenum Press, 1996.

Broder, David S. "Nonvoters: America's no shows", *The Herald*, October 10, 1999, pg. 5L.

Burgess, John, Pearlstein, Steven. "Protest Rattles Seattle", *The Sun Sentinel*, December 1, 1999, pgs. 1A, 29A.

Bussey, Jane, "Labor dispute nearing settlement in Guatemala", *The Herald*, March 21, 2000, pgs. 1C, 3C.

Carbonara, Peter, Shultz, Abby. "What Are You Worth?" *Fortune*, April 2000, pgs. 45-54.

Chardy, Alfonso. "Truckers clog roads to protest fuel prices", *The Herald*, February 10, 2000, pgs. 1B, 2B.

Cohen, Sharon. "Employees get millions when boss shares profits", *The Herald*, September 12, 1999, pg. 12A.

Cruze, Lawrence M. "White-collar workers back at desks after Boeing settles 40-day strike", *The Herald*, March 21, 2000, pgs. 1C, 3C.

Davis, Ann. "Treating On-the-Job Injuries as True Crimes", *Wall Street Journal*, February 26, 1997, pgs. B1, B5.

Denk, James. *The New York Times Special Report*, New York: Time Books Random House, 1996.

Dodds, Paisly. "Disillusioned chase 'American dream abroad", *The Herald*, September 10, 2000, pg. 21H.

Duboco, Tom, Townsend, Rosa. "Phantom road work uncovered", *The Herald*, November 2, 1997, pgs. 1A, 10A, 11A.

Fields, Greg. "Truckers strike takes heavy toll", *The Herald*, February 20, 20001, pg. 2E.

Fields, Greg. "Slick Justice", *The Herald*, September 26, 1999, pgs. 1L, 2L.

Fortune. "Big Labor Flexes Its Muscles", June 10, 1996, pg. 24.

Garcia, Bea. "Tobacco Lawyers set their sights on health care", *The Herald*, October, 10, 1999, pgs. 1E, 6E.

Golan, Andy. "Wage difference growing among working class", *Employment Digest*.

Green, Meg. "Meg Green", *The Herald*, November 5, 2000, pg. 3E.

Green, Meg. "Don't Count On Dividends", *The Herald*, November 5, 2000, pg. 3E.

Kripilani, Jasmine. "Women discuss life, work, 'solutions to situations'"., *The Herald*, October 12, 199, pg. 3B.

Lekachman, Robert. *Greed is Not Enough: Reaganomics*. New York: Pantheon Books, 1982.

Lowe, Janet. *The Secret Empire How 25 Multinationals rule the world*. Illinois: Business One Irwin, 1992.

Luttwak, Edward. *Turbo Capitalism Winners and Losers in the Global Economy*, New York: Harper Collins, 1999.

La Mendola, Bob. "Medical Group lacking cure" "Profit squeeze causes demise", *The Herald*, January 16, 2000, pgs. 1G, 12G.

Landers, Ann. "Our first patriots knew freedom is never free", *The Syndicated Columnist*, July 4, 2000, pg. 2E.

Lardner, James. "The Rich Get Richer", *U.S. News & World Report*, February 2, 2000, pg. 39.

Leibenberg, Maurice. "Size and Distribution of Income Since the Mid-Thirties", *The Review of Economics and Statistics*, February 1954, pgs. 16, 18.

Lewis, Sidney. *Strikemakers and Strikebreakers*, New York: E. P. Dutton, 1985.

Lewis, Diane E. "Bosses haven't kept their part of the new 'deal', workers say", *The Herald*, October 19, 1997, pg. 1G.

About the author

Amidst this new world order economy, with my full-time job as a professional pest control technician, and my wife now teaching full-time, we can only afford the bare necessities. We can no longer consider the purchase of a modest home in a modest neighborhood. We definitely will not consider living in a ghetto! We work too hard to settle for the scraps of society!!! We still can not live the quality of life we had back in the late 80s with my past good paying job, and my wife's past part time job. There is no residual income to eat out but once every couple of months. We now only own one car, and any dreams of me pursuing my leisure hobbies of boating, model airplanes, firearm marksmanship, are just that, dreams!

Another election year has come and gone, and campaign finance reform has once again been put on to the back burner. But as citizens we must realize that even if this subject was addressed, it is just the tip of a very, very big iceberg. We must take being civically involved very seriously. We have the power as consumers and employees to literally turn this plutocratic abomination up-side-down. But every single citizen has been exposed to the largest ideological social conditioning campaign by the power elites in the history of the free world. Whether this is a coordinated mass-cooperation amongst these elites, or a smaller un-coordinated individual effort, each with similar goals and plans that it appears to be a coordinated effort, we are not sure. Like a million birds suddenly taking flight, striving for self preservation at the crack of a hunter's rifle, the direction of the wind can be literally altered. Because of this we have become defeatist passivists, willing to accept our fate like trees before a hurricane without so-much as a peep of dissatisfaction. WE have played right into their hands. The battle has been won before it has been fought. However, we outnumber them twenty-to-one and like that flock of birds, whether as individuals with similar personal goals, or in a massive joint cooperative counter assault, we can once again turn the winds in our favor. Direct or indirect unity.

Therefore, as a family we will attempt to unify the people as a whole, or to unify their personal goals as individuals into similar directions snapping them out of their brain-washed stupor. We just might get enough birds pointed close enough to the same direction. When they take flight in their attempt to preserve their personal way of life from being changed forever, the winds will ultimately be reversed in our favor again. We will patiently show people how to become that proverbial employee and consumer from hell. How to make the elite's own dog turn on them and bite them back right back in the ass! We are not in this for a popularity contest and do not give a damn as to what the ramifications to our personal lives will be. The revolt of the commoners, proletariat, serfs, working-class, or what-have-you against this un-American, un-ethical, corporate and political plutocracy will go on!!!

At least we are no-longer dependent on our parents for every day necessities as my wife is now teaching. However, with two full-time incomes, we are still unable to prosper through hard work and loyalty as we have been taught by society. We just survive. There is just one thing! Society is in for a big surprise! We are not just a typical American family. ***Civic involvement is contagious, and so are we!!!!***

Coming from middleclass roots in Maryland, Jay T. Baldwin has witnessed his standard of living and income to cost ratio continue to decline into the new millennium. Once living the American Dream comfortably with a blue collar income in the middle to late 80s, now this Dream is becoming a distant memory. All in spite of taking up several blue collar professional trade career titles in a vane effort to maintain this American heritage, he and millions of his co-workers, once living a comfortable middleclass lifestyle are destined to become the new proletariat working class in a new two class society. As writer/author of Delight of The Overclass Demise of

The Middleclass, he continues his valiant struggle representing the average working American tradesman and company employee in Revolt Against The Plutocracy. He fights on behalf of the everyday working Joe/Jane, against the greedy American Plutocracy, and to take back the once easily accessible American Dream through pride, quality, loyalty in hard work, the traditional methods of accessing this heritage passed down from generation to generation.

Made in the USA
Columbia, SC
15 March 2022